CHANGING MY MIND, AMONG OTHERS

Books and Monographs by Timothy Leary

The Dimensions of Intelligence (M.S. thesis, Washington State Univ., 1946)

The Social Dimensions of Personality (Ph.D. thesis, Univ. of California, 1950)

The Interpersonal Diagnosis of Personality (1957)

The Existential Transaction (1960)

The Psychedelic Experience (with Metzner and Alpert, 1964)

The Psychedelic Reader (ed. with Weil, 1965)

Psychedelic Prayers from the Tao Te Ching (1967)

High Priest (1968)

Politics of Ecstasy (1968)

Jail Notes (1971)

Principles and Practice of Hedonic Psychology (1972)

Confessions of a Hope Fiend (1973)

Neurologic (with Joanna Leary, 1973)

Starseed: A Psy-Phi Comet Tale (1973)

The Curse of the Oval Room (1974)

Terra II (with Joanna Leary and L. W. Benner, 1974)

Future History Series:

Vol. I: What Does WoMan Want? (1976)

Vol. II: Exo-Psychology (1977)

Vol. III: Neuropolitics (1977)

Vol. IV: Intelligence Agents (1979)

Vol. V: The Game of Life (1979)

CHANGING MY MIND, AMONG OTHERS

Lifetime writings, selected and introduced by the author

Timothy Leary

Prentice-Hall, Inc., Englewood Cliffs, New Jersey 07632

For Barbara and Zachary

Book design by Joan Ann Jacobus
Art Director: Hal Siegel

Changing My Mind, Among Others:
Lifetime writings, selected and introduced by the author
© 1982 by Timothy Leary

Printed in the United States of America
Prentice-Hall International, Inc., London / Prentice-Hall of Australia, Pty. Ltd., Sydney / Prentice-Hall of Canada, Ltd., Toronto / Prentice-Hall of India Private Ltd., New Delhi / Prentice-Hall of Japan, Inc., Tokyo / Prentice-Hall of Southeast Asia Pt. Ltd., Singapore / Whitehall Books Limited, Wellington, New Zealand
10 9 8 7 6 5 4 3 2 1

ISBN 0-13-127811-8

ISBN 0-13-127829-0 {PBK}

Library of Congress Cataloging in Publication Data

Leary, Timothy Francis, date
        Changing my mind, among others.

        1. Leary, Timothy Francis. 2. Psychologists—United States—Biography. 3. Man—Addresses, essays, lectures. I. Title.
BF109.L43A37   128   81-17784

Homage to

Julien Offray de La Mettrie, 1709–51, French physician and philosopher who claimed, on the basis of personal observation, that physical activity is purely the result of the organic construction of the brain and the nervous system, and developed this theory in *Histoire naturelle de l'âme* (1745). Protests against his atheistic materialism were so strong that La Mettrie had to leave the country. He further alienated the public with *L'Homme machine* (1748), the final development of his mechanical explanation of man and the world. He lived in Berlin under the protection of his patron, Frederick the Great. His ethics, purely hedonistic, are set forth in *L'Art de jouir* (The Art of Play, 1751).

and

Christopher Columbus, genius navigator, indefatigable scientist, whose optimism, courage, interpersonal skill and sense of genetic mission produced the New Worlds in which new visions, new cultures, and new intelligence could emerge.

Contents

PART FOUR

THE POLITICS OF HUMANISM
(The successful scientist always upsets the hive)

PART FIVE

THE FUTURE OF SCIENTIFIC HUMANISM

INTRODUCTION

An Experiment in Intellectual Archeology

This book is a collection of scientific, scholarly, and political essays written over the last 33 years. The underlying theme is scientific humanism—the belief in the rapid evolution of intelligence in the human species and in the individual human being.

The Humanist strives (not always successfully) to be morally flexible, unique, changeable, open-minded, optimistic, utopian, progressive, funny, irreverent, tolerant, goofy. The Humanist chooses hopeful uncertainty rather than dogmatic past. Freedom over security. The humanist relies upon scientific intelligence for the solution of problems. The opposite of the Humanist is the person who relies on tradition and divine authority, who holds a pessimistic view of human nature.

This book is arranged in five chronological parts reflecting the interactions of these controversial libertarian ideas with the jittery custodians of our culture. Each idea is treated as archeological specimen and introduced by a commentary describing the cultural context in which it emerged. Thus we can see how the quaint psychological terms of the recent past have changed. We can watch humanist notions appear, become popularized, vulgarized (psychobabbled), and evolve in response to later events.

History cautions us that any work of art/literature/science becomes, in time, an anthropological relic like a Paleolithic stone knife—important and useful in its time, but unwieldy, primitive, even dangerous to the future unless understood in an evolutionary framework.

The researches described in this book are concerned with predictable change, metamorphosis, mobility, expansion, genetic escape.

In contrast to orthodox psychiatric and Judeo-Christian concepts that implicitly encourage dependence on authority, the aim here has been to develop a psychology that treats the human being as an independent agent with intelligent control of Hir* own neural and genetic equipment.

Part One describes early research (1946–60) that demonstrated how we humans fabricate the interpersonal-emotional realities we inhabit. These studies which demonstrate how we can understand and change our interpersonal roles were part of the "quiet revolution" in psychology accomplished by such anti-authoritarian thinkers as

---

*In order to avoid chauvinism, I use the terms "his," "man," "mankind," "he" to refer only to the male species. Where both male-and-female are referred to, the inclusive terms *hir, WoMan, humanity,* and *SHe* will be employed.

Benjamin Spock, Abraham Maslow, Rollo May, Carl Rogers, Harry Stack Sullivan. These men shared the brash, optimistic Emersonian belief in the changeability of human nature, inner-potential, self-actualization which became the Humanist Psychology.

Part Two takes us to 1961, when this Principle of Self-Determination was applied not just to behavior but to consciousness. In retrospect, does it not seem inevitable that the do-it-yourself, encounter-group, nondirective therapies of the '50s would lead to the self-administration of consciousness-expanding drugs? We shall survey the original papers on drug-induced brain-change which define the brain as the tool that carpenters the realities we experience.

In Part Three, the theory of imprinting and re-imprinting of the brain suggests how we can become producers of our own Reality Movies, direct the neural cameras, manage our bodies, use our heads. This bold step requires the personal assumption of those responsibilities formerly assigned to divinities by prescientific, superstitious people. My brain is god; your brain is too. Let's learn to practice the technologies of god with the grace, compassion and skill which the Judeo-Christian-Moslem Gods so obviously lack.

Part Four contains nine essays considering the politics of human evolution. Every survival technology naturally, instinctively struggles to perpetuate itself. Belief in centralized authority has helped get us organized to reach the present. Belief in human individuality and self-determination is also part of our genetic heritage.

It is the professional obligation of humanists to demonstrate in their lives and writings that the futures that they represent are safer and more attractive than the past that traditionalists urge us to perpetuate. This historical section illustrates the tactics used by the uneasy American establishment to harass, and thereby test, the new ideas presented in this volume.

Part Five, written from the vantage point of the future, discusses three genetic imperatives which will become the survival technologies of the 21st century—Space Migration, Intelligence Increase, Life Extension (S.M.I.^{2}L.E.). It is important to note that the inner-space explorations of the 1960's were occurring exactly during the time that our big outer-space adventures were happening. President Jack Kennedy was involved in both—no accident, really. Any sensible DNA scenario would have to plan it that way. Consciousness and intelligent narcissism surely must be expanded before our upstart species explores existence off the planet. The visions of Robert Goddard and Werner Von Braun teach us that inner launches must precede outer tripping. Our brains must master gravity before our bodies. A mass program of inner-voyaging will certainly shrivel into Ganges mysticism unless the visions can be precisely expressed in outer-space migration.

By 1982, the permanent Salyut settlements of the Soviets and the O'Neill-NASA blueprints for small High Orbital Mini-Earths (HOMEs) made it immediately practical to apply Self-Determination to construct HOME-steads aloft. We can now make our own planets (plan-its) aloft cheaper than building new cities down here. Like it or not, every new terrestrial shortage of oil, metal, jobs, hope, water, land, firewood presses us toward the escape-option, squeezes us inexorably outward (as pupal-butterfly presses against cocoon) up to the next High Frontier, where energy and raw materials are unlimited, where our winged hopes can create new fabric shells.

And by 1982 the explosion in genetics made possible—indeed, inevitable—the next area of self-responsibility: Genetic engineering. Here is the big leap in Self-Confident Singularity—we can decipher the RNA code for aging and death. We can correct chromosome dispositions towards somatic or neural inefficiency. We can innoculate ourselves against past viral strains and infect ourselves with new viral-repair agents. We can attain self-control over our own DNA. In these self-guided tours, we are working the frontiers, addressing ourselves to the most exciting options facing our species.

At the present time there are two problems facing our species—easily defined and easily solved:

1. There is an increasing number of increasingly dissatisfied people crowding this planet.

2. There is a decreasing amount of land, energy, raw materials, hope, and precise future planning.

Our politicians and political parties give us no solutions except to grab what we can and keep what we've got. Our religious leaders, similarly, do not even deign to address these two obvious challenges. Their only prescription is, understandably, to fall down on our knees and pray.

The application of human intelligence, expressed in the scientific method, is the only way that our evolution can continue. Humanism, freedom, individuality, self-knowledge, self-discovery, self-reliance, self-indulgence, self-confidence are the frontier American traits which have brought us this far. The researches described in this book were attempts to apply these Western genetic characteristics to the creation of the future.

At this moment (summer 1981) the forces of superstition and pessimism are riding high in the land. Wonderful—the choices are now made very clear. At this, the time when new visions, new hope, precise intelligence are waiting to be born, our oldest president tells us from his bully pulpit that evolution is an unproven and dubious theory. The Moral Majority (*sic*) has defined humanism, pride, self-confidence, intelligent optimism as the archenemies of their authoritarian dogmas. Good: the issues are well drawn.

This volume is offered as philosophic foundation, background support, and technical manual for those who believe in the freedom and responsibility of humanism.

PART ONE

ESSAYS IN NUCLEAR PSYCHOLOGY (The measurement of human movements and collisions in space-time)

In 1941, at age 21, I decided to become a psychologist, because, at the time, this profession appeared to be the sensible, scientific way of dealing with the classic human predicaments of boredom, ignorance, suffering, and fear.

To my young mind, it seemed logical that there could be no political-economic-spiritual solutions that were not based on the dramatic raising of:

enthusiasm
human intelligence
guilt-free happiness
individual self-confidence

From 1943 to 1946, I served as consultant psychologist in the U.S. Army Medical Corps and after the war enrolled as a graduate student at the University of California at Berkeley—which at that time was considered to have the best psychology department in the country (i.e., the world). For the first two months of graduate school, I performed routine tasks of surveillance—sitting in on the lectures of top professors, surveying their publications, collecting graduate school gossip (always the best source of information for an intelligence agent).

It was immediately apparent that the men who ran the Psychology Department were obsessed with minutiae of animal maze–learning (the analogy between students and rats was too painful to discuss openly) and uninterested in any experimentation on human behavior—especially research aimed at helping people or changing behavior.

These genial academicians had spent twenty years attaining acceptance and status by committing themselves to one or another theory of animal learning, however irrelevant they were to the fast-changing realities in the outside world.

There was, however, a new branch of "clinical" psychology which, benefiting from an enormous, sudden influx of federal money (which we later learned was CIA inspired) set up ambitious programs to train graduate students in the diagnosis and treatment of human pathology.

The conservative animal experimentors sagely complained that "clinical training" was simply teaching psychologists to become junior psychiatrists. Given the postwar prestige of Freudian psychoanalysis, however, even this subordinate association with the "couch mystique" was a matter of prestige to young psychologists.*

---

*Anthropological footnote: from 1940 to 1959, anyone who identified hirself in a social situation as a "psychologist" received a visible, delicious shudder of anticipatory fear:

In 1946, graduate interns in clinical psychology were assigned to clinics and hospitals, where they gave diagnostic tests and participated in the Grand Ritual of the Staff Conference—which interested me in that it was the High Mass of the New Religion and clearly reflected its preoccupations. At the head of the table sat the Chief Psychiatrist, flanked on either side by subordinate members of the Medical Caste. Next came the Ph.D. psychologists. At the bottom of the table clustered the Psychiatric Social Workers—usually females.

The "case" was presented. First the social worker spelled out the "patient's" social history. The psychologist then read his diagnostic testing report. In those cases where a psychiatrist had seen the "case," he contributed his impressions. Then, after a general discussion of the "case," the chief psychiatrist would pronounce a diagnosis and an administrative decision would be made about the patient: type of treatment, transfer to another ward or institution, discharge. The level of jargon was bizarre-baroque Freudian.

My first reactions of disbelief were followed by acute boredom. I sublimated my outrage with satirical remarks that made everyone laugh. Since then, I have often used humor as a philosophic tool to provide relativistic perspective.

In time my boredom turned to phobic despair. It was clear that few had much interest in the *patient's* point of view. The unfortunate human being called the "case" was treated as an abstraction around which whirled the most kinky sort of projections. Staff members routinely projected the contents of their own minds on the patient. In time, I saw the words of each clinician as strings of taffy emerging from their mouths covering the table, the floor and, at times, threatening to engulf the room. I impatiently longed for something tangible, measurable, real—to replace the speculation.

I saw then that success as a psychiatrist or clinical psychologist was in inverse proportion to the time spent in face-to-face interaction with the patient. The most prestigious and well-paid professionals spent the least time with patients and devoted the majority of their time to administration, consultation, and supervision in their offices.

It followed that if one wished to learn about the laws of

"Oooh, can you look within and spy my secrets?" Today, with 70,000 Ph.D.'s a year rolling off the assembly lines, the term "psychologist" elicits bored expectations of flaky self-importance. In the Woody Allen 1950's, "psychology" touched the same awe-change-magic that the word "drug" touched in later decades.

human behavior, it was necessary to spend no time in administration and to devote all one's time out there in the field, on the street, on the front lines. Over the last 33 years, I have tried to avoid having an office.*

During this early introduction to clinical psychology, I came to the conclusion that human behavior should be studied the same way that nuclear physicists study the behavior of atomic particles. (By contrast, Freudian orthodoxy operated with a 19th-century Newtonian thermodynamic engineering view of human personality.) To understand the behavior of human individuals, it was necessary to imitate the research techniques of 20th century nuclear physics: to create environments, cyclotrons, where human particles could be observed, recorded and measured.

A *psychlotron* is an environment, where human behavior is intensified, accelerated, charged with high-voltage: where the social-molecular structures are dissolved so that the individual's behavior and the collisions and interactions can more easily be observed and recorded.

For the last 33 years, I have been instinctively drawn to *psychlotron* places—high energy, high risk frontiers where human atoms are stripped from social bonds, free to operate according to internal gyroscopes interacting in clearly visible collisions with other free-spinning individuals. In my second year of graduate school, therefore, I used standard primitive political tactics to establish a psychlotron. I went to a popular political professor who specialized in group dynamics and asked him to sponsor a research project in the objective measurement of behavior of "patients" in groups.

To do this without medical supervision and outside the clinical environment was the exact political difficulty we faced twelve years later when we began to research drugs at Harvard without medical degrees. And as with the Harvard drug research, I solved this problem by finding a valuable ally outside the academic or medical communities—Dr. Raymond Cope, minister of the Berkeley Unitarian Church. In response to the commonsense practicality and good will of my proposal, he enthusiastically agreed to sponsor a series of group counseling sessions for members of his student congregation.

I then purchased a wire recorder (this was before tapes were

---

*Transactionalism, i.e., participant contact with subjects, is the application to psychology of the Heisenberg principle of indeterminacy. This approach is also used by ethologists who study natural behavior of animals—including humans.

invented), enlisted the collaboration of two other graduate students, and organized six counseling groups.

In 1982, it is hard to realize how eccentric and even illegal this was. We had essentially set up our own *ad hoc* clinic in which graduate students on their own time were "treating" 48 "patients" using a wildly radical technique—group therapy! In 1947, a medically trained psychiatrist considered group therapy as recklessly dangerous as requesting a group of patients to perform perilous surgical operations on each other. (In those primitive times, the unconscious was considered a primeval swamp of festering insanity).

We collected hundreds of hours of wire spools, which were transcribed by secretaries paid out of graduate-student fellowship stipends.

We considered each statement of each patient as a behavior trail, analogous to that of an electron in a cloud chamber. We attempted to classify these interactions in the same manner that nuclear physicists categorize the behavior of colliding particles, i.e., in terms of spatial coordinates: above or below, and positive (attraction) or negative (repulsion). Each statement of a patient was coded as to its effect of *putting down* or *elevating* the other person, and to its *affiliative* or *hostile* effect.

After several weeks, the validity of the scheme became obvious. We were able to code human interpersonal behavior reliably in terms of a two-dimensional grid. We were charting objectively recorded human interactions the same way a naval radar operator could track the movement of ships (see Figure 1).

We had made objective and scientific the classic ghost-in-the-machine of human psychology: *attitude.* We could now define *attitude* in the interpersonal context as the angle of approach to *another person.*

Once we had established the compass points of human interpersonal behavior, it was a simple matter to develop questionnaires that allowed therapists, diagnosticians, observers, even patients to describe their behavior in the same precise, calibrated language: "Patient X moved three points north (i.e., toward domination) in response to the therapist's southeast approach."

A breakthrough in human psychology is involved here. For the first time, interpersonal behavior of humans could be measured as objectively as nuclear-particle behavior, and *in terms of the basic parameters—spatial relationships.*

For the first time (1948) we could speak of Particle Psychol-

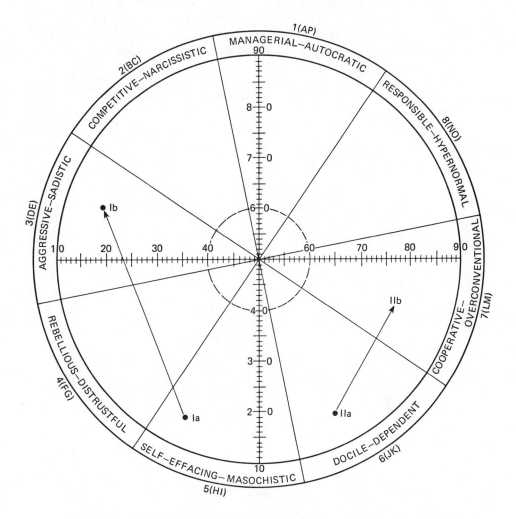

Figure 1. The tracking of the interpersonal behavior of two patients (I and II) during two group therapy sessions. Point I-a represents the mathematical summary of rated behavior of a patient during the first group therapy session. Her attitude—i.e., her measured angle of approach to others—was Self-Effacing Masochism.

Point I-b portrays her behavior during the second therapy session. She has become actively aggressive.

Point II-a represents the behavior of another patient during the first session. She was extremely Docile-Dependent. During the second session, she became much less dependent and more actively cooperative.

ogy or Nuclear Psychology—a psychology comparable to physics in that both disciplines study the movements of particles. (By 1979, the concept of personality classification in terms of one's own movements had led to such powerful concepts as swarming, population genetics, gene-pool migration, spin.)

1

The three doctorate theses resulting from the modest graduate-school research just described generated considerable interest. A new psychiatric clinic, connected with Kaiser Hospital, Oakland, California, built interpersonal diagnostic (tracking) methods into its operation. By 1957, thousands of patients had been diagnosed and treated using these approaches. Hundreds of clinics and research stations as far away as Czechoslovakia and Israel were using these methods. Even our own CIA had adopted them. Dozens of scientific papers confirmed that the Interpersonal Compass was calibrated correctly: that human interpersonal interactions could be charted as objectively as nuclear-particle collisions: and that such behaviors were of basic importance in human transactions.

In 1958, the experiments performed at the Kaiser Psychological Research Foundation (involving millions of recorded interpersonal particle collisions) were summarized in the book *Interpersonal Diagnosis of Personality.* In 1959, the *Annual Review of Psychology* called this "the most important book on psychotherapy of the year." Today, two decades later, this classic text is still actively in print.

The aim of interpersonal behavior was defined quite clearly: "To ward off anxiety and preserve self-esteem." This notion that the aim of human behavior was to maintain self-esteem—i.e., to feel good about oneself as an individual—was to become one of the major paradigms of the late 20th century. Previous theories of human destiny, all of European or Middle Eastern origin, stressed human submission to God or, in the cases of Freud and Marx, to society. This brash reference to "self-esteem," *individual* pride, was a patriotic attempt to bring American psychology in line with the Emersonian-Jeffersonian frontier ethos of our country. Previous attempts to Americanize psychology—the Horatio Alger Myth, Dale Carnegie, the John Dewey approach—attempted to encourage adjustment to the system, to the boss. Here, we state flatly that your basic responsibility is to yourself.

"Everyone makes their own interpersonal world." This was, for 1957, a radical notion. The reader is not urged to adjust to society. Adjustment-maladjustment is defined in terms of the individual, not Judeo-Christian conformity or Freudian stoicism. The advice here: Dial and tune your own behavior to get the results you want.

Consider the definitions: "Adjustment is characterized by an understanding of one's personality structure, by the development of mechanisms flexible enough to deal with a variety of environmental pressures, and by the management of one's behavioral equipment in such a way as to avoid situations where your mechanisms will be ineffective or damaged."

We present, now, an anthropological sample of a privately printed manual that outlined the clinical-technical steps in measuring human-particle collision behavior.

The tracking (i.e., diagnosis) of human behavior

The Interpersonal System of Personality, a complex combination of methods and measures for assessment of personality, is objective, employing reliable ratings of units of behavior manipulated by standardized statistical methods. The system selects for analysis those aspects of personality which concern a subject's relationship to others. The system is functional—since it is aimed at predicting interpersonal behavior in specified, crucial situations, particularly in psychotherapy.

This system is used to predict behavior. A set of sixteen interpersonal variables (i.e., the circular continuum described below) is used to categorize behavior at different levels of personality.

The interpersonal system is multi-level. It studies behavior at four levels. Level I considers how a person presents himself to or is described by others. Level II is composed of his descriptions of himself and his interpersonal relationships. Level III considers fantasy or "projective" material, and Level IV, his ego idea. Each of these general levels is divided into sublevels defined by the specific test stimulus or mode of expression. Thus, for example, dreams and waking fantasies comprise separate sublevels because they are different ways of expressing indirect, projective material.

The interpersonal expressions of the subject at all levels are scored in terms of the same sixteen spatial variables, given alphabetical code designations, and listed in a circular continuum. Figure 2 presents the sixteen-variable circle and items from the Interpersonal Check List which illustrate the meaning of each variable. An intensity dimension has been built into the circle and the check list: items increase in intensity in four steps as they move toward the perimeter of the circle.

This complex diagnostic system is designed to require no professional time or energy. The tests are administered, scored, converted into standard score indices, and plotted by technicians who need possess no psychological knowledge to produce a multilevel diagnosis of high reliability. The professional clinician is, of course, required to interpret and apply the meaning of the eight-digit code. The professional psychologist interprets the end product: but the routine summary of the diagnostic machinery is in the hands of the technical staff.

Variability Diagnosis

The essential, basic aspect of the interpersonal system is the multilevel conception which holds that personality is a relatively stable organization of different, conflicted interpersonal motives. We distinguish between three kinds of variability.

a. *Structural* (inconsistencies between conscious self-description, behavioral expression, and symbolic expression)

b. *Temporal* (inconsistencies in the same level of behavior over a time span)

c. *Situational* (differences in behavior in response to different social or environmental factors).

The multilevel structure of our model is a crude attempt to pay some respect to the complexity of human nature. Thus, once we have funneled the diffuse fluidity of human behavior into eight clusters, we next consider the relationship among these levels and measures. The organization of personality is defined (in this system) by indices expressing the kind and amount of variability or conflict among the levels and areas of personality. These interlevel relationships we call variability indices—objective, numerical indices which reflect discrepancy or concordance among the establishments of personality.

Figure 3 presents the descriptive summary points for two patients whose behavior has been diagrammed. The two summary indices place patient S in the octant 6; they thus become a simplified and numerical summary of the circular diagram. The vertical and

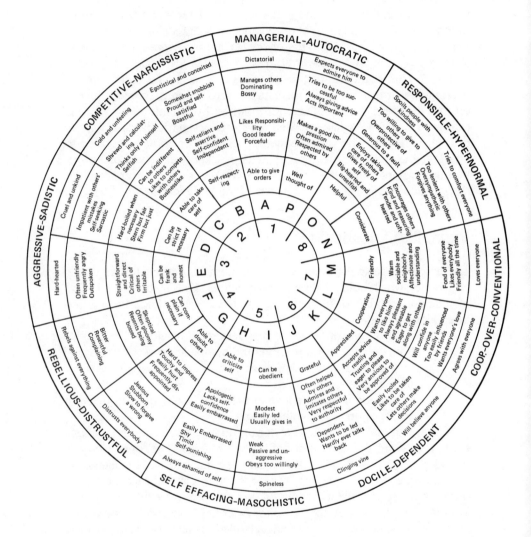

Figure 2. Interpersonal Check List illustrating the classification of interpersonal behaviors into 16 variable categories.

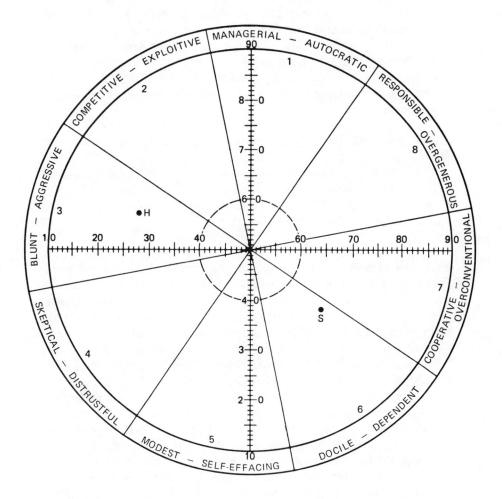

Figure 3. Multilevel diagnostic summary points for two illustrative patients.

horizontal lines represent varying discrepancies from the center point of the circle. We obtain in this manner the summary point of the patient's interpersonal behavior as rated by the 16 variables in relationship to 800 randomly selected psychiatric clinic admission patients. Our subject S is considerably more docile and dependent than the average clinic patient.

The great advantage of the circular grid is that many summary points can be graphed on the same diagram, facilitating comparison among levels of any individual's personality or among different individuals. In Figure 3, patient H claims to be friendly and docile while her private fantasies stress sadism.

Linear distance between the summary points for Level II and Level III indicates the kind and amount of private feelings which are denied conscious self-description.

These discrepancies—interpersonal or interlevel *Variability Indices*—are, in some respects, operational redefinitions of certain Freudian "defense mechanisms," since they systematically indicate the conflicts among different levels.

Worthy of historical note is that the title: "multilevel" was not new. Freud had lifted this notion from Fliess and the German Romantics in the late 19th century, but "measurement" is a psychophysical concept alien to Freudians. Every word on the Interpersonal Check List has been "measured" in a series of computer studies. These words, when emitted from a test-subject, turned out to be highly predictable "particles." If you checked yourself as being "helpful" on this list, it was possible to predict with high probability how you would check any other word. Treating "words" as emissions, the frequency and variety of which were of crucial importance to a "word-manipulating species," followed Zipf as a breakthrough in nuclear or particle psychology. Another innovative contribution is the discussion of variability —changeability as an important dimension of human behavior.

The credits were amusing. The four intelligent women who produced this book were nonprofessional high school graduates —prelude to the "humanistic" sixties in which the trade-union monopoly of the professional psychologist-psychiatrist was broken—and everyone was challenged to become hir own life-doctor.

This chapter from *Interpersonal Diagnosis of Personality* represents an important lurch in my evolution as a scientist. Written in 1955, it is an amazing forecast of what I would be writing 25 years later—and, more to the point, a precise forecast of what best-selling prophets of the Sartrian me-generation would be saying in the 1970's/1980's.

      The essay presents the concept of personal responsibility for the effects of one's behavior. Self-Determination: your moment-to-moment interpersonal signals pull, fabricate, create the personal environment you inhabit. You don't blame your parents, your race, your society. You accept responsibility for your behaviors—which in turn elicit the response you get from your world. This point of view, which seems so clichéd today, was shockingly heretical to the orthodox Freudian-Marxist determinists of the primitive 50s.

The principle of self-determination

The Interpersonal Reflex

What a person does in any social situation is a function of at least two factors: (1) set: his multilevel personality structure and (2) setting: the activities and effect of the "other" person with whom he is interacting. We determine the interpersonal meaning of any behavior by asking, "What is this person doing to the other? What kind of a relationship is he attempting to establish through this particular behavior?" The answers to these questions define the subject's interpersonal impact. For example, "He is boasting and attempting to establish superiority"; or, "He is rejecting and refusing to help." A father may employ one or 1,000 words to refuse his child's request. The mode, style, and content of his expressions may be very different, but their interpersonal effect —rejection—is the same.

In a large percentage of interactions, basic motives are expressed in an automatic reflex manner, so that they are often at variance with the subject's own perception of them. This facet of behavior, often unverbalized and so subtle as to escape articulate description, is therefore difficult to isolate and measure. Sometimes these interpersonal communications can be implicit: Grandfather talks incessantly about the lack of initiative of modern youth in order to impress others that *he* is a successful, self-made man. Grandmother talks incessantly about sickness, calamity, and death to remind others that her time may be short. Behind the superficial content of most social exchanges it is possible to determine the naked motive communications: I am wise, strong, friendly, contemptuous; as well as the concomitant messages: you are less wise, less strong, less likable, contemptible.

Jung has described the "persona" as a masklike front behind which more basic motives exist. We are dealing with similar purposive behavior, but in emphasis something more important than a social facade—closer, perhaps, to the "character armor" concept of Wilhelm Reich, or the "conversation of gestures" developed by George Herbert Mead.

How a Poignant Woman Provokes a Helpful Attitude. A patient reports to a psychiatrist a long list of symptoms (insomnia, worry, depression) and unfortunate events (divorce, unsympathetic employer, etc.). Whether her expressions are scored separately or summarized, we derive a clear picture of a JK approach—"I am weak, unhappy, unlucky, in need of your help."

The psychiatrist is under strong pressure to express sympathetic, nurturant communications. Helpless, trustful behavior tends to pull assistance; that is, JK tends to provoke ON. Further, the patient-therapist situation lends itself easily to the "needs help/offers help" relationship. There exists a tendency for the psychiatrist to express openly (or much more likely, by implication in his bearing, attitude, his very quiet competence) that he knows how the patient can be assisted. But actually, the "nurturant interpreter/trustful follower" situation exists not in what the participants *say* but in what they *do* to each other.

The Penitentiary Trains the Prisoner for Criminal Aggression. Many cultural situations have interpersonal implications so built in that a flexible, collaborative relationship is impossible. In prison psychiatry, for example, it is virtually impossible to shake off the institution's implicit contempt for the inmate. Every nonverbal cue tells the prisoner that he is a dangerous, untrustworthy outcast. The prisoner often responds by accepting the interpersonal role he is being trained for. That is, BCD pulls EFG. Long duration human relationships tend to be selective on both sides. Thus, the recidivist criminal is least anxious and most self-confident when in passive rebellion against a strong punitive authority who feeds and beats him.

Automatic role relationships function to minimize anxiety, setting up smooth-flowing reciprocal interactions. When the pattern of interpersonal reflexes breaks down or is ambiguous, considerable distress generally results—manifested in symptoms of anxiety. Some prisoners are made uncomfortable by a guard who refuses to assume the authoritative role. Symbiotic marriage partners can panic when the implicit assumptions of power, guilt, and dependence on which they rest are temporarily threatened. Factory, department store, office, university —all have complex networks of routine, unverbalized evaluation through which power, prestige, contempt, punishment, acceptance, etc., are expressed. Investigations will very likely reveal that individuals tend to select jobs and occupational roles in accord with their interpersonal techniques for anxiety reduction and self-esteem.

How Professor and Student Train Each Other. Professors are so addicted to the stereotyped teaching reflex that they often cannot inhibit the didactic response. One psychology professor's lecture developed the thesis that teachers should stimulate the student to seek answers himself: "Don't let them become dependent on you; make them think for themselves." As soon as the lecture was over, a graduate student (well trained to the dependency reflex) rushed up with a question: "In my undergraduate teaching section, the students are continually asking me to solve their personal problems and demanding answers. What shall I do?" The professor responded, "You'll always find your students tending to trap you into solving problems that they should work out for themselves. Now what *I'd* do if I were you is . . ." The verbal context of an interaction can be quite divorced from its interpersonal meaning.

How a Sullen Patient Teaches Others to Reject Him. A 30-year-old man complained of depression, general immobilization, and social isolation. After intake interviews and testing, he entered a psychotherapy group along with four other patients. All group members were strangers when they met. The interpersonal actions of the subject and fellow group members during the first eight sessions were summarized, combined into octants, and plotted on a circular profile (Figure 4).

This diagram tells us that in a group, the subject complained, demanded, accused, withdrew in a bitter, distrustful manner (FGH). His fellow patients reacted to him with critical, unsympathetic, rejecting

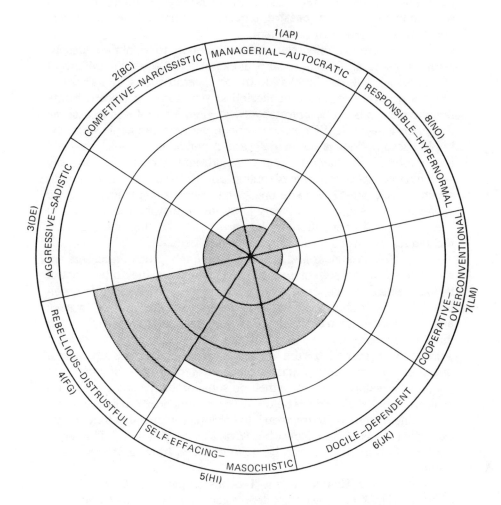

SUBJECT

Figure 4. Summary of interpersonal interactions between an illustrative subject and four fellow group members.

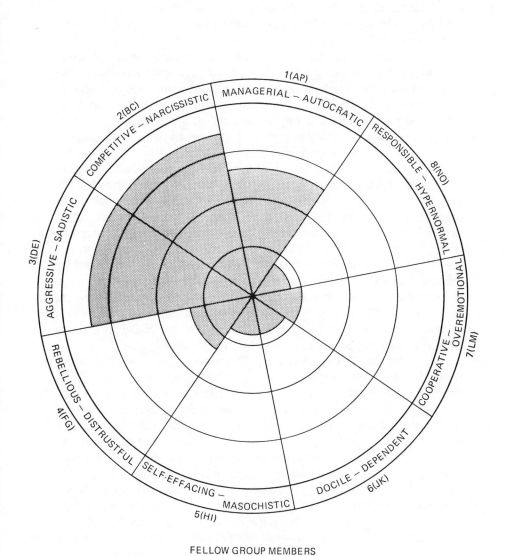

FELLOW GROUP MEMBERS

exasperation (BDE). After eight sessions in the group, the patient had virtually duplicated the suspicious, isolated pattern that had originally brought him to the clinic!

These interpersonal automatic, involuntary nature reflexes, makes them most resistant to therapeutic change. The more the psychotherapy group members tried to explain to the subject *why* he irritated them, the more he protested his feelings of injury. Later, he developed intellectual insight and cooperative, self-confident behavior, but during many months of treatment, spontaneous reactivity brought a return of the original responses.

The involuntary nature of these reflexes demands continual emphasis to keep them from slipping out of focus. This hidden dimension of behavior is so basic it is taken for granted. Consider this analogy: A physician may ask the patient to report any pertinent psychological events noticed during the previous day. The patient might remember a feeling of depression at the office, worry over bills in the evening. It is inconceivable that he could report that he conveyed by gesture, bearing, tone of voice, and verbalization a consistent message of pessimism and resentment: that the "others" he regularly interacts with have been trained to respond to him in an irritated and rejecting manner. Nor would he be able to indicate that his ability to express tender or affiliative purposes is crippled and inhibited.

Routine Reflex Patterns. The average adult is challenged, pleased, bossed, obeyed, helped, and ignored several times a day. Thus, the flexibly functioning person can demonstrate the sixteen interpersonal reflexes many times in any one day. A small percentage of individuals get "others" to react to them in the widest range of possible behaviors and can utilize a wide range of appropriate reactions. Many, however, do not react with consistent appropriateness or flexibility. One might respond to the pleasant stranger with a disapproving frown. Each subject shows a consistent preference for certain interpersonal reflexes; others are very difficult to elicit or entirely absent. Most individuals train "others" to react to them within a narrowed range of behavior patterns, and in turn show a restricted set of favored reflexes. Some show a very limited repertoire of two or three reflexes and reciprocally receive an increasingly narrow set of responses.

The individual may be quite unaware of these spontaneous tendencies—to complain to his wife, be stern with his children, boss his secretary, depend on the office manager. When he *consistently, routinely* favors certain mechanisms with one individual significantly more than chance and tends to pull certain responses from the other to a similar degree, then a role relationship exists. Most durable relationships tend to be symbiotic. Masochistic women marry sadistic men—who tend to marry women who tend to provoke hostility. Dependent men tend to seek nurturant superiors, who in turn are most secure when they have docile subordinates to protect.

Take the oversimplified example of a man who reacted to his wife with the reflex of grumbling reproach (FG) to an inappropriate extreme. His voice took on a tired, whiny quality the minute he entered the house. He could often be jolly, firm, or protective with his spouse, but as we pile up the thousands of interaction ratings, the trend towards mild complaint becomes increasingly clear. He does not *deliberately* inject the hurt, tired note in his voice, or plan the slight droop of the shoulders. He may not be aware of the continuous mild passive irritation. It might take some weeks of therapeutic exploration for him to verbalize the private feelings for his bitterness: (1) that he is a defeated genius whose wife caused his failure, (2) that he could be a success today if *she* had not persuaded him to marry and leave engineering school. More intensive analysis would, of course, trace the roots of these feelings back even further to genetic predispositions.

This man is within essentially normal limits because he maintains a reasonably flexible range of interpersonal behavior: Over time, we would see all sixteen reflexes. But he favored or overemphasized passive complaint and distrustful, realistic hesitancy. This man entered a therapy group (psyclotron) along with four other strangers. Over eight sessions, he lectured, argued, helped, cooperated, but the mechanism he spontaneously favored and manifested a significant majority of the time was passive resistance. At the same time, a summary was made of the fairly flexible interactions this man pulled from the others. The group listened to him with respect, deferred to him, accepted his help, liked him, respected him, but *on the whole,* felt a mildly critical superiority (BCD) in reaction to his grumbling approach.

In seven sessions of brief interactions, this subject succeeded in duplicating his life situation with four strangers. This man, it must be remembered, is essentially *normal.* His wife and his friends, very likely, understand and adapt with humorous (and sometimes irritable) impatience.

Patients as Diagnostic Instruments. By allowing the patient to react with others in a group therapy situation, we enable him to demonstrate, directly and openly, his repertoire of interpersonal reflexes. He tends to accomplish his *own* interpersonal diagnosis.

The therapeutic group serves as a small subsociety, a miniature world. When we ask members to rate each other's interpersonal behavior (on a checklist of the sixteen generic variables) we obtain a valuable diagnostic estimate of what each patient has done to the others. Clinicians are not supposed to admit that they like, fear, or look up to a patient; their ratings, indeed, are supposed to be divorced from personal reactions. Naive, untrained fellow patients do not "psychologize"; they generally judge each other in terms of direct reactions.

Interpersonal reflexes operate with amazing power: many maladaptive subjects can provoke the expected response from a complete stranger in a matter of minutes. Chip-on-the-shoulder defiance, docile, fawning passivity, timid, anxious withdrawal can pull the reciprocal reaction from the "other one" with unfailing regularity. Severe neurotics—with limited ranges of reflexes—are incredibly skilled in drawing rejection, nurturance, etc., from the people they deal with. In many cases, the "sicker" patient is likely to have abandoned all interpersonal techniques except one—which he handles with magnificent finesse. (Most clinicians will testify that so-called catatonic negation is a powerful interpersonal maneuver.) We say, "He trained or provoked the group members to reject him," rather than, "They rejected him." We take the subject as the focus of attention and as the focus of responsibility. But this point of view plows headlong into the most cherished beliefs of Western philosophy—from Sophocles (who stresses fate) to the modern mental hygienists (who overemphasize parental behavior). The average man bases his security and self-esteem on the traditional procedure of externalizing blame. It is easy to accept that the successful, self-made person makes the grade and that humans strive and bargain for the interpersonal goals reflected in half the spectrum—independence, power, popularity, affection. It is often less comprehensible that humans should actively seek the other half of the circular continuum—dependence, weakness, distrust, and self-effacing modesty.

How Two Human Beings Got What They Bargained For. A patient poignantly reports: "I want a dependent, feminine mate, but my three ex-wives were bossy, exploitive tyrants." At the conscious level this man may "want" a feminine girl, but his behavior—immobilized, distrustful, and masochistic—forces the most neutral woman into exasperated activity.

Another patient states, "I want a strong, successful husband to take care of me; but all I attract are penniless artists and dreamy bookworms." This woman may consciously wish for a strong husband; but the strongest man would feel smothered and alienated by her automatic, deeply ingrained mothering reflexes—to which dependent men are drawn with mothlike fascination. What human beings *consciously* wish is often quite at variance with the results their reflex patterns automatically create for them. Voluntary intentions, resolutions, even insights are feeble compared to the ongoing 24-hour-a-day involuntary interpersonal reactions.

Why do human beings limit their social machinery and provoke a restricted set of narrowed-spectra reactions from others? Why do some individuals have no ability for realistic, modest self-criticism and compulsively express only narcissistic self-enhancing mechanisms? Why do others cling to retiring modesty and eschew self-confidence? Most puzzling of all (to the Western mind): Why do some masochistically court interpersonal humiliation—doggedly provoking rejection and isolation?

Harry S. Sullivan defines personality as the pattern of interpersonal responses employed to reduce anxiety, ward off disapproval, and maintain self-esteem. In general, humans experience less anxiety in a familiar situation, when employing familiar responses. Reciprocal relationships with crucial "others" develop quite naturally. The more anxiety-provoking the individual's world—particularly his parental home—the more likely he is to select the familiar, narrow, certain, response, and to avoid promising but uncertain potentialities. But the more an individual restricts his actions to one narrow sector of the interpersonal spectrum, the more he restricts the social environment. The man who continually employs submissive reflexes tends to train people to boss him and thus discourage people from looking to him for forceful leadership. The submissive man's interpersonal world tends to become more and more lopsided, putting pressure on him to obey and not command. He thus comes to a restricted but stable relationship with his environment.

Reciprocal Relations Are Probable, Not Inevitable. Aggression *usually* breeds counteraggression. Smiles *usually* win smiles. Tears *usually* provoke sympathy. In specific cases, however, aggression can win tolerant smiles, tears can provoke curses. If you walk up and aggressively shove a stranger, the largest percentage will mirror your aggression—and probably shove back. Your counterresponse then becomes the issue. You might apologize, or retreat, but your statistically probable response is to shove back, perhaps harder. *Interpersonal reflexes tend to initiate or invite reciprocal interpersonal responses from "others" that lead to a repetition of the original reflex.*

A normal, fairly flexible person can use any interpersonal response the situation calls for. He is less committed to (and less skillful) in the use of any *particular* reflex. So the sicker you are, the more power you have to determine the relationships you have. A maladjusted person with a crippled set of reflexes tends to overdevelop a narrow range of one or two interpersonal responses expressed intensely and often. *When two individuals interact, the "sicker" person determines the relationship.*

We meet here a lowest-common-denominator process, a Gresham's law of interpersonal collisions. Sick people control the interpersonal interaction. The "sicker" (i.e., the more maladaptively rigid), the more power to determine the nature of the relationship. Invariably all normal social games stop when someone acts inappropriately. In social situations, this dilemma is solved by simply avoiding the "scene maker": "We'll never invite *her* over again."

In politics, however, the situation is more ominous. A country is a closed system, and you can't avoid the troublemakers —particularly since they usually have the weapons! Throughout most of human history, countries have been controlled by violent, suspicious, unpleasant men whose behavior would be considered criminal or psychotic if expressed in situations that they could not control by force. Only in the Western democracies can a precarious system of checks and balances prevent the reciprocal interpersonal process of one bad turn invites another.

3

The following essay, originally titled "The Diagnosis of Behavior and the Diagnosis of Experience" and written as a chapter for a book on psychodiagnosis, became the first systematic attempt to define a psychology that was methodologically and philosophically coordinate with nuclear physics. The essay begins by applying basic principles of modern physics (relativity and Heisenberg indeterminancy) to the study of human behavior—defined as movements in space-time. It then proceeds to "resolve" the classic philosophic paradoxes of mind/body, inner/outer, art/science, subjective/objective.

In psychology, the classic polarity of inner-subjective and outer-objective can be solved in the same way as in the physical sciences: through a continuum of visibility that runs from nuclear-particle behavior to chemical-molecular to microscopic to macroscopic. Traditional divisions of philosophy are redefined in terms of inner (i.e., neurological) and outer (neuromuscular) behavior. The essay then proceeds to discuss methods for measuring movements in space. Ways of classifying and measuring "inner changes within the nervous system are mentioned (but detailed discussion is postponed to Part Two).

By 1981, the remarkable explosion of research in psychopharmacology, microgenetics, brain-localization, and the increased sophistication of our classification of the circuits, levels, and stages of neurological evolution demonstrated the prescience of this early, primitive essay.

Basic philosophic principles for a science of human behavior (ethology) and of human experience (neurology)

I am convinced of the need for a science of psychology that is existential and transactional. By *existential* I mean a concentration on flexible concepts and methods that grow out of the unique changing situation. By *transactional* I refer to an open collaborative attitude between the psychologist and the person studied. Exactly how can post-Einsteinian ingenuity be applied to human problems? How can we use our brains to do good, to do good well, and to do good *measurably* well?

1. Why not study natural events as they occur, rather than artificial situations (e.g., tests, experiments) arranged in our offices?

2. Why not use a conceptual language arising from the data, rather than imposing upon the situation our own favorite, prefabricated variables? We should be more flexible and eclectic in selecting concepts, recognizing the semantic "flimsiness" of verbal abstractions.

3. Since behavioral transactions are continually changing, why not continue to collect natural records throughout the term of the transaction? Why not expect our techniques and concepts to change as our subject matter changes?

4. Since behavioral transactions are not standardized, but always unique, why do we routinely rely on our own tests? Why not let the natural transaction produce its own records, which we can measure and interrelate? If and when the need for standardized tests grows collaboratively out of this natural situation, why not construct, revise, or design a measuring instrument for this unique situation?

5. Why ignore or blur the difference between consciousness and behavior? Why not develop maps, models, and measures for describing inner events and relate them to separate models and measures for describing external behavior? Imposing our favorite stan-

dards, concepts, and symbols on the situation is a form of intellectual narcissism that Western science has held up as the ideal. I am implying rather a collaborative adaptation, a yielding to the unique data, a calculated and sensitive passivity to idiosyncratic facts. I suggest we select from the enormous storehouse of available verbal abstractions those that seem to fit the human situation we deal with. Let the situation determine the variables.

Can we make our endeavor transactional, i.e., emotionally realistic? We must treat our fellow man as what SHe is, a human being piloting a 30-billion-cell brain, and not as an object to be dissected, manipulated, controlled, predicted.

The problem we study should not grow out of our own professional preoccupations, but should rather be a collaborative decision between the subject and ourselves. The patient helps define the variables. When feasible and relevant, the subject should help design and construct the record-collecting devices or test forms.

The subject should be treated as the phenomenological equal of the psychologist in the collaborative research. The patient, after all, is the world's leading authority on his own life and the transactions in which he is involved. If we depersonalize patients, they will depersonalize us back. If we keep secrets from them, they will keep secrets from us. In the sort of research I am endorsing, subject and therapist, collaborators in the joint research agree on goals, and then both work to meet the forecasted standards.

We each live an inner life of consciousness and an outer life of behavior. Consciousness is the blueprint for action. What we rarely are aware of, we rarely do. People will share their inner blueprints with you when it is reasonable, feasible, and relevant *to their interests* to do so. They are eager to collaborate, but reluctant to yield.

The Philosophy of Internal and External

Western psychology has never satisfactorily resolved the tension between internal-subjective and external-objective phenomena. We have consistently imposed the method, language, and goals of the external upon the internal continuum. The two can be related only if their difference is kept clear. First, we must distinguish between two different approaches to reality.

Science is the study of movements, behavior, events external to the nervous system; the study of recorded movements and the communications of these movements to others. *Art* is the study of experience, events registered by communication systems within the body—and the communicating of these experiences to others. Art can be just as precise, disciplined, systematic as the symbol systems of external science.

Existential-transactional therapy requires that the psychologist teach the patient to be a scientist in observing his behavior and an artist in describing his experience.

Failure to distinguish between the recorded external and the neurally experienced internal leads to a variety of confusions. Only external events (recorded behavior) can become part of a scientific (game) contract. Internal events (sensory, somatic, cellular, molecular experience) require an explicit, artistic contract between the "one-who-turns-others-on" and the "one-who-is-to-be-turned-on." The patient must become an artist who cares enough about the psychologist to turn-him-on to his experience.

When we set out to study consciousness and such elusive altered states as ecstasy, there is the observer's "subject matter" and there is the subject's "reality," and usually these have no relation. The psychiatrist may see hebephrenic psychosis, while the subject may be experiencing hedonic ecstasy. The outside observer has an entirely different view from the experiencing person. The psychiatrist asserts it a "fact" that the subject sat in a catatonic state for two hours, refusing to talk; the subject knows the "truth" to be that he was spinning far out of space-time into an ecstatic dance of neurons which made words inadequate and irrelevant. Of course, both are "right." But the conflict in perspective leads the patient to feel misunderstood, and the psychologist to feel frustrated. Observer logic and neurologic cannot communicate; so the patient is committed to the mental hospital.

Science needs languages and measurement methodologies for external movements in space-time. Art develops detailed languages and methodologies capable of paying respect to the flowing complexity of the internal, the countless levels of neurological decoding, the many levels of consciousness.

In order to develop a science of behavior, our present schemata are inefficient because they confuse internal-external. They jumble together the evaluations of the experiencing scientist, with narrow measurements of the subject's behavior. For example: three Parisian behavioral diagnosticians, André, Marcel, and Pierre, walking through the Bois de Boulogne, run across an undressed couple making lively movements on the grass. André, age 6, exclaims, "Look, they are fighting." Marcel, a sophisticated 8, replies, "Oh, no, André, they are making love." Pierre, a true Parisian at 10, adds, "Yes, and very badly too." Empirical studies of psychiatric diagnosis suggest a similar difficulty in labeling and evaluating behavior in experiential terms.

Classification of Space-Time Elements of Behavior: The Proximity Option

The first step in diagnosing behavior is to determine where the subject spends his time, how long, how frequently, and with whom. Location in space-time is a relatively straightforward task and is basic to any psychological evaluation.

The most direct measures of interpersonal behavior would be based on continuous recordings of movements. For about one-tenth the cost of psychoanalytic sessions, one could tape twelve electrodes the size of a dime to one's body and obtain patterned read-outs of one's muscular behavior that would produce profiles of one's behavior so unique, so precise as to be embarrassing. A behavioral fingerprint. There is no one in the world who uses throat plus hip plus hand-muscle movements like you. Psycho-physiologists don't provide us with these mirror-measurements because we're not ready to learn this much about ourselves—yet. So for practical diagnostic purposes it is useful to collect observational samples of behavior. For a two-week period in 1962 I carried a kitchen timer with me throughout the day. On waking in the morning I would set it to ring every ten minutes and continued to reset it for ten-minute intervals until retiring in the evening. The bell allowed a time-sample of my movements in space-time during the day. At each shrill jangle I would enter on a sheet: (1) the time, (2) the place, (3) a description of my behavior, (4) my posture, (5) number of others present, (6) posture of others, (7) a code of my behavior according to a game-classification (see Figure 5).

Such summary sheets reveal with humiliating clarity my behavioral characteristics during this period. I note that five times more units were spent with daughter than son (Oedipal factors?); 60% of my posture involved a chair (chairman behavior? power motives?); 41% of the time was spent alone (introversion? alienation?).

A very powerful and ridiculously simple tool is thus available to the person interested in self-discovering. Humanist diagnosis involves the subject studying hir own behavior. This leads to the practical conclusion: To change your behavior, start by changing your space-time locations. How you park your auto-mobile body. My interpersonal relations could easily be changed by spending more time with my son, more time sitting on the floor looking up at others, and so on. (Changes in consciousness must go along with alterations of behavior to avoid robotization.)

The diagnosis of interpersonal behavior is tremendously facili-tated by the space-time location system. Here again we ignore tempting variables and focus simply on the basic questions: What space do they share? What time do they share? We thus define a powerful variable we might call intimacy, commitment, involvement, attitude, *i.e.,* angle of approach. We might hazard a definition of love as the amount of space-time shared.

The basic interpersonal issue is how much space-time will you share with another? Your office? Home? Bedroom? Body? What kind of time will you share? Day or night? By appointment only? The fact that the husband and wife spend thirty years together day and night is considered much more important than the emotional game they play (fighting, submitting, cooing, dominating).

If you want to change someone's behavior—share space-time with hir. Your space-time is the most valuable and potent instrument you have. If you understand this simple principle, you have attained a liberating direction of your life. Following this hypothesis we should

Figure 5.

Time	Place	Movements	Posture	Others Present	Other's Movements	Other's Posture	Movements Indexed According to Game
9:30	Bed	Sleeping	Lying	0			Body maintenance
9:40	Bathroom	Washing	Standing	0			Body maintenance
9:50	Bedroom	Dressing	Standing	0			Body maintenance
10:00	Kitchen	Cooking	Standing	4	Eating	Sitting	Body maintenance
10:10	Kitchen	Cooking	Standing	4	Eating	Sitting	Body maintenance
10:20	Bedroom	Dressing	Standing	0			Body maintenance
10:30	Car	En route to church	Sitting	3	En route to church	Sitting	Religion
10:40	Church	Listening	Sitting	35	Listening	Sitting	Religion
4:00	Son's room	Watching TV	Sitting	1	Watching TV	Sitting	Recreation
4:10	Son's room	Watching TV	Sitting	1	Watching TV	Standing	Recreation
4:20	Daughter's room	Helping with homework	Standing	1	Homework	Sitting	Intellectual

expect that mother-child relationships (nine months of internal body sharing) and marital relationships (extended duration of internal body sharing) are the most potent change situations. College lectures and doctor-patient interviews are the least potent. This suggests that if you can't "mother" or marry them, the best way to influence behavior is to engage in reciprocal home visits or meet regularly in extra-work locations (bars, restaurants, beaches). The most successful programs for dealing with social "problems," like Alcoholics Anonymous, scrupulously avoid the power-loaded environment of the scheduled office interview. The first functional issue in behavior change is presence. Will the patient continue to come? How can we change him if he won't share space-time with us?

In the prison, space-time factors become dramatically obvious. Consider a young "delinquent" sentenced to prison at age 19. Who is going to shape his behavior? Other prisoners with whom he shares cell, meal, table, shop bench, yard time (and often body space). Next to other convicts, he will share most time with guards. The middle-class professional calls the convict into the prison clinic and spends thirty to forty minutes a week with him. According to the space-time formula, such well-intentioned interventions are pitifully limited.

The space/time (proximity) option implies that we should tell dissatisfied persons to hang out with people whom they emulate. Be a reality groupie. Tested by 4 billion years of unicellular evolution, the proximity principle works. You become like (absorb the characteristics of) the organisms you associate with. This is the unfailing law of personal reality-creation. Imagine, for example, the change in your life if you were to hang out for three days with the President or the Pope or Elizabeth Taylor. Result #1: you would become a minor celebrity yourself.

Proximity determines your *Preality*—the reality you prefer, pre-fab, program. Think of your body as a *Star Trek* spaceship which you constantly propel into situations where no HuMan has gone before. But Preality is not limited to physical proximity. Electric communication tremendously increases our Preality options. If you could pick up the phone and talk to the President or the Pope or Elizabeth Taylor anytime you wished, the effects on your Preality would be profound.

Our Preality options are limited by time. The change-agent simply cannot share the amount of time necessary to alter the movements of clients. Hours on the couch are an inefficient and ineffective ploy. The behavior-changer's role thus becomes that of a navigational consultant helping the dissatisfied person understand and get control of Hir own proximity movements.

Measuring Movements

When our three youthful French diagnosticians leave the Bois de Boulogne and report to the folks back home, no records exist of the movements they observed. Their report is subjective. What exists is their memory. This points up a basic issue, often overlooked. From the scientific point of view, we never study raw behavior—a jumble of observed movements in the grass—only records of behavior. We observe movements, but we measure and index records.

There are four kinds of records of behavior:

1. Records of muscle movements, physiological or cinematographic.
2. Records of vocal movements (tape recordings).
3. Nonverbal artifactual records of behavior (Greek vases, drawings, things made).
4. Records of verbal behavior (written or spoken).

Since 1955 I have been developing schemata for counting and measuring records of natural behavior. Behavior can be described in terms of indices based on objective counts. A tape recording of verbal behavior during a ten-minute period yields up one hundred indices (counts, not ratings) which can be charted as they vary over time. The molecular units are simple counts. How many words spoken? How many references to self? How many to mother? Interpersonal collisions are charted by comparing the patterns of participants sharing the same space-time.

The comparisons of the simplest counted indices provide revealing evidence of the interchange. Figure 6 presents verbal movements made by a patient and therapist during twelve hours of psychotherapy. Notice that the patient refers to herself only 10% of the time during the first session and continues to avoid herself as subject until the 9th session. From this time on, her verbal noises refer to herself at least 50% of the time.

When we consider the therapist's profile, a more meaningful pattern emerges. Notice the extreme discrepancy. In the first session, the therapist is concentrating on little else than the patient (87%). Her low indices now take on greater significance. She refuses to discuss his topic—her. The therapist is not following her conversational lead.

This measure of the free natural movements of persons sharing space and time are invariably revealing, obvious, simple to index, and loaded with relevant meaning.

Notice that we score and index the therapist's behavior as well as the patient's. Most psychologists routinely rely on tests and experi-

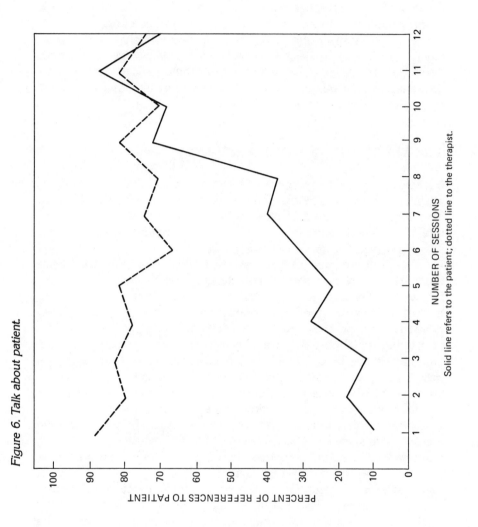

Figure 6. Talk about patient.

NUMBER OF SESSIONS

Solid line refers to the patient; dotted line to the therapist.

PERCENT OF REFERENCES TO PATIENT

ments that measure the movements of only one member of the transaction—not very democratic. Whenever feasible and reasonable, we collect records from all participants—in free, natural recordings. Patients, clients, subjects are diagnosing us professionals all the time. It is only good sense to include the patient's diagnoses of us.

The subject-object, doctor-patient relationship is undercut. Figure 1 ruthlessly profiles the movements of both participants without distinction of role or status. The approach automatically forces us to recognize that all our contexts are interpersonal and that we always study a patient-in-hir-interpersonal-field.

The Diagnosis of Consciousness

Consciousness is energy received by structure. Structure is energy in transitional state. There are as many levels of consciousness as there are neurological, sensory, anatomical, cellular, molecular, and atomic structures within the human body—a galaxy of communication systems, and energy patterns, being sent and received.

When a psychologist sets out to define levels of consciousness, SHe usually comes up with mental abstractions that tell only about hir own trip. Thus, Freud defines the conscious as routine, conventional, normal awareness; the unconscious as unthinkable, naughty (repressed); the superego as highly valued. Freud is simply listing symbols of differing social meaning. Such listings differ from culture to culture. Our knowledge of consciousness, a biochemical process, must be based on our understanding of neurochemical process.

Before the discovery of the microscope, medicine was based on crude macroscopic observation. Before the discovery of neurotransmitter chemicals, psychology and psychiatry were in the same state. We are now able to define different levels of consciousness in terms of the neurotransmitters which produce them. We can study them systematically, and replicate our observations.

Psychological diagnosis (except in the most administrative sense) cannot be carried out unless the diagnostician is aware of the level of consciousness (or combinations of levels) of the other. The diagnostic question is: "Where is your head at?"

At our present crude and primitive level of understanding it is appropriate to consider eight levels of consciousness-intelligence.

1. Autonomic nervous-system: mediating physiological satis-
factions and warnings (pain-somatic-pleasure)
2. Mid-brain: mediating mammalian emotion, aggression,
territorial instincts, power, security
3. Left-brain (dominant hemisphere): mediating thinking,
manual dexterity, language, symbolic learning, manufacture
4. Domestication-socialization circuits: mediating cultural behavior, sex-role-impersonation, moral-ethical behavior necessary for acceptance by society
5. Right-brain and sensory-somatic circuits: mediating awareness of body-function, rhythm, pattern, erotic-hedonic, aesthetic behavior
6. Meta-programming circuits: allowing consciousness of the
brain as a bio-electric loom, fabricating realities
7. Neurogenetic circuits: allowing consciousness of Brain-
RNA-DNA communication and direct deciphering of genetic
blueprint
8. Frontal-lobe circuits: permitting direct awareness of and
communication with electronic-atomic information, e.g.,
brain-computer linkups

These levels are listed in order of the age, speed, power,
complexity, expansiveness, and planful wisdom of the energy structure.

Notice that each level of awareness can be *produced*. Each of
these neural circuits can be turned on by neurotransmitter chemicals
—naturally produced by or introduced into the body.

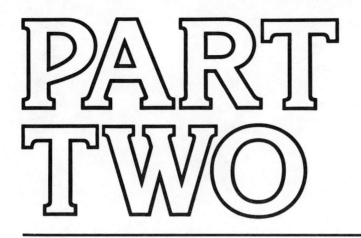

PART TWO

How to Change Your Brain

In 1960–61, a group of some 35 professors, instructors, and graduate students organized what later became the Harvard Psychedelic Research Project. Core members of this influential task force included Walter Houston Clark, Houston Smith, Richard Alpert, Gunther Weil, Ralph Metzner, Walter Pahnke, Aldous Huxley, Alan Watts, George Litwin, Frank Barron. Among the part-time participants and advisors were Allen Ginsberg, William Burroughs, Arthur Koestler, Ken Kesey, Andrew Weil, Stanley Krippner, Al Hubbard, Gordon Wasson, Gerald Heard, Charles Olson, Jack Kerouac, Neal Cassady, Ken Babbs.

Vectored into the attitude of this extraordinary company were scientific enthusiasm, scholarly fervor, experimental dedication. Statistical morale was consistently high because the numbers looked so good!

Over 400 "subjects" shared high-dosage psychedelic experiences with the researchers in an atmosphere of esthetic precision, philosophic inquiry, inner search, self-confident dignity, intellectual openness, philosophic courage, and high humor. The historical impact of this "swarm" of influential scholars has not yet been recognized by the still-timid press—popular or scientific. The "Bloomsbury biographies" await the next generation.

The experimental methods and attitudes used were more important than the drugs. These neurological experiments were the first wide-scale, systematic, deliberate application to human behavior of the relativistic theories of particle behavior. Our research picked up precisely where the giant founders of experimental psychology —Wilhelm Wundt, Gustav Fechner, William James, Edward Titchener —left off a long generation before. Our aim, like theirs, was the precise correlation of objective-external differences with internal conscious reactions.

Forgotten in the later hysteria of the 1960's was the exquisite design of the early Harvard experiments. Rarely in the short history of psychology was such elegant, complex, socially influential research conducted! At the same time that the CIA was furtively dosing unwitting Harvard students for purposes of control and destruction, we were operating with the books wide open. No secrets, careful record keeping, pre-post testing. Triple-blind designs, total collaboration, the intensive training of "guides." The extensive publication of results in scientific journals—including that impressive model of scholarly innovation we called the *Psychedelic Review.*

From the first we were preoccupied with the classic question: Who gets to go? Who can select the brain-drug option?

Our first answer as scientists was simply to publish our results and let individuals, in dialogue with society, wrangle over the answer. But it was clear, immediately, that every pressure group wished the control-decisions to be made by itself. Physicians insisted that only those with M.D.'s . . . police said no one . . . the older wished drugs kept from the younger.

Our second answer was that any and every informed adult democratic American should decide who and what to put in hir own body. The question: Who should take acid? was a repeat of the familiar, Who should have sex with whom? Who can smoke nicotine? Use alcohol? Wear bikinis? Drive a pleasure car? Transmit radio waves? In democracies, these personal decisions are made by individuals and cannot be ceded to officials, too eager to meddle in individuals' affairs.

At Harvard, these decisions were not made quickly. Many of our advisors urged that the drugs should remain exclusive. Gerald Heard, of blessed memory, was the most outspoken elitist: "These sacraments are powerful tools for the guild of philosophers." On the other side of the debate was Allen Ginsberg, the crusader for democratization, even socialization, of the drugs. Ever the worrying, nagging revolutionary, Allen howled his 1950's anarchic chant—"Turn on the world!"

There was a middle position: Play ball with the Hive Establishment. Stay on government or institutional payrolls (with tenure) and reassure the commissars that psychedelic drugs can somehow produce more efficient, well-adjusted, serene soviet workers. Use the drugs to advance our positions in the bureaucracy. On to HEW! On to Stockholm!

Curiously, the Harvard group never even considered this "mature" position. The most influential of our number were freelance gentlemen-scholars not dependent on any bureaucracy: Huxley, Alpert, Metzner, Heard, Ginsberg, Olson, Leary, Clark. And with few exceptions, our younger graduate students made the courageous decision to work outside the academic system. Another thought-provoking fallout from the Cambridge research: almost none of the graduate students "grew-up" to become conventional, tenured, academic pensioners.

As the world came to know, our 1963 decision was to expand our experimental design from selected laboratory samples of hundreds to field studies involving millions. We human ethologists, activist anthropologists, left the Ivy Tower to live with the domesticated primates.

The major theme of this book, repeated in every chapter, is neurologic, or neurophysics—the "scientizing" of internal experiences which, in the pre-scientific past, have been called psychological, spiritual, mystical, visionary, subjective, mental, sensory, esthetic-erotic, emotional, or religious.

From the first paper in 1946, my obsession has been to objectify inner experiences, to demystify the software of human existence. How? By relating changes in external behavior, systematically and lawfully, to changes in the brain. Why? To give the individual, the Human Singularity, power over Hir own internal experiencing (i.e., Hir brain) and of Hir external behavior.

This required that we work the tissue frontiers, the membrane borders where the External traffics with the Internal; where the outside world interfaces the antennae of the nervous system. For example, when we gave 100 micrograms of LSD to a subject (often one of ourselves), we were observing the effects of this measurable stimulus administered in a specified external setting on the receptive nervous system. We could not "see" the changes in the brain (yet), but we could infer them during the acid-trip by measuring reactions in the form of questionnaires, reports, behavior. And, on the broader social scale, we could observe the effects on American culture of 7,000,000 people dropping acid. We observed the effect on those who tripped and those who did not—and the collision between the two swarms.

In pursuing this goal of relating external stimuli to reports about internal-neural change, we were, paradoxically enough, following the *most* orthodox tradition in psychology (see Figure 7). For performing experiments which the forgotten founders of scientific psychology would have understood and applauded, we were thrown out of Harvard and subjected to the Semmelweis Treatment.

Current psychological priesthoods ignore the fact that the profession of psychology was originated by Gustav Theodor Fechner, a physicist who recognized that the key to understanding human nature was the relationship between external stimuli and the brain.

Scientific attempts to bridge the external and the internal were begun by Sir Isaac Newton, a recognized, eclectic master of the sciences of his day. When the University of London was closed for two years (1664–66) during the plague, Newton "withdrew" from the outside world and discovered the laws of gravitation, the calculus, and the theory of the light spectrum. Shortly thereafter, Newton lost interest in measuring external events and turned most of his energies "towards alchemy, theology and history, particularly problems of chronology." In other words, at the peak of his scientific triumphs,

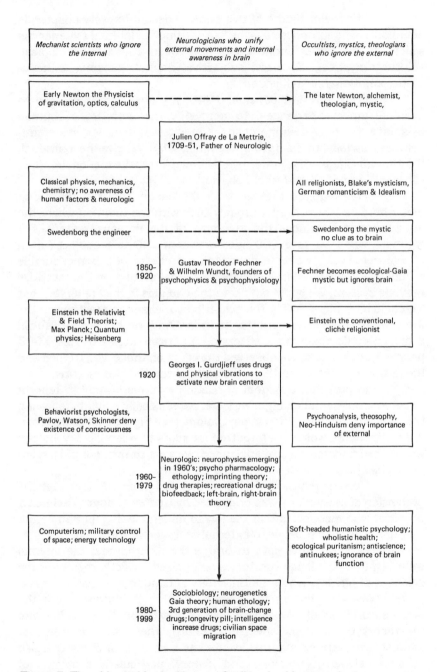

Figure 7. The old mind-body dilemma finally solved by neurologic.

Newton became a "head," a student of the inner spiritual world—or in modern terms, a neurologician. Modern physicists do not dwell on this dramatic life-change in their hero.

After Newton's attempt to relate the external-material and the internal-spiritual, physics and chemistry became mechanistic. German idealism (Immanuel Kant), British mysticism (William Blake), German Romanticism (including Schopenhauer's renovation of oriental passivity) reacted with revulsion from the scientific and tended to deny the importance, relevance, or even the existence of external movements. Thus the brilliant significance of Fechner's attempts to apply the rigor of mechanistic and mathematical science to the richness of the subjective-inner-neurological.

Since the book you are now reading (and my life) is a faithful, dutiful, follow-up to the work and life of Fechner, it may be useful to summarize this philosophic giant's extraordinary career.

Gustave Theodor Fechner (1801–87) became professor of physics at Leipzig in 1834, but ill health forced him to leave in 1839. His "illness" was clearly neurological or psychosomatic. He lay in bed for a year, unable to see, communicate, or locomote. This "sensory-social deprivation" ended one day when he rose, walked to the garden, looked around, and announced that all life was a unity. The rest of his career was devoted to "scientizing" the internal ineffable. Two of his most important books were *Zend-Avesta* (1851) and *Elementen der Psychophysik* (1860). He maintained that life is manifested in all objects in the universe.*

Note that the origins of scientific psychology were called psychophysics; that Fechner wrote a book on psycho-esthetics. The importance of these concepts has been ignored by the mechanistic psychological bureaucracies that have domesticated psychology for the last 60 years. The book you hold in your hand cannot be understood unless you grasp that the recent history of philosophy-science is nothing less than the ancient struggle to relate body and mind, i.e., the external-mechanistic with the internal-neurological.

Brass-instrumented laboratories popped up in Germany, England, and America. Psychology was called "introspectionism." The subject used in experiments was a "trained introspectionist," i.e., one who could purify hir mind of extraneous thought and concentrate on "J.N.D.'s" (Just Noticeable Differences) in external stimuli. Which

---

*This statement is a brilliant anticipation of the Gaia theory proposed by Lovelock and Margulis in 1978, and of the exobiological researches that were to transform science in the late 20th century.

weight felt heavier? What were the discriminated units of perceived taste, smell, kinesthetic sensitivity? Sensational psychology. But during the 1920's, Ivan Pavlov and John Broadus Watson glorified raw-radical mechanistic behaviorism and denied the existence of consciousness as a scientific datum. At the same time (and these polarities seem to be perfectly synchronized according to laws of cyclical development), Freud and his diverse followers focused on consciousness and unconsciousness.

Socialism, communism, and liberal-rationalism tended to stress the material. Right-wing thinkers stressed the romantic-spiritual. The caricature extremes of this polarity is illustrated by Hitler—a romantic vegetarian, a student of the occult, who believed in race, blood, soul, genetic-chauvinism, social Darwinism, destiny, drugs, vision. And on the other side, Stalin who killed 20,000,000 in the name of dialectical materialism, socialism, and economic progress, and Mao who killed 40,000,000 for the same cause.

By 1960, both the psychoanalytic and the socialist-materialist dreams began to fade. Psychophysics boomed back with a bang—although now called *neurophysics*, more commonly known as the "head-trip." Almost everyone began popping brain-change pills to alter moods, perspectives, realities. From middle-class Valium addicts, to "reward-yourself-with-a-light-beer-after-work" drinkers to pot-heads, over 80,000,000 Americans caught on that brain function can be changed by one simple behavior—put a specified chemical into your body.

Predictably enough, most of those who used drugs during the 1960's and 1970's glorified the drugs and raved incoherently about inner experiences, but failed to realize that the brain was the key. The very term "consciousness-expanding" (or "consciousness-altering") drug is a primitive, prescientific concept. The precise terminology is "brain-change-drug." We often preferred the term "brain-*reward*-drug." These verbal distinctions are not petty or pedantic; the Brain is the key. The Brain is the source. The Brain is God. Everything that humans do is Neuroecology.

4

In the fall of 1959, I taught behavioral psychology at the University of Copenhagen by day, and by night learned experiential psychology in the port-town's psychlotrons. Eighteen months later, respectably perched at Harvard, I received a letter from a friend, a professor of psychology in Denmark: Copenhagen had been selected as host city for the 1961 convention of the International Association of Psychology. My friend confided that Danish psychology was suffering from an inferiority complex in relation to medical psychiatry, and that the Psychology Department fervently hoped that the international congress would establish the credibility and respectability of psychology —thus resulting in increased federal funding.

The conference was scheduled in smorgasbord style —visiting psychologists had their choice of some 20 seminars or presentations at any time—except for the first day, which was devoted to three general convocations. Could I help in suggesting keynote speakers for the three plenary sessions? Sure thing, Bjorn.

We quickly agreed on a slam-bang opening day. The conference would open in the morning with a lecture by Harvard Professor Harry Murray—elegant, courtly, romantic, high cultural dean of personality psychology. For the afternoon plenary, my suggestion of Aldous Huxley was enthusiastically accepted. The distinguished British author was a favorite of the anglophile Danes who knew him as sophisticated novelist. (As it turned out, the genial Danes were unaware that Huxley's recent books were devoted to consciousness-altering drugs.)

The evening plenary session, chaired by me, focused on new methods of psychotherapy. In addition to my major lecture, there would be contributions by my brilliant, innovative friend-mentor Frank Barron, who had introduced me to the use of psychedelic drugs. Also scheduled was Richard Alpert, my partner in the Harvard Psychedelic Drug Project.

A few weeks before the conference, Professor Murray walked into my Harvard office with the congress schedule in his hand, chuckling: "You've subverted this sedate, boring conference into a wild bohemian drug session, haven't you?" I smiled and nodded. "In that case," replied the suave Professor Murray, with a twinkle in his eye, "I guess you better guide me through one of your visionary trips. I can't be left behind by romantic-literary upstarts like you and Huxley." And so it came to pass that Professor Murray came to my home and, propelled by psilocybin mushrooms, voyaged to uncharted realms of his own neurology.

Professor Murray opened the congress by announcing that after taking a psychedelic trip he had shelved his prepared lecture in favor of a new topic: New Visions for Psychology's Future. Not a bad beginning! In the afternoon, Aldous Huxley took the enormous gathering of solemn-faced academicians through *The Doors of Perception.* As we left the Queen's Palace Auditorium, three members of the Danish psychology faculty rushed up to me complaining bitterly and waving newspapers. One top headline read: *I WAS THE FIRST SCANDINAVIAN REPORTER TO TRY THE POISONOUS MUSH-ROOMS FROM HARVARD.* Covering the front page was a photo, magnified to 12 gleaming inches, of Richard Alpert's eye, dilated, popping out wildly. Underneath, the photo's caption read: *"'I can control my insanity,' says Professor Alpert of Harvard."* It seemed that Richard Alpert (in later years, to become a Hindu holy man, name of Baba Ram Dass) had the night before been partying with some members of the press and had been persuaded to turn on a reporter.

"You are making fools of us," shouted the Danish psychologists. "You Americans don't understand. Denmark is a very little, cozy, quiet country. Scientists are not supposed to perform experiments that are reported on the front page." I reassured them that the evening's program would be impressive and history-making. And I promised them that during the congress, Richard Alpert would not turn on any more Danes.

That evening I delivered the following lecture, which subsequently was reprinted in psychology textbooks and several reference volumes. It is considered a classic, influential work because it introduces the notion that human behavior can best be understood in terms of "games." For example, the position "husband" in the Game of Marriage is seen as comparable to a position of, say, "outfielder" in the Game of Baseball. The Game Theory is a very subversive, meta-social concept. It implies that you are not just the role that you-and-society have fabricated for you. It encourages flexibility, humorous detachment from social pressures. It allows you to change "games" and positions without the shame-stigma of being unreliable or undependable. It allows people to study and even measure their performances, and to seek coaching. It endorses change-ability and an amused-cynical liberation from "hive" pressures. The Game Theory subtly undermines the cultural authoritarianism that forces people to play rigid parts in games that they themselves do not select.

Another "historic" contribution of this essay: it presented, for the first time, the notion that in order to change behavior (external performance), it is necessary to change your inner experience, i.e., your neurology. Here you will find an archeological curiosity: the first advocacy of brain-change drugs, not as medicines to cure disease, but as self-employed instruments to improve, change, and manage one's consciousness.

After scholarly presentations by Professor Frank Barron and another respectable psychologist, Richard Alpert walked to the podium and shocked the audience—me included!—by announcing that the visionary experience *was an end in itself,* that the drug-induced religious-mystical trip produced love, Christian (*sic*) charity, and the peace that passeth understanding. This final straw broke the back of scientific respectability. Psychiatrists leaped up and, in seven languages, denounced nonmedical psychologists discussing drugs, and berated the notion of drugs used for growth instead of cures for disease. For the angry psychiatrists, there was much applause.

At our hotel suite later we were joined by three Danish psychologists who looked at me with melancholy reproach. "You have set Danish psychology back twenty years."

"Not at all," I cried, filling their glasses with aquavit and their brains with positive electricity. "You have just hosted the most important congress in the history of psychology. The annals of our science will record that in Copenhagen, psychology became a true science of brain change. I'll bet you a bottle of champagne that in twenty years this conference will be compared to those moments in history when Newton and Darwin spoke before the Royal Society." We continued abusing the dangerous Danish drug and left on good terms.

Two weeks later—September 1961—further history was made at the annual meetings of the American Psychological Association. Acting as a moderator of a symposium on altered states of consciousness, I assembled a panel that included Alan Watts and William Burroughs in his first American public appearance. A crowd of young psychologists listened and went home to use drugs to alter consciousness.

The following essay reflects, perhaps, the innocence and excitement that motivated these first proposals to change behavior by altering the brain with neurotrophic drugs.

How to change behavior

Except for reflexes, instinctual reactions, and random muscular movements (which fall into the province of physiology), all behavior is imprinted by and conditioned by social pressures. Behavior sequences which are culturally determined might be considered game sequences. The listener may think I refer to "play," but I also consider stern, serious, real-life activities as "games." A game is defined as a learned cultural sequence characterized by six factors: Roles, Rules, Goals, Rituals, Language, and Values.

Like baseball and basketball, the behavior that psychiatrists label as "disease" can be considered games, too. Dr. Thomas Szasz suggests that "hysteria" is a certain doctor-patient game involving deceitful helplessness. Psychiatry, according to this model, is a behavior-change game.

Far from being frivolous, many so-called sports, or "play-games" are superior in their behavior-change techniques to psychiatry and psychology. The "game" of American baseball is superior to any so-called behavioral science. Baseball officials have classified and reliably record molecular behavior—bit sequences (strikes, hits, double plays, etc.). Their compiled records convert into indices for summarizing and predicting behavior (RBI: runs batted in; ERA: earned-run average, etc.). To judge those rare events that are not obviously and easily coded, baseball employs well-trained umpires. Baseball experts have devised another remarkable set of techniques for bringing about desired results: coaching. Baseball shares time and space with learners, sets up role models, feeds relevant information back to the learner, for endless practice. Baseball is clean and successful because it *is* seen as a game. You can shift positions. You know how you are doing. You can quit, or declare yourself a free agent.

Cultural stability is maintained by preventing people from seeing that the Roles, Rules, Goals, Rituals, Language, and Values of society are game structures. Cultural institutions encourage the delusion that games have inevitable givens, involving unchangeable laws of behavior. Most cultures treat the family game as implicit contracts limited in time and space. It is treason not to play the nationality game, the racial game, the religious game.

The currently popular method of behavior change is called

psychotherapy—a medical game that interprets confusion and ineffi-ciency in game-playing as illness. Consider the football player who doesn't know the rules. Perhaps he picks up the ball and runs off the field. Shall we pronounce him sick and call the doctor?

Not understanding the game nature of behavior leads to confusion and eventual helplessness.

The science game, the healing game, the knowledge game, are our proudest game accomplishments, but only as long as they are seen as games. When they go beyond this point, the trouble begins: the emergence of experts, professionals, priests, technocrats, status-bound engineers. At this point, games that began with the goal of decreasing human helplessness end up increasing it.

When people come to us and ask us to change their behavior, we can find out what games they are caught up in, what games they want to commit themselves to. Expose them to models of successful game-playing, feed back objective appraisals of their performance.

How do you care for them? Share time and space with them. Sounds simple enough, doesn't it?

The most *effective* approach to behavior change is applied mysticism.* Identify the game structure of the event. Make sure that you do not apply the rules and concepts of other games to this situation. Move directly to solve the problem. A person who can stand outside or above his or her culture can often cut through games-rules to what is most relevant to survival and peace of mind.

How can we Westerners see that our own potentials are much greater than the social-hive games in which we are so blindly trapped? Once the game structure of behavior is seen, change in behav-ior can occur with dramatic spontaneity. The visionary brain-change, consciousness-altering experience is the key to behavior change.

All the learned games of life can be seen as programs that select, censor, and thus dramatically limit the available cortical response. Consciousness-expanding drugs unplug these narrow programs, the social ego, the game-machinery. And with the ego and mind unplugged, what is left? Not the "id"; no dark, evil impulses. These alleged negative "forces" are, of course, simply taboos, anti-rules. What is left is something that Western culture knows little about: the uncensored cortex, activated, alert and open to new realities, new imprints.

Why is this brain-activating experience so strange and horrid to Western culture? Perhaps because our Western world is overcommit-

---

*The term "mysticism" is an ineffective archaism. By the 1970's we would refer to "applied neurologic" or "self-programmed brain-change."

ted to objective, external behavior games. This is a natural opposition and a healthy one: "the game" versus the "meta-game." Behavior versus consciousness, the universal brain-body versus the local cultural mind.

But this old paradox should be made explicit if it is to be fun. What should provoke intense and cheerful competition too often evokes suspicion, anger, impatience. Intelligence increase stimulated by brain-change is, to me, one of the greatest challenges of our times. In three hours, under the right circumstances, local games that frustrate and torment can be seen in the broader, evolutionary dimension. But in the absence of relevant scientific rituals to handle the drug experience, physicians seek to impose their game of control and prescription. Bohemians naturally impose their games of back-alley secrecy. Police naturally move in to control and prosecute.

In our research endeavors we developed 11 egalitarian principles to determine role, rule, ritual, goal, language, value, and to define the real, the good, the true, the logical. Any contract between humans should be explicit about any temporary suspension of these equalities. Two research projects attempted to put these egalitarian principles into operation.

In one study we administered psilocybin, in a naturalistic supportive setting, in order to observe the rituals and language Americans impose on an intense brain-change experience quite alien to their culture. One hundred and sixty-seven subjects—43 females and 124 males—were given psilocybin. Of these, 26 were scholars, artists, medical doctors, professional intellectuals; 21 were nonprofessional normals, 27 were drug addicts (psychological or physical); and 10 were inmates of a state prison. The drug was given only once, under informal (non-laboratory) conditions, with no attempt to be therapeutic or problem oriented.

Seventy-three percent of our subjects reported the psilocybin experience as "very pleasant" or ecstatic; 95% thought the experience had changed their lives for the better. Three out of four reported happy reactions. The most common reaction reported was the sudden perception of the effects of abstractions, rituals, learned-game routines: ecstatic pleasure at being temporarily freed from these limitations.

You cannot sensibly talk about the effects of a psychedelic drug without specifying the set of the subject and the environmental context. If both are supportive of self-discovery and aesthetic-philosophic inquiry, a life-changing experience results. If both are negative, a hellish encounter can ensue. Of course, people tend to impose familiar games onto the psilocybin experience. If the drug-giving person is supportive, flexible, and secure, then the experience is almost guaranteed to be pleasant and therapeutic.

Many of the 167 subjects in our study were already involved in rewarding games to which they could return with renewed vision and energy. But many of our subjects came through the psilocybin experience with the knowledge that they were involved in nonrewarding games, caught in routines they disliked. Many of them moved quickly to change their life games. For others, the "therapeutic" effect of the experience did not last. They were left with pleasant memories of their visionary journey and nothing more.

The second experiment involved 35 volunteer prisoners in a maximum security prison. The recidivism rate is 80%. Twenty-eight would be expected back in prison within a year. In baseball terms, 80% is the error percentage our team attempted to lower.

The drug was given after three orientation meetings with the prisoners. The psilocybin session was followed by three discussions, then another drug session, then more discussions. In some 100's of hours of mind-blown interaction, there was not one moment of friction or tension. Pre-post testing demonstrated dramatic decreases in hostility, cynicism, depression, schizoid ideation; definite increases in optimism, planfulness, flexibility, tolerance, sociability. The psilocybin experience made these men aware that they had been involved in stereotyped "cops and robbers" games—of being tough guys, of outwitting the law, of resentful cynicism. "My whole life came tumbling down, and I was sitting happily in the rubble." said one prisoner.

The group has become a workshop for planning future games. Some prisoners are being trained to take over the functions of a vocational guidance clinic—preparing occupational brochures for inmates about to be released, making plans to act as rehabilitation workers after their release and to organize a halfway house for ex-convicts. Other prisoners are using their time to prepare for the family game, the old job games to which they will return.

Of course, our new game of allowing criminals to take over responsibility, authority, and prestige brings us into game competition with the professional middle class. If criminals are no longer criminals, where do the rest of us stand? People are upset when their games are changed.

Those who talk about the games of life are invariably seen as frivolous anarchists tearing down the social structure. Actually, only those who see culture as a game can appreciate the exquisitely complex magnificence of what human beings have done.

Those of us who play the game of "applied mysticism" respect and support good gamesmanship. You pick out your game, learn the rules, rituals, concepts; play fairly and cleanly. Anger and anxiety are irrelevant, because you see your small game in the context of the great evolutionary game which no one can lose.

5

Historically, creativity is often associated with psychosis, alienation, and delinquency: The flaky artist, the mad scientist; even Einstein as lovable, absent-minded clown. Whenever 20th-century literature or film portrayed a brilliant mental giant who fabricated wonderful new realities, he was invariably a bad guy! Recall the classic movie stereotype of the genius who builds gleaming cities under the sea, who outwits and neutralizes both the Soviet and American military (God knows we have all longed to do *that*!), who constructs luxurious cities in space filled with genetically superior women and men (as our landlocked NASA bureaucrats should have done, ten years after Apollo II). These handsome geniuses, always in loving collaboration with slinky, well-dressed ladies, are the enemy (!) whom James Bond (a macho, unprincipled, ruthless Gordon Liddy-type CIA agent) is sent to destroy!

But the ultimate in superstitious, Ayatollah-type future-fear is the Frankenstein myth: a scientist of the primitive 19th century who created life! And now the name of Frankenstein, to the easily-spooked natives of America, is synonymous with "monster." The historic origin of this hatred of the creative, this phobic taboo against change is, of course, the Prometheus myth. SHe who has the confidence and heroic daring to seize the future for humanity is punished by paranoid, jealous, frightened Gods.

These negative, eerie images of the creative person are not accidental. The cultural distrust of the innovator is genetic in origin. Species survival logically requires that the large majority of the genetic castes (see Part Five) necessary to keep the gene pool moving through time-space be docilely reproductive. An anthill or beehive would be weakened if too many ants came up with bright new ideas. Before the individualistic American republic, no human tribe, nation, or race has allowed a high percentage of creative deviance.

And until recently, no psychologist could explain why genius emerges and how it could be nurtured. Or, even more unthinkable, how genius could be *produced*—because this implies improving the species beyond the level of the hive leaders. The next paper (written in the barbarous period circa 1962) emphasized one's choice over one's own behavior and brain changes. Today, *ethology* (which represents our genetic confidence and skill in open, direct, observation of human behavior) and *neuro-logic* (our readiness to tamper with the brain) allows us to define creativity as a process easily amenable to change. Anyone who wants to, can be coached to behave more creatively. And you can learn how to alter your brain function to experience in novel ways.

Creative performance and the creative experience

The Four Choices You Make in Managing Your Own Creativity

Type 1. You can choose to be noncreative (reproductive) in your behavior and noncreative in your brain activity, acting and experiencing within the narrow confines of your local culture or hive. (If you are a bank teller or a young psychologist with ambitions, this is the better part of wisdom.)* Call this TYPE 1 Reproductive-Reproductive—no novel behavior, no fresh experience. In a fast-moving frontier niche like America this docile, normal cast probably comprises only 75% of the population.

     Type 2. The Reproductive Creator can be more inventive in behavior, and yet remain docilely stereotyped in experiencing. A crafty skill in producing new combinations of old cultural stereotypes can be developed. Here we include artists, designers, entertainers, packagers who recycle old fads or add new wrinkles to the classics: "Hey, let's make Romeo and Juliet black and gay!" "Let's have the good guy turn out to

---

*Actually, one's ability to change social role (caste) and to change one's brain is determined or limited genetically. Each gene pool probably produces members of the four creative castes in the exact proportion necessary to keep the gene pool surviving at any particular (ecological niche) and time. At times of migration, more creative performers and brain changers are obviously needed.

be the bad guy!" "Let's raise the hemlines next year!" "Let's throw long on first down!" Wow! What creativity!

In a wide-open, mobile society like America, perhaps 12% of the population operates at this level. In a static society like Saudi Arabia, you will, of course, be drawn and quartered for suggesting even the slightest change in hemlines or in good-guy roles.

Type 3. The Creative Reproducer is an interesting and little-discussed human caste: psychics, visionaries, *idiot savants*, those with unusual talents, Bobby Fischers, people with perfect musical pitch, mental calculators, intuitives, natural artists, "oddballs." In some past cultures, these people, whose brains are wired differently from the species norm, who see things differently, were recognized, tolerated, even rewarded. In most closed societies, these "strange ones" are ridiculed, ostracized, even punished. Demographic statistics on deviance suggest that 12% of any gene pool are exceptionally endowed. Their brains have activated futique circuits that would be optimal in some future or different niche, but which, in the present, put them naggingly out of touch.

Although Type 3 brains are fabricating original realities, they use conventional-reproductive behaviors to express their visions. An Inquisition zealot looks through Galileo's telescope and declares that Satan's work is on display! A worried cardiologist takes LSD, activates ecstatic visceral circuits, and shouts that he is having a heart attack. Obviously, there is a natural tendency to impose the language and rituals of the past upon new experience. As an inevitable fallout of my profession (as encourager and stimulator of creative singularity), can you imagine the range of letters I receive in any week? From freaky, tormented prophets and visionaries in Kansas City, Nome, Melbourne, and Cape Town—souls who "see," "experience," "know" certain truths, and who breathlessly describe these revelations in tired vocabularies, using CIA conspiracies, UFO visitations, and reincarnation clichés (invariably Egyptian), to threaten whoever fails to accept the valid new connections perceived by their mistimed, out-of-phase futique brains. If you have altered your brain to new revelation and are running around using traditional metaphors, you are undoubtedly Type 3. If you have a sense of humor, you are a joy and a delight. If lacking in whimsy, you are a social bore and pious irritant. In either case, you are advised to move to:

Type 4. The Creative-Creator possesses an activated brain and has accepted the Heisenberg Determinacy (your brain is God the Fabricator) and can carpenter new realities in harmony with the fast swirl of current evolution. The Creative-Creator fuses-uses appropriate clichés of the past, the trendiest waves of the present, technologies of the future. As suggested in our discussion of Type 3, access to "special" brain circuits is, for the most part, genetic. Genius does come from the genes.

A person in any of these four quadrants of creativity can be seen as effective or as incompetent by his culture—and, for that matter, by cultural subgroups.

If we divided each type into those labeled by their contemporaries as (A) effective and (B) ineffective, we obtain the eight categories presented in Figure 8. These two-dimensional circular grids can plot test scores or content-analysis indices along the two coordinates in order to diagnose the individual. This system leads itself to the same variety of multilevel applications as the interpersonal circle.

The Development of Creative Behavior

In most of life's crucial games we stumble in the dark, not knowing how we're doing. The first step in behavior change, then, is explicit definition of the game, learning the rules and strategies. You need some way of scorekeeping and to be at the proper space-time ballpark, hanging around people who are adepts at the game. It is disappointing to come thundering over the goal line for a touchdown only to be greeted with yawns because the gang is playing tennis. (I have spent a good part of my professional life doing this.) Get a good coach. Behavior, being movement in space/time, is not changed by words or by repeating mistakes. And practice is needed.

In 1961 Frank Barron, William Meyers (at that time a Harvard graduate student), and I initiated a creativity-change project which allowed a preliminary crude check on these hypotheses. By matching pairs of students on faculty ratings of creativity, 40 volunteer subjects of the junior class at the Rhode Island School of Design were divided into groups A and C, whose creativity ratings had equal means and equal standard deviations. IQ scores were available on all subjects.

First, both groups were administered, under identical conditions, the Guilford Unusual Uses Test and the Barron Originality, Independence of Judgment, and Preference for Complexity questionnaires, in that order. Then, after an intermission, the groups were separated. Group C was asked to "play the role of an extraordinarily original and creative person"; Group A, the role of a highly intelligent authoritarian person. Both groups then repeated the tests. The results indicated that Group C (creative) improved in performance relative to

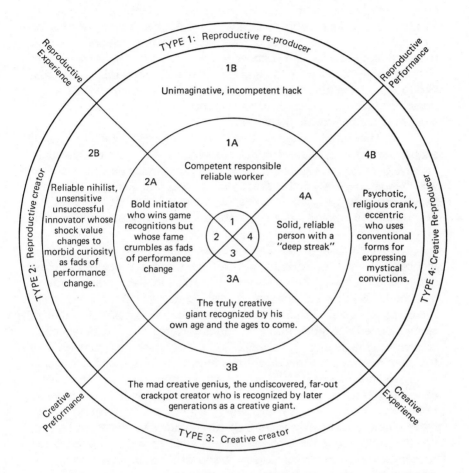

Figure 8. Schematic diagrams of social labels used to describe types of creativity. (Inner circle illustrates positive social labels and outer circle negative labels.)

Group A on ability to think up ideas. This indicates that the creative set increases creative performance and the authoritarian set decreases creative performance. We may conclude that creativity can be increased. It also suggests that role playing, or set-taking, is a specific mechanism for increasing creativity. Creativity has a social aspect as well, as shown by the results on the three Barron questionnaires that measure interpersonal and social attitudes. With the creative set, Group C increased its scores over its earlier scores with standard instructions. Group A, with the authoritarian set, decreased its scores on the Barron questionnaires. Mind sets affecting creative performance also affected interpersonal and social orientation.

The results suggest that (1) creative behavior is a game sequence; (2) people have considerable voluntary control over their creative behavior; and (3) if the game contract is made explicit, behavior will change drastically in the direction that roles and goals demand. The experiment also suggests that people automatically shift rituals, adjust new rules, and employ the appropriate language once the commitment is made.

A sample of 50 juniors was selected (at random) for a feedback study. Barron and I met with each subject, opened the test folder, and explained the creativity test results. In every case we found that the student's creativity scores and ratings of originality by faculty members checked closely with the stated game goals. For instance, teachers rated one student with low originality scores as solid, responsible, but unimaginative, consistently indicating close identification with middle-class family values. From this student's subsequent discussion emerged this message: "I'm a normal, conventional person looking forward to a steady, interesting job and a happy family life. I've no desire to be a tortured genius, sacrificing a good income for risky bohemian independence." There seemed little discrepancy between the level of creativity and professional goals selected. Painters and sculptors scored higher on independence of judgment, spontaneous flexibility, and social deviance than architects or industrial designers.

The Activation of Creative Awareness

Researchers administered psilocybin to more than 400 persons, many of whom were financially dependent on being creative. Artistic and literary folks respond ecstatically and wisely to drug experience. They tell us this is what they have been looking for: new, intense, direct confrontation with the world about them. Poets and painters have always tortured themselves to transcend space/time boundaries by every means possible, and at certain historical time-places—invariably when political-economic security allows breathing space from survival pressures—entire cultures "get high" on brain-change techniques. In the Khajuraho culture (c. A.D. 1000) an entire society collaborated in constructing enormous temples covered with erotic carvings. The Konarak culture (c. 1250) again mobilized the energies of a generation in constructing acres of sexually explicit temple sculpture. A similar thing happened during the Mogul period, 17th century, in north India, when the Taj Mahal and other esthetic-erotic constructions dominated social consciousness. The prevalence of mind-changing drugs (several Mogul emperors were notorious hashish-opium smokers) and mind-changing yogic methods undoubtedly stimulated these amazing peaks of artistic expression.

More than 100 psilocybin sessions run in a maximum-security prison demonstrated that creative vision and mystical illumination are a function of the cortex when it is temporarily relieved of word and ego games. More than half our semiliterate prisoners reported in blunt, nonabstract words what have to be interpreted as mystical experiences. A lower-class, uneducated criminal can, via psilocybin, experience what Blake saw in his visions. It's all there in the cortex after all. But the convict does not have language or literary skills to communicate his vision: "Yeah, Doc. I saw all these flames of fire, and, wow, I knew it meant the end of me, but then, I realized it can't really hurt because we're all part of the same thing anyway so I relaxed and went into it, and. . . ." Reports like this come from the most verbal of our prisoner group. The majority just look us in the eye, shake their heads in awe, and say, "Gee, Doc, those mushrooms are really something out of this world."

We obviously cannot wait fifteen years while the prisoner finishes graduate work in English Literature and learns the literary game. But we can coach him in the creative production of new combinations. I think it is possible to get deep creative insights into whatever behavior sequence or professional occupation you are involved in. Creativity is not a function of lucky heritage or elite training. There are more visions in the cortex of each of us than in all the museums and libraries of the world. There is a limitless possibility of new combinations of the old symbols.

A true democracy of creativity—experienced and performed —is close at hand. Intensely close relationships develop among most people who have had this experience together. In the past, when these visionary experiences were accidental, a Dominican Father in Spain had his experience in one century, and a Hindu on the bank of the Ganges in another century: communication did not exist. And because disciplined mystic experience involves a withdrawal from games and social interaction, your monastic or hermit doesn't have people around. The group drug experience allows this to happen.

In 1964, the first commercial book summarizing LSD experimentation was edited by David Solomon, an early pioneer in psychedelic drug research who, at the moment of this writing (1980) is in an English prison, serving a cruelly long sentence for manufacture of LSD. The British judge who sentenced Solomon justified the Turkish barbarism on the grounds that Solomon had influenced millions of minds *through his writings* about drugs. This 20th-century scholar is in jail for his ideas!

Many ethologists have noted that in dealing with cultural change, British and Western European countries run about ten years behind America. The bourgeois hysteria about recreational drugs that convulsed the United States during the Nixon administration has now moved eastward to 19th-century Europe, where police officials and moralists have a new victimless crime to persecute.

Reflect for a moment on the melancholy fact that a pioneer scholar is languishing in prison for, among other things, publishing the book for which this essay was the introduction. The essay itself made three important contributions to neuro-logic. 1. The motto: TO USE YOUR HEAD YOU HAVE TO GO OUT OF YOUR MIND solves the classic dilemma of prescientific psychology and philosophy: we cannot study the brain (the instrument for fabricating the realities we inhabit) using the mental constructs of the past.

2. An even more important advance spelled out in this essay is the discussion of *imprinting*—first discovered by animal ethologists. Almost all we learn about human nature has and will come from our study of other species. We had to understand evolution of other species before we were bold enough to say (and how many dare say it today?) that humans evolve and that individual humans evolve at different rates. In the following essay, the concept of *imprinting* was applied for the first time to human development. As the human being matures, different neural circuits are activated and the following neurotechnologies emerge in a predictable sequence: sucking, biting, crawling, walking, muscular domination, nonverbal social communication, imitation of symbols, invention of symbols, cooperative symbol communication, adolescent sexual-mating, parenting, and aging/security-seeking. (Other more advanced neurotechnologies will be considered in a later section.)

As each brain circuit is activated, it blindly imprints the environmental cues that happen to be present. When the verbal imitative circuits are turned on around ages three to four, the language and mentation skills of the parents and custodians is imprinted. If the child is Chinese, a Chinese mental reality is in-habituated. The first powerful sex object has an unshakable effect on further sexual conditioning. Even more interesting is the suggestion that imprints can be suspended and changed. *Serial Imprinting* means that you can use your own brain as a movie camera to "shoot" the realities you inhabit.

3. *Set and Setting* is the third epic contribution of this essay. Before the 1960's, physicians and experimenters administered drugs in a most primitive, naive manner. It was assumed that each drug acted mechanically to bring about a specific physiological result. The *placebo* effect was recognized as a terrible stumbling block in the neat-precise mechanical science of determining how drug X influenced organ Y. Subjects given a sedative and told it was an energizer ran around restlessly and couldn't sleep. Subjects given energizers and told they were sleeping pills proceeded to nod out. These results used to plague researchers working for the big drug firms. The influence (indeed, the dominance) of the nervous system as managing biocomputer was unheard of.

The hypothesis we developed at Harvard suggested that the effect of any psychoactive drug was almost entirely due to the drug-taker's expectations and subjective assumptions interacting with the pressure of the environment. Even at this primitive moment (1964) we were coming to realize that the brain is a robot computer perfectly designed to *fabricate any reality we program it to construct.* If you believe that LSD is lethal poison, even your ecstatic sensory orgasm will feel like a death convulsion. If, at that vulnerable sensitive moment of imprint suspension, the environment tells you that you are sick or in danger, your robot computer will so react.

Set and Setting and the *placebo* effect demand that psychology get hip to the Heisenberg principle of determinancy. *If what we expect affects what happens in our brain, then let us precisely program the suggestions our vulnerable brain will realize.* If the setting also affects what happens in our brain, let us make sure that the environment is the reality we wish to inhabit. The brain is not a blind, reactive machine, but a complex, sensitive biocomputer that we can program. And if *we* don't take the responsibility for programming it, then it will be programmed unwittingly by accident or by the social environment.

Three contributions to psychopharmacological theory

Visionary plants (the peyote cactus, the divine mushrooms of Mexico; divinatory vines and roots) have been used for thousands of years. Today's technology provides synthetics of the active ingredients of these ancient and vulnerable concoctions. These foods and drugs produce ecstasy, the most sought after and most dread experience known to man. *Ex-stasis* means, literally, out of, or released from a fixed or unmoving condition. Some theorists like to suppose a steady growth in human consciousness; others, especially Eastern philosophers, point to alternating cycles of expansion and contraction and warn that man's awareness may contract down to the robot-narrow precision of certain overorganized species of life. The anthill and the computer remind us that increased efficiency does not necessarily mean expanded awareness. I believe psychedelic drugs and their effects should be viewed in the context of this emergent philosophy of evolution of intelligence.

The Renaissance-Reformation mythos would have us believe man is the chosen lord of all species. But in the last few decades, scientific instrumentation has confronted man with visions, vistas, and processes that have thoroughly dissipated hir philosophic securities. Astronomers speak of billions of light years, physicists of critical nuclear-process structures that last only microseconds. The genetic blueprinting strands are so compact that the seed of every human being on earth today could be contained in a box 1/8 inch on a side. The new scientific data define man as an animal only dimly aware of the energies and wisdom surrounding and radiating through hir.

We can use our rational faculties to change our instruments and language, invent new mathematics and symbols to deal with processes beyond our neurological scope. But then comes the neurological implosion. Rational consciousness is *a fragile, tissue-thin artifact easily blown away by the slightest alteration of biochemistry, by the simplest external stimulation—for example, by a few microvolts strategically introduced into specific areas of the brain, or by the removal of accustomed stimulation.*

The potential of cerebral association is of the order of thirteen billion to the twenty-five-thousandth power, *per second.* But we think rationally at a maximum rate of three concepts—ten phonemes—a second. Our present mental machinery cannot possibly handle the whirling, speed-of-light, trackless processes of our brain, our organ of consciousness itself.

The paradox: to use our heads, to push out beyond words, space-time categories, social identifications, models and concepts, it becomes necessary to go out of our generally rational minds. If we at times seem uncertain, too ready to spin out unproven hypotheses, this is a sign of *the preliminary, rapidly changing speculation that inevitably characterizes a new breakthrough in the realm of ideas.*

That our research provokes fierce controversy suggests that man's accepted view of himself is coming into collision with new concepts.

The Stable World That Used to Be

It is useful to see all cultural institutions as expressions of the epoch's basic mythos; each discipline simply reorchestrating underlying themes of the age. What fails to fit the mythic harmonic tends to be heard as disruptive dissonance. Thomas S. Kuhn describes how scientific activities are determined by paradigm—a distinctive world view, defining the problems and methods of any era. Science cannot go beyond the paradigm's limits without risking being seen as eccentric, even "unscientific." During the last fifty years our basic world view seems to have been undergoing another of these gigantic struggles of ideologies of which the current controversy over psychedelic drugs is but a minor skirmish. *The older, classic world view concerns itself with equilibria among forces that are visible, external, predictable, measurable, manageable by man, within the realm of macroscopic consciousness. The religious expression of this mythos is Protestantism, with its emphasis on behavior, achievement, balancing, and rationality. Democracy, communism, parliamentarianism, all emphasize the macroscopic, visible aspects of behavior.* Classic physical science emphasized the orderly; God the master engineer balancing the clockwork equilibrium of material forces. But the metaphorical interpretations we impose betray our implicit, basic (usually unconscious) commitments: God runs the universe the way a good Christian runs his business; the way Andrew Mellon ran the country. Like a factory.

Psychology again fits the dimensions of the myth. Behaviorism (a scientific movement invented and manned by Protestants) recognizes only visible actions. Human personality is pictured as ruled by conservation principles—ego, id, superego—pushing toward equilib-rium. There was much more to Freud than this; but the Hasidic, expansive, and mystical aspects of Freud's thinking have not survived the post-Freudian Protestantization of the theory.

The Emergent-Root Myth

Evidence from every branch of science testifies to energies and structures which, though fantastically potent, are microscopic—indeed, invisible. The good old macroscopic world is a rather clumsy, robotlike level of conception. Structure becomes process. Matter becomes a transient state of energy. Stasis becomes ex-stasis.

The same exponential mythos appears in other institutions. Overproduction, overkilling, overpopulation, automation, remind us that older economic, political, religious, artistic, psychological views of man, defined in externals and behaviorals, are reaching an agonizing end-point.

Psychology, man's view of his nature, is always the last to adapt a new world view. From the standpoint of established values, the psychedelic process is dangerous and insane—a deliberate psychotiza-tion, a suicidal undoing of the equilibrium man should be striving for. *With its internal, invisible, indescribable phenomena, the psychedelic experience is incomprehensible to a rational, achievement-oriented, conformist philosophy.* But to one ready to experience the exponential view of the universe, psychedelic experience is exquisitely effective preparation for the inundation of data and problems to come.

Each of us possesses around 30 billion brain cells, several times the number of human beings in the world. Each brain cell is a computer capable of relating with as many as 25,000 others. The number of possible associations is of the order of 30 billion to the twenty-five-thousandth power, a quantity larger than the number of atoms in the universe. This electrical-chemical complexity is the *ana-tomical* structure of consciousness.

Into the brain, each second, there pour something like 100 million sensations. The brain itself fires off around five billion signals a second. Yet we are aware of only the millionth fraction of our own cortical signaling. Huge areas of the brain (neurologists call them "silent areas") are blocked off from consciousness. Reflective neurologists pose disturbing questions: ". . . has man, perhaps, more brain than he knows what to do with? Is his huge 'neo-pallium' like a powerful engine in a decrepit automobile that can never utilize more than a fraction of the available horsepower?"

Imprinting and Re-Imprinting

Little is known about the learning processes by which the brain's enormous potential is limited and contracted. According to psychologist Clifford Morgan,

> [Konrad Lorenz] happened to be present when some goose eggs in an incubator hatched. For this reason he was the first large moving object the goslings saw. Much to his surprise, the goslings began following him about as though he were their parent. The young goslings, in fact, would have nothing to do with their mother goose and insisted on his constant company. This learning takes place very rapidly and without any specific reward. . . . The imprinting phenomenon . . . can take place only during a short interval (a few hours or a day or two) and at a certain time (usually shortly following birth). It also seems irreversible; difficult to alter through subsequent learning. However, some true learning [may be] connected with it. Young goslings, for example, at first follow any human being [who] has been the first object contact after hatching. A few days later, however, they learn the individual characteristics of the person who ordinarily leads them to food and shelter, and then they will follow no one else. Thus imprinting may be a natural stage in maturation.

Here is a sudden irreversible learning, which seems independent of motivation, reward, conditioning—a sudden, shutterlike fixing of the nervous system. Once taken, the picture then determines the scope and type of subsequent "lawful learning." Imprinting, a biochemical event, sets up the chessboard upon which slow, step-by-step conditioning takes place.

One awesome aspect of imprinting is its unpredictable, accidental quality. In another experiment, young birds were presented with a Ping-Pong ball at the critical moment and spent their remaining lives pursuing plastic globes. This amusing and frightening experiment reminds us that each of us perceives the world through biochemical-neurological structures accidentally laid down in our earliest moments. We may be chasing the particular Ping-Pong ball which, at those sensitive moments, has been imprinted on our cortical film.

Certain alkaloid molecules (psychedelic drugs) dramatically suspend the conditioned, learned aspects of the nervous system. Suddenly released from its conditioned patterning, consciousness is flung into a flashing loom of unlearned imagery, an eerie, novel landscape where everything seems possible and nothing remains fixed. Might we consider the psychedelic effect as a temporary suspension of imprinting?

Some current neurological research already indicates that serotonin is a key factor in the transmission of nerve impulses. There is a difference in serotonin metabolism between infants and adults and between "normal" and schizophrenic persons. LSD also affects serotonin metabolism. Marplan, a drug, "builds up the brain's stockpile of serotonin," has a tranquilizing effect on mental patients, and blocks the action of LSD.

Serotonin might contribute to the imprinting process necessary for "normal" perception. The shifting, unfixed imagery of the involuntary (and unpleasant) psychotic state, and the voluntary (ecstatic) psychedelic state, are associated with a change in the body's serotonin level. Psychedelic drugs may provide the possibility of reimprinting—a neurological restatement of the "death-rebirth" experience so often reported during psychedelic moments: during the psychedelic session, the subject's nervous system is in a disorganized flux closely analogous to that of infancy. And here we come to the accelerated personality change, rapid learning, sudden life changes so regularly reported by psychedelic researchers.

The Psychological Situation

A most confusing aspect of psychedelic drug phenomena is the wide variation of responses. There is the common factor of going beyond the imprinted, learned structure, but the specific content of what comes next is always different. LSD, mescaline, and psilocybin simply do not produce a generally predictable sequence of responses.

Psychedelic substances have negligible somatic effects. Their site of action is the higher nervous system. Once "normal" modes of awareness are suspended, specific consciousness changes occur due to set and setting.

Set refers to what the subject brings to the situation, his earlier imprinting, learning, emotional and rational predilections, and, perhaps most important, his immediate expectations about the drug experience. *Setting* refers to the social, physical, emotional milieu of the session.

Most important is the behavior, understanding, and empathy of the persons who first administer the drug and who remain with the taker while the drug is in effect. The psychedelic controversy itself is a broad social confirmation of the set-setting hypothesis. The extreme suggestibility, the heightened vulnerability to internal or external stimuli—which leads some to paranoia, others to cosmic ecstasy—points to the critical importance of expectation and environmental pressure.

The Problem of Communication

Words are inadequate to describe the speed, breadth, and shuttling flow of a 30-billion-cell cerebral computer—and the fears aroused by the very nature of the topic. Not long ago I spent an afternoon with Dr. Richard Alpert and Dr. Ralph Metzner, lecturing to the staff of The Hudson Institute, one of the country's most respected think tanks. About thirty-five scientists were present, and in closing the meeting, the chairman—a well-known physicist who had taken LSD several times—questioned the possibility of verbal communication about the psychedelic experience. "Those who have taken a psychedelic drug realize it can't be talked about, and those who haven't naively assume that it can be talked about with the current vocabulary."

After the meeting, we met with four members of the institute who had previous experience with psychedelic drugs. Three were strangers, but without any social niceties, these men immediately plunged into a frank, avuncular coaching process, as though Alpert, Metzner, and I were rookie pitchers being instructed by four veterans; as though all seven of us were meeting to figure how to explain to earthlings the procedures and events of our totally different world.

Each coach had a different strategy. One said we should make our psychedelic lectures completely personal: "Tell concretely what happened to you." "Nonsense," said another. "Be strictly objective and scientific. Rely only on published data." A third disagreed: "Make it practical. Tell the audience about the dosage, how long it lasts, what people say and do during sessions." The fourth was the most psychological: "Recognize the fears of the listener. Anticipate his objections. Be humble. Stress the dangers and problems. Don't put him on the defensive."

But all four advisors were unanimous in criticizing my central metaphor: " 'You have to go out of your mind to use your head,' is guaranteed to scare rational, intellectual people. Use a positive, familiar jargon. Talk about creative reorganization or perceptual reintegration."

But psychedelic drugs *do* take us beyond our normal conceptual framework. Most of the great religions have taken this disturbing goal of ex-stasis as their central program.

Fear of the Potential

Experienced psychedelic veterans recognize certain fears generated by the psychedelic process:

1. Cognitive: loss of rational control; fear of disorientation and confusion.

2. Social: doing something shameful or ludicrous; the loss of social inhibitions.

3. Psychological: self-discovery; finding out something about yourself that you do not want to face.

4. Cultural: discovering the painful truth about the institutions with which one is identified; seeing through the tribal shams; becoming disillusioned with one's social commitments and thus becoming irresponsible.

5. Ontological addiction: finding a new dimension of experience too pleasant; perhaps all men share the hunch that normal consciousness is a form of sleepwalking and that somewhere there exists a form of "awakeness" from which one would not want to return.

This fear of losing the social-ego identity is based on an illusion. One who has the courage to undergo the shattering of the illusion will die, but in the mystical sense, "so that he may live again." A Zen koan (paradox) says: "Be dead, thoroughly dead, and do as you will." The healing process, which Paul Tillich describes as "taking a walk through hell," brings the transcendence that lies beyond.

Like other forms of anxiety, these five fears are related to deep yearnings and potentials. For each terror, there is a corresponding liberation. Terror is a negative desire. The terror of seeing yourself is the negative aspect of the ecstasy of really seeing yourself.

7

The next chapter, published in 1965 in *ETC*, a journal of semantics edited by S. I. Hayakawa, deals with the problem faced at the beginning of every new science. A science is born when a new tool is discovered for expanding the human sensorium—a new extension of the brain.

The discovery of brain-change drugs has been compared to the discovery of the microscope. New forms swim into perception. It is a truism that you cannot impose the ethics and language of the past upon subject matter revealed by a new extension of the senses. Galileo was arrested for describing what he saw in his telescope. The Inquisition would not bother to look through the lens. When Janssen, Galileo, Hooke, Leeuwenhoek, and Malpighi expanded human perception with the microscope, they realized that new languages, new theories were needed to use the new information. The following essay tried to demonstrate the need for a new language to describe the expanded brain vistas triggered off by psychedelic drugs.

By the way, S. I. Hayakawa, editor of *ETC*, hated this article. He wrote a solemn preface in which he claimed that his normal, routine perceptions were so full of sensation and freshness that he needed no expansion. He subsequently made fame and fortune politically espousing his conservative opposition to change. Sleepy Sam is one of the few psychological philosophers able to apply his knowledge of semantics and mass consciousness to real-life situations. More power to him!

Languages: Energy systems sent and received

Mobile, far-ranging mammals have to pilot themselves through widely differing environments. Their complex machineries depend upon discrimination of cues and the learning of elaborate behavior sequences.

Consider the mammalian body as an enormous ocean liner with billions of passengers and crew—a completely self-contained, integrated, harmonious system of energy exchanges. But a look-out is required—of course—the so-called "waking consciousness," the mind.

While milllions of signals flood the mammalian cortex from all parts of the nervous system, one level of awareness has to be directed to the immediate external environment—to be alert to neighborhood changes, to distinguish between rewards and punishments, to select what is to be avoided and pursued. This neurological "fixing" on external cues is based on imprinting and subsequent conditioning.

Symbols—The Language of Imprints

Imprinting, a biochemical freezing of external awareness, is confined to definite brief periods in individual life, and to a particular triggering set of environmental circumstances. Once accomplished, it is very stable—perhaps irreversible. It is often completed long before the specific behaviors which the imprinted pattern establishes. Imprinting is the selection of triggers that automatically activate inborn characteristics of the species.

As the result of eccentric imprinting, fowl attempt to court humans; lambs desert the flock and follow their keepers; goslings attempt to hatch watermelons; buffalo calves attempt to mate with huntsmen's horses; zebra foals attach themselves to moving cars; ducklings reject the mother in favor of orange basketballs. The rather terrifying implication is that early, accidental, and involuntary events can tenaciously couple human instinctual machinery to entirely *in*appropriate stimuli. (Which orange basketball imprinted you?) Another possibility is that all subsequent learning centers around the original imprint. Mental life is limited to associations relating back to the original imprint. The human being is "hooked" to the specific external stimulus. Sensory deprivation experiments suggest that the human cut off from his addictive "supply" of external stimuli shows all the symptoms of a "dope fiend"—restlessness, discomfort, anxiety.

The brain is a motion-picture camera capable of shooting millions of frames a second. The imprint system is one of these frames, stopped—one static model, years out of date, kept current only by slow conditioning and association. The "dead," "removed" quality of man's thinking has interested philosophers for centuries, and has been described most effectively by linguists and semanticists, especially Ludwig Wittgenstein, Edward Sapir, Benjamin Whorf, and Alfred Korzybski. What happens, outside or inside, we perceive in terms of our mental imprint system. We live in a frozen world—cut off from the flow of life and energy.

Imprinting equips us, cues us to maneuver around the neighborhood, determining attractions and repulsions. The genetic blueprint plays a statistical game. In spite of the occasionally freaky nature of many early imprints, enough of us do imprint appropriate stimuli that we reproduce, keep the hive-society going, and care for our young—the crucial genetic issues. That the consciousness of prescientific humanity was limited to a tunnel vision may be of no consequence in the evolution of intelligence. When it's backbone time, it backbones. When it's brain-change time, species learn to reimprint.

Suspension of Imprints

All neurological processes are biochemical, and many experiments have demonstrated that imprinting can be postponed, altered, or prevented entirely by tension-reducing or tranquilizing drugs.

This chemical resuscitation of the frozen symbol systems is not a recent development. In every culture in recorded history, men have used chemicals of vegetable origin to alter consciousness. Members of cultures with primitive technologies and distribution systems will drop any activity in order to "get high." The same is true of cultures where primitive legal or moral sanctions make it difficult to obtain brain changers. During American Prohibition, a mass mania sprang up around liquor. The same is true in penitentiaries or in military servitudes.

Alcohol is primitive, crude, and dangerous; its worldwide popularity is probably due to European engineering methods for mass production and distribution. Alcohol, by the 18th century was available; other competing mind-changers were relatively rare.

The global popularity of chemical mind-changers is due to their producing ecstasy, perceptual change, fresh sensation. Ecstasy means to break out of the verbal prisons, suspend your imprints, see things anew, perceive directly. With freshened perception goes the feeling of liberation, insight, the exultant sense of having escaped the lifeless net of symbols. Men drink, smoke, chew, or fast to escape the tyranny of words, the limits of the imprint; to regain what they have lost in socialization. The ecstatic is wordless. Try to describe even the mundane effect of getting "tight" at a cocktail party.

Reimprinting

But what happens after the neurological liberation? How is it integrated back into life?

Hinduism and Hinayana Buddhism flatly urge their devotees to reach a state of detached nirvana and stay there. Other philosophers have argued that ecstasy must lead to liberated return. Christian mystics, Mahayana Buddhists, and many Hindu sects insist that the person liberated from his neurological straitjacket will be known by his works and his actions. But until recently, very few persons have actually attained freedom from imprints. Breathing exercises, monastic withdrawal, prolonged meditation, mantras, mudras, mandalas can produce a state of quietude and serenity, but only rarely do non-drug adepts report the blinding illumination, whirling inundation of accelerated sensation, unity through multiplicity, that characterize direct neurological confrontation. Today, by ingesting a psychedelic drug, temporary freedom from imprints is almost guaranteed.

But again, so what?

These compounds produce *new* imprints. During a psychedelic session, the nervous system, stripped of all previous learning, is completely vulnerable. Powerful attachments and repulsions develop during psychedelic sessions. Here is the danger and promise of psychedelic drugs—the development of new symbol systems and the refocusing of old systems.

Language Systems Available to Man

Our bodies plod through complex energy fields, incapable of absorbing the largest part of the messages surrounding us. But even so, the nervous system is still capable of a much wider range of awareness. Tantric Hinduism, for example, suggests that a universe of awareness exists at each of seven chakras, or nerve centers, in the body. For centuries Oriental psychologists have been developing methods to activate these chakra levels.

Our restriction of consciousness is, of course, no setback to the genetic blueprint. Life (DNA) is transmitted by us, through us, even though we sleepwalk. Perhaps the duties of the hive require a blindness to broader meanings and rapturous vibrations. In *All and Everything,* Georges I. Gurdjieff suggests that if man saw his true position in the evolutionary sequence, he might in despair quit playing his role. In order to keep man chasing externals, Gurdjieff speculates, the Kundabuffer organ—clearly a brilliant anticipation of the concept of imprinting—was introduced into the nervous system to keep man attached to external striving and cause him to see reality upside down.

The absurdity of language is now clear. Each of us labors under the illusion that our imprint board is reality—a situation beautifully described by Plato's Cave, or the parable of The Blind Men and The Elephant. When two human beings attempt to communicate, the absurdity is compounded: my chessboard interacting with your Monopoly game.

Those who live at the same time and in the same anthill share enough consensual codes to preserve the illusion of communication. That fraction of our language that refers to visible events in local space-time is reasonably efficient. We can communicate about static externals and materials, but little else.

Three Possibilities for Improving Man's Linguistic System

1. Increase our current imprint's efficiency by recognizing clearly what we have imprinted, recognizing our chessboard's limitations and dimensions, and developing new chains of association to open up the imprint board, without brain-change drugs.

2. Suspend the imprint with drugs, and tune in on the internal and external energy accessible to the human nervous system. Western psychology recognizes no methods or possibilities for getting off the imprint board. We must work within the tribal, temporary, accidental limits.

3. Note that suspension of imprint is *temporary.* No one has yet demonstrated the possibility of remaining "high" indefinitely. The

problem of reentry, return to externals, must always be met. We can reimprint carefully, selecting the new chessboard, choosing the persons and externals to which we will become *voluntarily* hooked.

Before the addicted "dope fiend" or alcoholic can be cured, he must recognize his affliction. The first step, therefore, is to recognize that our consciousness is totally hooked to certain externals; recognize the limits and directions of our imprints. Some forms of psychoanalysis aim to do this. Long chains of associations are laboriously traced, step by step, to the original imprint situation. A new sequence of associations is attempted, centering on the person of the analyst (transference). But, as Freud saw, verbal interaction in the consulting room cannot duplicate the impact of the original biochemical structuring. Each external imprint is uniquely located in space and time.

We can learn from the physical sciences, which keep their language system in tune with the processes they measure. A chemical formula is a functional shorthand that words can never reproduce. The linguistics of the chemical formula allow us to make changes in the formula that parallel changes in molecular structure. As Ilya Prigogine suggests, evolution involves dissipative structures. Nature is an open system, and any denotation describing nature should strive for openness as well. The philosophic advances stimulated by the physical sciences will inevitably filter down and be incorporated into a culture's communication. Everyone now babbles about "feedback" or "noise" or "input." This may improve communication about external affairs, but not the problem of communicating the internal, the experiential. When we deal with the neurological, we dip our cups into the rushing stream of experience. "Reality" is always subjective, unique, and irreplicable; "truth" subjective, unique, and fleeting. Since language determines experience, we must design a language that distinguishes the external from the neurological experience. If our language is closed, so will be our experiencing, perception, and thinking.

But *some* system is necessary. If our linguistic structure is chaotic and haphazard, then so will be our thinking and experiencing. The recent popularity of YMCA-Hindu-Buddhist babble is an ominous example of mushiness.

To describe internal neurological events, three types of experiential languages are possible:

1. Use external symbols to describe our experiencing, but only when consciousness is completely externalized, tied to external references—only one very limited type of experiencing.

2. We can combine external symbols in novel subjective forms—creative, imaginative, fantasied, visionary thinking. Such experi-

encing is pathological if involuntary (hallucinations, delusions); highly valued as poetic, when voluntary. We experience in terms of familiar-external symbols, but combine them in novel ways.

3. Bypass symbols completely. Communicate in terms of the energy recorded by our nervous system. We communicate these experiences by selecting and directing audio-visual energy sources that stimulate the nervous system of the person to whom we are communicating. In developing an experiential vocabulary we can include all the terms of the "old language," but the words no longer denote external movements in space-time. They are buzzwords with no external reference, just metaphorical noises, that activate an experience and hopefully communicate my buzz to someone else. Don't worry about external logic when you are metaphorically describing experience: the sentence, "It was a solid-gold, billion-dollar orgasm" does not involve a transaction that your stuffy banker will honor. (If you are describing an external game sequence, you must, on the contrary, be prudishly conscientious about the semantics of movements in space-time.) If you plan to communicate internal states metaphorically, using external symbols (including words), you must smash through linguistic conventions —alter sequences, turn words upside down, cut up and reassemble verbal sequences from all relevant sources.

To describe externals, you become a scientist. To describe experience, you become an artist. The old distinction between artists and scientists must vanish. Every time we teach a child correct usage of an external symbol, we must spend as much time teaching him how to fission and reassemble external grammar to communicate the internal.

The training of artists and creative performers can be a straightforward, almost mechanical process. When you teach someone how to perform creatively (i.e., associate dead symbols in new combinations), you expand his potential for experiencing more widely and richly.

Johnny is assigned an essay on "A Day at the County Fair." He writes an essay like a police-evidence report. Accurate observation tells him about external movements on the fairgrounds. He is then assigned to write: "My Experience at the County Fair." Here he reassembles the jumble of smells, sounds, memories, images in the style of James Joyce or William Burroughs.

Every word in the dictionary can be combined in endlessly new sequences. Every paragraph in the encyclopedia or any other publication becomes a paint pot in which we can dip our experiential brush. Photographs, paintings, objects, can be reassembled into new forms to express an experience nonverbally. The work of Bruce Conner, the eccentric garbage-can assembler is a good example; on his painting board, Conner nails a burlesque poster, a worn-out brassiere, a faded hat-feather, a tattered perfume ad. He covers the whole with transparent nylon hosiery and communicates the poignance of sexual disillusionment. This technique could be taught in primary school. In art class, Johnny is told to describe a flower; then is asked to cut up and reassemble to communicate his *experience* of the flower. This binocular approach to education teaches the philosophic distinction between "subject matter" and "reality," between objective, consensual "fact" and subjective "truth."

Experiential Language Must Go Beyond External Language

The vocabulary of external reference covers the most prosaic and game-limited fragment of experience. We play with a very limited set of Sears, Roebuck symbols. Korzybski suggested increasing semantic breadth and accuracy by a numerical code: instead of "apple," we have apple^1, apple^2, etc. Combining and reassembling words also multiplies their expressive potential, but we are still left with a lexicography basically designed for describing visible, objective space-time movements.

But experience is widely subjective. It transcends games. In constructing a vocabulary and grammar of internal reactions, where do we begin?

One starting place is the language of games that claim to be transcendental or experiential. Philosophies of the East are concerned with the internal, i.e., the neurological. Their onotologies, epistemologies, and logics are the despair of the Western scholar attuned to an external philosophy. We are told that Sanskrit, compared to English, contains about forty times the number of references to experiential events. It is no accident that most non-psychiatric researchers in the psychedelic field found it useful to borrow the terminology of Oriental philosophy. But it is pointless to teach our children experiential Sanskrit, because it is still a language of words, far removed from the speed and flow of experience.

To experience directly, we must transcend the verbal-symbol imprint, experience energy-flow *directly,* receive energy messages *directly.* The future language of experience will be based directly on the concepts and technology of light, sound, cellular movement, sympathetic and parasympathetic nervous system imagery: direct replication of energy flow.

Consciousness is a biochemical neurological decoding that

takes place at many levels of the nervous system. Units of the language will be based on units for measuring and describing these energy transformations. In the next century, we shall all talk like physicists. Communication about external events is science. All men are good or bad scientists when they describe external events. But men must become artists to describe internal events. In developing systems for communicating experience, how can we transmit energy patterns to "turn on" the receiver—i.e., directly stimulate the nervous system, bypassing the receiver's symbol system? Most of us are terrified by free neurological energy. We resist being turned on. We ostracize those who try to turn us on—by social isolation, censorship, and legal restrictions.

The consensual symbolic hallucination must be maintained. Any rent in the hive symbol system threatens the structural delusion. While the illustrator is welcomed, the buzz-shock artist—who turns you on—is anathematized by the conventional hive member.

The creative artist's aim is the same as the scientist's: accurate recording of the dance of energy transformations. The scientist observes the external, the artist the experienced. The engineer manipulates the external, the illustrator portrays it; neither are artists.

Three Artistic Language Systems

1. *Reproductive Art* focuses only on the external, hive-consensual, static symbolical structure—the game. Great illustrators (Norman Rockwell, Dürer) succeed in communicating the revealing epiphany moments of game culmination.

2. *Visionary (or neosymbolic) Art* attempts to translate the energy dance in terms of unique combinations of static symbols. Hieronymus Bosch, Lenora Carrington, Goya, the Surrealists, Dali, John Cage, Antonio Gaudí.

3. *Transcendental Art (Tranart)* avoids reliance on familiar symbols or external forms and directly transmits sensory energy. Abstract art is a step in this direction.

Physics, biology, biochemistry, genetics, and Tranart all express the same message: Beyond the hive imprint all is one dance of electrical energy; of cellular process. Science and art have the same aim: to record the process.

We have been taught to narrow our awareness to a fantasy world of symbol solids. But that's not how it really is. All matter is energy—everything is whirling change, even you! Look at your baby pictures. Look in the mirror. You are a dramatically changing process.

Imagine a mile-high camera taking a picture of your city every six months. Run six hundred frames through your projector. Representative art plays the delusionary game with familiar static categories. Visionary art invents its own categories. Tranart attempts to get back to the cortical flash. Op art, for example, attempts to return to the retina, freezing the naked, patternless mosaic. Your Persian rug (the Islamic artist is forbidden to reproduce forms) is static Tranart, an unstained experiential slide of retinal sensation. Have you seen a cross-section of retinal tissue? A many-layered technicolor swamp of rods and cones, interlaced with capillaries. No Sears, Roebuck images there! Imagine your Persian rug undulating, each unit in motion, a swirling rock-and-roll of color. That's what the original rug designers had in mind. The rug contains the message, the reminder.

Reproductive art reminds only that man can share static symbols. Illustrative painting and photography freeze the symbolic. Abstract painting and microscopic photographs freeze the process. (*Moving* pictures help keep the hallucinatory process going and duplicate the imprinted "reality" delusion.) In the last few years we have witnessed the emergence of psychedelic Tranart attempts to communicate nonsymbolically, to cut through hallucinations to the direct sensation, to produce the direct sensation of flowing process, a reproduction of the microscopic event.

Psychedelic drugs provide creative experience—suspending verbal governors so that the neurological motor operates at high speed. To communicate a psychedelic experience, you require psychedelic Tranart, which tries to keep up with the speed and breadth of direct sensation. After psychedelic training, we accustom ourselves to the pace of the nervous system. We experience a flood of new worlds. Tranart requires new technical means, based on the machines now used by scientists, to record (1) the life process, (2) the energy dance. Instead of the brush and the Leica, psychedelic artists use the electromicroscopic camera, random analog projectors, multiple films and tapes, polarized light, chemically treated slides, the oscilloscope, the telescopic camera, lasers, computer animation, sci-fi special effects.

Conventional visual art techniques involve the surface (canvas or paper), the paint (or covering substance), and the instruments to shape the design (pallet knife, brush). Tranart employs the same three media—(1) the screen, which can vary in shape and texture; (2) the energy source: these always-changing energy patterns are called Direct Process Images (DPI's); (3) symbolic representations, called Learned Form Images (LFI's).

DPI's externalize representations of the flow of direct

sensation-experience. Flowing, unstructured, unidentifiable, they are communications of the experience of direct energy.

LFI's are representations of learned and artifactual perceptual forms: objects, things, organisms, events, bodies, chairs, flowers. Both DPI's and LFI's may be auditory or visual, internal or external, depending on whether they represent experiences bubbling out of the lower nervous system or coming from without. Thus, visual internal DPI's are moving magnificatious of retinal processes—cellular or subcellular events (organic DPI's). Visual external DPI's are moving pictures of energy processes at the atomic or subatomic level: waves, interacting planes of light, images of inorganic processes continually moving, flowing, dancing.

There are also auditory DPI's—recordings of sounds heard from inside of the body (internal); recordings of sounds registered in the brain without cognitive patternings, unstructured natural, white noise (external).

Visual LFI's are representations of "things" if they are consensual, of "hallucinations" if idiosyncratic. Traditional moving pictures and filmed sequences are visual LFI's. Symphonies are auditory LFI's, game sequences for the trained ear. Auditory internal LFI's are representations of experiences generally considered psychotic: hearing "voices" or "meaningful" sounds inside your head.

Thus, we have three kinds of art, communicating three types of experiences: (1) "reality-oriented": storytelling, reproductive, realistic art; (2) old images combined into new patterns, blending incongruous sequences—montage, assemblage, the movie "cut-up" method used by Bruce Conner in which he recombines dozens of old newsreels; Salvador Dali's surrealistic combinations of organic and inorganic forms; John Cage's chance combinations of sounds and noises; (3) *Neurological Tranart*, recording the mixture and interweaving of direct process with learned game form; Van Gogh's skies contain energy vortices. Tchelitchew's "Hide and Seek" has mysterious faces moving out of capillary streams and organic networks. Visionary Sufi miniatures have rocks in the backgrounds which, when you look closely, seem to have mysterious faces hidden. Bruce Conner's *Cosmic Ray* movie has pulsing abstract forms out of which emerge now a naked woman, now marching soldiers, now parachutes, now Mickey Mouse. Visionary Tranart is LFI's imposed on or woven into DPI's; game concepts superimposed on the energy process.

Pure Tranart attempts to record pure, symbol-free energy. Jackson Pollock's paintings are indistinguishable from retinal cross-sections. Persian rugs are only slightly more symmetrical. To represent visual internal DPI's, we used recurrent film loops of microbiological processes. When projected, these uncannily reproduce the psychedelic vision. Cells dance through technicolor swamps. Ciliated protoplasm flails down undulating channels. Membrane spheres bounce across vague tissue landscapes, flowing without cease. "What is it?" That's the point, of course! You can't label the microscopic process with macroscopic terms. The cellular life signals never stop. The film keeps moving.

The DPI Library

Tranart requires a wide variety of paint-color or sound-notes. A library of visual DPI's is a collection of slides and films of energy and microbiological life processes. Just as the painter knows the range of available pigments, so the Tranartist knows the range of available DPI's representing direct, formless sensations.

After your visions, you select from the DPI film catalogue the closest representation. No DPI comes close to direct sensation, of course, but it comes closer than words. The very existence of a DPI lexicon lets you know where to go for a more exact representation. Microbiological film technicians and physics-lab technicians thus become the philologists of the new DPI's language.

The LFI Library

In neosymbolic or visionary Tranart, structure is provided by LFI's —films or tape-recordings of structured events, objects, people.

Researchers at the Castalia Foundation have developed a code system for every cultural, personal, biological, and chemical event. When a structured (consensual hallucination) sequence—visual, auditory, tactual—is needed to add form to a Tranart communication, a filmstrip is located in the LFI library, or created.

An ever-increasing library of catalogued DPI's and LFI's is thus assembled. With infinite combinations of experiential images, it is possible to express any experience of noncultural energy, life process, or visionary creation. To record a visionary experience (a mixture of primary process and cultural sequence) requires Visionary Tranart —LFI's imposed on or woven into DPI's.

A vision of undulating streams or bouncing spheres (not recognized as blood cells) convert (as an LFI is imposed on the primary process) into uncoiling serpent-flow, which changes to a network of

Chinese Communist soldiers, which shifts into the florid, pulsating face of a leering Oriental dictator which flickers into the portrait of one's feared stepmother.

A blood-circulation DPI film loop is set running on one projector. Then the subject finds an LFI sequence of uncoiling serpents. They are green, so he imposes a red filter. The DPI projector starts running; after a minute the red-filter-serpent LFI projector is snapped on—out of focus. Gradually, the LFI strip is brought into focus and the vision slowly shifts from pure DPI to DPI-LFI vision. The LFI filmstrip is then spliced to newsreel film of marching Chinese columns, and then the picture of Chou En-lai. A still photo of Stepmother is inserted in a slide projector with a veined red filter completely out of focus and slowly focused at the appropriate second.

The Tranartist experiments until he gets the flowing sequence he wants, with LFI's fading in and out of focus—with the pulsing DPI stream always flowing, flowing in the background. Then he adds sound. The pump of a heartbeat fades into the thud of marching feet, to shouted commands in Chinese, to Stepmother's voice screaming "You'll never amount to anything." The sound sequence is adjusted to the visual barrage and speeded up: 30 seconds of the Tranart representation of a psychedelic vision.

Perceived forms swim into focus out of the swirling, unformed wave process: a fact of perception. Visionary Tranart makes it possible to duplicate this as an expressed communication. In principle, there is no limit to the range of DPI-LFI communication. Tranart is based on the raw records of science, which become part of a new and vastly expanded basic language of experience. Language approaches the speed and extension of the neural network, an increasing percentage of which becomes available to consciousness, communication, and conceptualization.

PART THREE

HUMANIST INTERPRETA- TIONS OF THE RELIGIOUS EXPERIENCE (Your Brain Is God)

In 1966, the Harvard-Millbrook psychedelic researchers decided to exploit the religious metaphor in order to encourage people to take charge of their own brain functions. Our own commitments and role-models were always scientific. For example, we succeeded in training illiterate prisoners to perform the functions of (and to talk like) psychologists. And our summer training camps in the Hotel Catalina in Zihuatenjo, Mexico, effectively taught a wide range of intellectuals how to reimprint their own brain programs.

Our logic seemed clear: brain-activating drugs expose people to powerful, mind-blowing experiences that shatter conventional ideas about reality. If left alone by society, our International Foundation for Internal Freedom (IFIF) would have succeeded in training several thousand neurologicians who, in their own communities, could have trained hundreds of thousands of Americans to use their own heads.

But wisely or foolishly, we got scared off this scientific approach. After being expelled from Harvard, Mexico, Antigua, and Dominica in four months (May–August 1963), we cravenly decided that the authorities were not ready for the 21st-century concept: *Every Citizen a Scientist*. So we fell back to the familiar historical turf upon which most earlier freedom movements had fought the battle —religion.

Though it might be against the law for responsible American citizens to use psychoactive plants and drugs to change their brains, surely 400 years of Western civilization must support the right of Americans to worship the divinity within, using sacraments that worked for them. We studied the meaning of the word *sacrament*, usually defined as something that relates one to the divinity. One of the most offensive, flaky characteristics of 1960's acid-users was their compulsion to babble about new visions of God, new answers to the Ultimate Secret of the Universe. For thousands of years individuals whose brains were activated had chattered about "ultimate secrets" in the context of mystical-personal religious revelation. We were forced to recall that for most of human history, science and philosophy were the province of religion. And most specifically, all references to what we would now call the psychoneurological were described in religious terms. Our political experiences at Harvard also pushed us in the direction of the religious metaphor. When it became known on campus that a group of psychologists was producing revelatory brain-change, we expected that astronomers and biologists would come flocking around to learn how to use this new tool for expanding awareness. But the scientists, committed to external manipulations, were uninterested. Instead we were flooded by inquiries from the Divinity School!

I must confess that I was uneasy about falling back on the religious paradigm. For 40 years I had been conditioned to respond negatively to the word "God." Any time someone started shouting about God, I automatically expected to be conned or threatened by some semiliterate hypocrite. We tried to avoid this insidious buzzword. God knows, at one point we talked about LSD as a "brain vitamin" or dietary supplement—but this more accurate label sounded dodgy. Self-control of one's diet was not to become respectable until the holistic medicine of the 1970's.

Our problem—typical of time-travel agents dealing with primitive cultures—was that a dramatic change in neurology must be gently introduced in the language a culture traditionally uses for those "mysterious, unknown, higher powers" which its science has not yet explained. A review of 20th-century literature showed that there was obviously a strong taboo against "brain-change." By 1960, indeed, the brain had replaced the genitals as the forbidden organ that must not be touched or turned on by the owner. The only way in which consciousness-change experiences could be discussed was in terms of philosophic-religious. Even Buddhism, an atheist method of psychological self-control, allowed itself to be classified as a religion.

So religion it was. I recall the moment of decision: During a wild, all-night LSD session in our mansion in the Boston suburbs, Richard Alpert came up to me, eyes popping, and announced, "The East! We must go back to the wisdom of the East!" *Go back?*

The lawyers agreed. There is apparently nothing in the Bill of Rights to protect scientific freedom. The Constitution was written in a horse-and-buggy pre-technological era. But there *was* a First Amendment protection of Freedom of Religion. After all, Catholic priests were allowed Communion wine during Prohibition. So I agreed to the religious posture on the conditions that there was to be no kneeling down, no dogmas, no holy men, no followers, no churches, no public worship, no financial offerings. . . .

8

This chapter began as an invited address delivered at the 1963 meetings of the American Psychological Association. The inviting group was the Association of Lutheran Psychologists, who had taken a night off from the more secular events of the convention to listen to some comments about "The Religious Experience: Its Production and Interpretation."

This was four months after my being fired from Harvard University, so the Lutherans were inviting controversy. I had (1953–59) administered psychological screening tests for most of the younger ministers in the Lutheran Church, and so my contributions to the faith were, perhaps, being recognized. The paper attempted to scientize myth and mythologize science. We were trying so romantically to heroicize-sanctify our lives, their lives, life itself.

I have been working on this essay for the last 18 years, refining and updating. It is my *summa theologica* in that it attempts to translate classic issues of theology into the language of modern science. It may be the first comprehensive philosophy to deal with evolution, both species and individual, both past and future.

The original essay was widely reprinted in several languages and probably contributed to the current blossoming of young visionary scientists who are now, aged 30 to 45, pushing out the frontiers of physics, chemistry, and biology. It is safe to estimate that over a hundred young Ph.D. physicists and a like number of biologists read this paper at some point along the way. When you read this chapter, imagine yourself an impressionable, brilliant college student, circa 1964–70, searching, experimenting, dreaming the dreams of grandeur and idealism and splendor that characterized that more utopian optimistic period.

It is an activist, do-it-yourself theology. God is defined in terms of the technologies involved in creating a universe and engineering the obvious stages of evolution. Anyone interested in playing the God-game is given suggestions for activating the various levels of intelligence in hir own brain and DNA and expressing them through the tools of modern science. Any human being who wishes to accept the responsibility is offered the powers traditionally assigned to divinity.

The eight crafts of God: towards an experiential science of religion

Many years ago, on a sunny afternoon in a Cuernavaca garden, I ate seven so-called sacred mushrooms given to me by a scientist from the University of Mexico. During the next five hours, I was whirled through an experience which was, above all and without question, the deepest religious-philosophic experience of my life. And it was totally electric-cellular scientific, cinematographic.

Personal reactions, however passionate, are always relative and may have little general significance. Next come the "Ho Hum, questions, "Why?" and "So what?"

Many predisposing factors—physiological, emotional, intellectual, ethical-social (i.e., financial)—cause one person to be ready for a dramatic mind-opening experience and lead another to shrink back from new levels of intelligence. The discovery that the human brain possesses an infinity of potentialities and can operate at unexpected space-time dimensions left naive me exhilarated, awed, and quite convinced that I had awakened from a long ontological sleep.

Since my brain-activation-illumination of August 1960, I have repeated this biochemical and (to me) sacramental ritual several thousand times, and almost every subsequent brain-opening has awed me with philosophic-scientific revelations as convincing as the first experience. During this period (1960–68) I have been lucky enough to collaborate with several hundred scientists and scholars who joined our various search and research projects. In our brain-activation centers at Harvard, in Mexico, Morocco, Almora, India, Millbrook, and in the California mountains we have arranged transcendent brain-change experiences for several thousand persons from all walks of life, including more than 400 full-time religious professionals: about half professing Christian or Jewish faiths and about half belonging to Celtic, pagan, or Eastern religions.

In 1962, an informal group of ministers, theologians, academic hustlers, and religious psychologists in the Harvard environment began meeting once a month to further these beginnings. This group was the original planning nucleus of the organizations that assumed sponsorship of our consciousness-expansion research: IFIF (1963), the Castalia Foundation (1963–66), and the League for Spiritual Discovery

(1966). That our generating impulse and original leadership came from a seminar in religious experience may be related to the alarmed confusion we aroused in secular and psychiatric circles of the time.

The study, sensationalized in the press as "The Miracle of Marsh Chapel," deserves further elaboration as a "serious," "controlled" experiment involving over 30 courageous volunteers and as a systematic scientific demonstration of the "religious" aspects of psychedelic experience. This study was the Ph.D. dissertation research of Walter Pahnke, M.D., then a graduate student in the philosophy of religion at Harvard University, who set out to determine whether the transcendent experience reported during psychedelic acid sessions was similar to the mystical experience reported by saints and religious mystics.

As subjects, 20 divinity students were selected from a group of volunteers and divided into 5 groups of 4 persons. To each group were assigned 2 guides with considerable psychedelic experience —professors and advanced graduate students from Boston-area colleges.

The experiment, believe it or not, took place in a small, private chapel at Boston University, about one hour before noon on Good Friday, 1962. The dean of the chapel, Howard Thurman, was to conduct a public 3-hour devotional service upstairs in the main hall of the church. He visited our subjects a few minutes before the start of the noon service and gave a brief "inspirational" talk.

Two subjects in each group and one of the two guides were given a moderately stiff dosage (i.e., 30 mg.) of psilocybin. The remaining two subjects and the second guide received a placebo that produced noticeable somatic side effects (hot-cold skin flashes), but which was not psychedelic. The study was triple-blind: neither the subjects, guides, nor the experimenters knew who received psilocybin.

If you ever run a double-blind study with these drugs, you must not have controls around experimental subjects because no one will be fooled. I knew immediately that two subjects in my group had nicotinic acid; I could tell by their red faces and their restless "game" activity. But thinking they were on the verge of a mystic experience, they started winking, "Isn't this great? The poor fellows in the other room are being left out of it." Later, after we had been in the chapel and saw other subjects reclining on the floor, obviously completely out of this world, the two called me and said, "Let's go back into the other room." They started playing the drug game again: "How long has it been?" "Gee, I thought I had it." "Now what did you feel exactly?"

A door banged open, and a man walked in, looked out the

window, and said, "Magnificent." He turned without looking at us as he walked out. We all knew who was placebo and who was mystical.

Typically, 9% of LSD subjects reported unpleasant experiences; most of these fought the experience. In the Good Friday experience, for example, one divinity student fought it all the way, repeating: "Now when is it going to get over? I'm just not in control of myself. Didn't you say it would last four hours?"

There is a magnificent selectivity operating here, because people committed to controlling themselves sense ahead of time that the notion of ego transcendence or loss is threatening. They don't volunteer; don't show up, or postpone it. Of course, courage is the key to creativity or to any relinquishing of ego structure.

Our studies, naturalistic and experimental, demonstrate that if the expectation, preparation, and setting are Protestant-New England religious, an intense mystical or revelatory experience will be admitted by 40 to 90% of subjects ingesting psychedelic drugs. These results may be attributed to the bias of our research group, which has taken the rather dangerous ACLU position that there are "experiential-spiritual" as well as secular-behavioral emotional-political potentialities of the nervous system. Five scientific studies by other investigators yield data which indicate that (1) if the setting is supportive but not spiritual, between 40 to 75% of psychedelic subjects will report intense and life-changing philosophic-religious experiences and (2) if the set and setting are supportive and "spiritual," then from 40 to 90% of the experiences will be revelatory and mystico-philosophic-religious.

How can these results be disregarded by those concerned with philosophic growth and religious development? These data are even more interesting because the experiments took place in 1962, when individual religious ecstasy (as opposed to religious piety) was highly suspect and when meditation, jogging, yoga, fasting, body-consciousness, social-dropout-withdrawal, and sacramental (i.e., organic) foods and drugs were surrounded by an aura of eccentricity, fear, clandestine secrecy, even imprisonment. The 400 professional workers in religious vocations who partook of psychedelic substances were responsible, thoughtful, and "moral," highly moral, individuals, grimly aware of the controversial nature of drugs and aware that their reputations and jobs might be undermined. Not bad, huh? Still the results read: 75% philosophic revelation. It may well be that, like the finest metal, the most intense religious experience requires fire, the "heat" of police constabulatory opposition, to produce the keenest edge. When sacramental biochemicals are used as routinely and tamely as organ music and incense the ego-shattering, awe-inspiring effect of the drugs may be diminished.

What Is a Religious Experience?

The religious experience is the ecstatic, jolting, wondrous, awe-struck, life-changing, mind-boggling confrontation with one or all of the eight basic mysteries of existence. The goals of an intelligent life, according to Socrates, is to pursue the philosophic quest—to increase one's knowledge of self and world. Now there is an important division of labor involved in the philosophic search. Religion, being personal and private, cannot produce answers to the eight basic questions. The philosopher's role is to ignite the wonder, raise the burning issues, inspire the pursuit of answers. It is science that produces the ever-changing, improving answers to the haunting questions that religious wonder poses.

First let us list the questions which any fair survey of our philosophic history would agree are most fundamental to our existential condition:

1. Origins: *Questions of Genesis.* How, when, where, why did the life come from? How has it evolved?
2. Politics: *Questions of security, power, control, and territory.* Why do humans fight and compete destructively? What are the territorial laws that explain conflict? How can humans live in relative peace and harmony? How, when, where, and why do humans differ (among each other and from other mammalian species) in aggression, control, cooperation, affiliation?
3. Epistemology: *Questions of truth, fact, language, knowledge, communications, manufacture of objects, artifacts, and symbol systems.* How, when, where, and why does the mind emerge (in the individual and species)? And how, when, where, and why do humans differ in their ability to process information, learn, communicate, think, plan, and manufacture?
4. Ethics: *Questions of good and evil, right and wrong.* How, when, where, and why do humans differ in their moral beliefs and rituals? Who decides what is good and right?
5. Esthetics: *Questions of beauty, pleasure, luxury, sensory reward.* How, when, where, and why do humans devote their energies to decoration, hedonism, art, music, entertainment?

And how, where, when, and why do they differ in modes of pleasure?

6. Ontology: *Questions about Reality and its (their) definition.* How, when, where, and why do humans differ in the realities they construct and inhabit? How are realities formed and changed?

7. Teleology: *Questions of evolution/de-evolution of life.* What are the stages and mechanisms of evolution? Where, when, how, and why has evolution occurred? Chance? Natural selection? Natural election? Creation? If life is created and evolution blueprinted, who did it? Where is life going?

8. Cosmology: *Questions of galactic evolution, of ultimate power and basic structure.* How, when, where, and why was matter-energy formed? What are the basic units and patterns of matter/energy? What are the basic forces, energies, and plans that hold the universe together (or don't) and determine its evolution? Where are we going?

Now it is true that most human beings spend little time thinking about these issues. Mundane questions about how to get fed, how to avoid irritable neighbors, which career to follow, which girl to marry, who will win the Super Bowl obsess the normal consciousness of most humans.

The religious-philosophic person is defined by hir concern for the great navigational question. The answers, we recall, come from the listening posts which we set up to obtain from nature the signals which will increase our knowledge about what nature is up to.

The Current Scientific Answers to the Eight Basic Questions, and the Success of Religions, Both Ancient and Modern, in Anticipating and Decoding These Answers

The last century has been one of considerable religious disarray and confusion. On the one hand, the old creeds have obviously not succeeded in producing survivally-safe answers. When the Catholic church threatens eternal damnation for believers who do not follow St. Paul's 1st century taboos against birth control—at a time when starvation and overpopulation are endemic in Catholic countries—a certain nervousness develops. When the 1,000-year-old warfare between Christianity and Islam erupts again in the 87th crusade—Rockefeller vs

Khomeini-Khadafi—again, sensible people wonder what these aging religious fundamentalists really have in mind for the future of our species.

Suddenly there is an explosion of new scientific insights —nuclear physics, astrophysics, genetics, neurology, ethology—which produce data requiring drastic changes in our conceptions of human nature. We face the splendid, glorious, possibility that, now, for the first time, our species can not only answer the basic questions but take over the technologies for running the universe, the planet, the genetic future. It is surely time for a global celebration! Finally our species is on the threshold of living, not in helpless fear and ignorance, but in confident, loving hope!

Are the religious folks listening?

As we survey these new findings which allow us to learn and practice the eight technologies of God, we are delighted to discover that certain ancient religions (mainly the pagan) in millennia past had anticipated what our scientists are now discovering. And as Americans we are proud to point out that the 1960's drug-culture's giddy, wild, confused eruption of philosophy and spiritual anarchy played an important role in stimulating and provoking the new Scientific Paganism of the 21st century. The new scientific answers provide us with eight new definitions of God as designer/technologist of the universe. And they suggest how any serious-minded intelligent person can begin to master these Eight Crafts of Divinity.

1. Origins: God the Protozoan. Our fundamentalist Judeo-Christian friends assure us that life was created by a stern, omnipotent, judgmental condominium-owner named Jehovah and that our destinies follow His impenetrable plans.

Most religions throughout history have offered metaphorical or poetic myths which, unfortunately, developed in prescientific days before Copernicus, Darwin or Galileo. Giordano Bruno was not the only one to be killed for suggesting that the universe is a big, wild, place filled with other centers of intelligence.

During the past fifty years, astronomy, exo-biology, and genetics have produced wondrous scenarios of Big Bangs, Black Holes, alternate universes, accidental or directed panspermia (seeding of planets from space), and the ultimate cosmic unifying principle, that every atom in our bodies has come from the supernova explosions of far-distant stars.

For us, as a species momentarily stranded in a landlocked terrestrial stage, life began locally in the ocean, in unicellular form. We clumsy, heavy bipeds, clinging like barnacles on the grasping 1-G surface of an embryonic planet, tend to overestimate our status and function in the evolutionary web. The unicellular state is the first, the most basic, the omnipresent triumphant form of intelligent life.

Everything that we now possess as physiological or neural equipment was built into the original design of the first protozoan cells.

Individually, too, we began as a single cell at the moment of our conception. Only recently have we begun to understand the seed-complexity of our beginnings. The single cell handles more transactions per day than do the nine million primates of New York City. As we decipher the tactics and intelligent operations of the single cell, we shall begin to understand how our own lives can be better arranged. This is especially obvious when we consider that our original germ cell contained the blueprints for designing the equipment which makes it possible for us to write, edit, print, distribute, buy and read this book.

Mystics and psychedelic drug users have commented eloquently on the unicellular pageantry and wisdom that accompanies transcendent moments. Much of visionary-drug art is protozoan—from Bosch to Sufi rugs to acid-rock light shows. Our LSD subjects regularly report accessing those large circuits of our brain that are tuned into cellular traffic.

At the most down-to-earth level, we cannot move into outer space until we realize that life-on-earth is a giant unified cellular entity. The Gaia Theory (which we shall consider at later stages of theo-technology) reminds us that the space capsules in which we will escape from this planet will inevitably be based on unicellular design. Is it not clear that the launch-out from the planet will require us to fabricate self-sustaining capsules that must be capable of performing the most rudimentary unicellular behaviors?

God #1 is thus the Single-cell Intelligence, the collaborative brain that knows how to run a simple protozoan. The First God is the one-celled God. The First and original craft of God is Protozoan.

2. Predator-Prey Politics: God the Emotional Mammal. Most religions play on home-territory sentiments and seek to establish political–military–police–predator control. Position in the pecking order had always been influenced, if not determined, by religious status. (Until 1960, only a predator Protestant could become president of the United States.) Religions activate midbrain centers that mediate mammalian, emotional territorial behavior. Dumb religions stimulate defense of home turf: aggression-control and submission docility. The smarter religions stimulate migration. Judeo-Christian–Moslem, Marxist religions glorify conquest, expansion, and murder of nonbelievers. The deliberate incitement of chauvinist-partisan fear-and-rage is a standard tactic in most human theologies.

Ethology and sociobiology observe the behavior of animals in natural habitats and study the reflex methods of social organization used by other species: territoriality, caste division of labor, bluff, slavery, gestural communication, olfactory signaling, migration, hierarchy. There seems to be no social problem discussed in the Judeo-Christian Bible that has not been solved more harmoniously and intelligently by social insects.

Eastern religions (non-urban and thus more in tune with nature) have developed ecological sensitivities that are in agreement with the recent insights of sociobiologists. Surely it is time for grim, suspicious, fear-rage mammalian Islamo-Christian sects to adapt a more genial, tolerant perspective of interspecies or intraspecies collaboration. The psychedelic drug experimentation of the 1960's produced one wonderful bi-product: a pagan love of nature, a hippy sense of alienation from man-made anthropocentric philosophies. Is it not clear that the ecology movement owes its birth to barefoot acid-pagan concern for nature?*

Here again, we see that brains activated by psychedelic drugs readily accept the findings of modern science, restate the Oriental life-affirming philosophies of Buddhism, Jainism, Hinduism; and make possible the Scientific Paganism of the 21st century.

Psychopharmacology, particularly in its use of the tranquilizers, has introduced the notion of "turning off" irrelevant or inappropriate emotion, thus giving medical respectability to the Hindu and hipster notion of being "cool." Let us consider a dictionary definition: "emotion:

---

*When I was studying mammalian theology at Folsom prison in 1973, it was my custom, during the clear, blue-sky, desert-hot summer months, to walk barefoot in the prison yard. One day the leader of the Hell's Angels, his name was James "Fu" Griffin, approached me.

"Hey, man," he said, "how come you walk barefoot in the prison yard? Don't you know that's dangerous?" We were the best of friends and his question was solicitous, not hostile. He wanted nothing but the best for me.

"Why is it dangerous?" I asked.

"Well you're exposed. Like to germs and all. You know all these animals spit on the ground here."

"Yeah, I know. But here's how I look at it. When you walk barefoot, like undefended, you are very alert about where you put your feet. I'm more alive, like a wild animal, when I'm barefoot. And, come to think of it, I believe it would be better if more prisoners here stopped spitting on the yard and joined me walking barefoot."

"I see what you mean," said James "Fu" Griffin.

He subsequently got a degree in anthropology from Berkeley and is, at the time of this writing, a country-Western promoter in San Francisco.

agitation of the passions or sensibilities often involving physiological changes. Rage, fear, greed, desire, gratitude, jealousy, self-pity." Is this any way to run a species? Why do these loco-motions play such a visible part in human life?

Personal emotions are poetically considered to be a diagnostic symptom of humanity. Mr. Spock, of *Star Trek,* is "alien" because he does not break down in irrational outbursts, fits of temper, or sentiment. If, now and then a tiny little tear of self-pity would appear in Spock's eye we would consider him one-of-us. To be human is, for many psychologists, to be honestly irrational. One shows one's "real nature" when some unpleasant feeling is revealed.

This romantic view of human nature is clearly Mediterranean. Now that our species is ready to send advanced probes into space it is a matter of amusement that our species-identity is influenced by a bunch of semi-illiterate Bronze-Age Greeks, Italians, and Semites. Saint Augustine was a fanatic, superstitious Libyan. Aristotle was an Athenian living in a barbarous era when treachery, ignorance, fanaticism were endemic. Old Testament drama, vulgarized by Italian opera and homogenized in our modern prime-time soap opera, has insidiously glorified emotions —mammalian, male-macho meanness, and self-pity. Even today this humorless, jumpy fanaticism arises from the Mediterranean basin like an adrenaline smog.

Romantic poetry and fiction of the last 2,000 years has quite blinded us to the fact that emotions are a low mammalian form of jungle consciousness. Emotional *actions* are the most contracted, dangerous form of fanatic stupor. Any peasant, any child can tell you that. Beware of emotions. Watch out for the emotional person, the heavy-breathing lurching Latin lunatic. The emotional person is turned off sensually. His body is a churning robot; he has lost all connection with cellular wisdom or atomic revelation. Emotions are addictive, narcotic, and stupefacient. Like an alcoholic or a junkie, the frightened person activates his favorite mammalian circuit.

Moods such as sorrow and joy accompany emotions. Like a junkie who has just connected, the emotional person feels good when he has scored emotionally, i.e., put someone down or been beaten down.

Conscious love is not an emotion; it is serene merging with yourself, with other people, with other forms of energy. Love cannot exist in an emotional state. The great kick of the mystic experience is the sudden relief from emotional pressure. The only state in which we can learn, harmonize, grow, merge, join, understand, is the absence of emotion called security, attained through fine-tuning the emotions.

Why, then, if emotions are so painful, demanding, and blind-ing, are they built into the human repertoire? For a basic survival purpose. Emotions are emergency alarms. The organism at the point-of-death threat or territorial invasion goes into a paroxysm of frantic activity, like a fish out of water, like a cornered animal. But the sensible animal avoids situations that elicit fear. Your wise animal prefers to lay back relaxed—using his senses, tuned into his delicious body-organ music, closing his eyes to drift back in cellular memory. Dogs and cats are high, i.e., alertly cool, all the time—except when bad luck demands emotional measures.

Evolution works through recapitulation, adding new somatic-neural circuits to the old, requiring each individual to repeat the evolutionary stages of the species. Each of us has a mammalian midbrain geared for territorial security, physical safety, offensive. In order to perform any of the "higher" functions of intelligence, we must satisfy the midbrain. We must arrange our lives so that we feel "at home," cozy, safe in a territorial niche, with adequate food supply.

It is also part of survival wisdom to check out, dry-run, our animal emotional repertoire. Flick through the paranoia dials regularly. What would I do if an armed robber stole into the house at midnight? What would I do if jumped by some hoods in the parking lot? What would I do if the Blacks break out of the ghetto or the rednecks invade the ghetto?

Like all our divinities, the presocial, wily-animal god of emotion-locomotion resides within our nervous system, ready to pour out flight-fight endocrine juices. Politicians and priests deliberately play on our fears and exaggerate our dangers for their own profit. This is the National Security ploy. The intelligent human being has learned to turn-on-and-off the emotions, the way you navigate the other circuits in your brain. The Second Craft of God is intelligent access to and control of emotions.

3. Epistomology: God the Semanticist. How do we know? Why do we think and believe what we think and believe? How do we determine what is true and what is fact? Why will people believe even the most bizarre notions? Why do people, especially establishment priests and scientists, deliberately refuse to learn lessons basic to survival and happiness? How come people believe fanatically in such different and opposing ways? Why are brains equipped or programmed or condi-tioned to perform such different functions? Why do minds work the way they do? That these questions still remain unanswered after 3,000 years of Eastern-Western philosophy reflects the primitive, primate nature of our species.

Many religions include an epistemological theory of truth-fact. Most assert that truth was revealed once and for all by an inaccessible Deity in the form of Sacred Writings. And most religions nominate priesthoods (a lawyer-scribe caste) who arbitrate, interpret, and enforce (with violence) the Divine Truths revealed in the Bibles, Korans, Torahs. In cultures where truth-fact are tied to religious dogmas, then science wanes, practical investigation languishes, and thinking is subordinated to submissive belief.

But once again, we see that some Eastern religions (Zen, for example) and some Western philosophies—particularly the semantic —have understood the crucial difference between the map and the territory, between the avalanche of raw data processed by the brain and the pitifully few abstractions which we use to label reality. More recently, linguists and cognitive psychologists and ethologists have produced data that help us understand how the cognitive function emerges in species and in individual humans.

Around the age of 6 in the individual human (and around 25 million years ago in the age of our species) the Evolutionary Intelligence arranges to activate frontal lobes. Only when our primate ancestors had learned to walk on two feet, thus freeing their mouths for oral signaling, could the new laryngeal-manual circuits of the brain emerge.

Obviously people are born with different brains. A key factor in the evolution of intelligence is socialization. Division of labor. Gaia works with gene pools, which produce specialized castes, individuals genetical-ly geared to perform the different functions that contribute variously to the needs of the group. Sociobiologists have ruminated obsessively to explain *altruism* in social animals. Why does one bird give the alarm signal when the hawk is sighted? This seems to violate the "selfish gene" principle of natural selection. By drawing attention to himself, the flock "crier" risks his own reproductive future.

One possible answer—that of inborn caste difference—has so far eluded the ethologists. Some birds are caste-equipped with nervous systems geared to scan more restlessly, and to react with speedier alarm-signalry. Other birds in the flock are equipped with nervous systems caste-calibrated for more accurate homing, food selection, or for just plain old dull following, thus adding population mass, in swarming numbers, to the gene pool. Surely commonsense observation of human heredity shows us that genius brains can emerge from the dullest-normal of the kith-kin.

A human group requires a variety of brain castes to perform the highly specialized and complex acts necessary to keep the collective unit going. People are born with different minds, equipped with brains designed to be better at certain mental functions. Our minds are "made up" for us at the moment of conception. Twentieth-century mass-education methods disastrously assumed that equal Ivy League education for all was the neurological goal of a democratic or even a socialist society. But mass education has not worked. Millions of Johnnies now find themselves in college, still unable to read, because a majority of brains today are not designed to process abstract symbols rapidly, pleasurably, obsessively. Probably not more than 10% of Americans' brains are geared to comfortably handle symbols, i.e., to read and write. Most legally literate people read only when necessary, and then with discomfort. Many highly successful nonreaders have learned in parrot fashion to recognize and rote-repeat symbol combinations. But they are incapable of producing personal original verbal communication. Writing ability cannot be taught. Those who are called "writers" or "literary" may make up a special small caste, necessary to provide specified functions in the social hive. My God, if everyone were a "literary writer" no one would be left to manage the store.

So genetics and sociobiology give us one basic answer to the question: How are our minds made up? The secondary answer to the epistemology question is linguistic-neurological. Each child (and gene pool) is permanently "fixed" in a mental-linguistic style of thinking, during the critical period when the linguistic circuits of the brain are being activated. The 6½-year-old imprints the sign-systems and signal attitudes that happen to impinge on his nervous system. The mental-complexity level of the home, neighborhood, and cultural *Zeitgeist* determines the texture of one's mentation.

Many a Newton and Einstein has lived and died in dumb cultures that could not provide the vulnerable brain with the level of symbol complexity required. Teachers—a critical aspect of the "mental environment"—are, of course, themselves members of a mental caste, crucial genetic agents designed to perpetuate unquestioningly the hive culture. Their function is to instill, in rote manner, the symbols and thinking-modes of the society. They succeed with that large majority of students, themselves bred for unthinking hive performance. But teachers often run into problems with young members of the "thinking" caste, neurally geared to invent, originate abstractions. It is sufficient only that this caste be exposed to the current symbol techniques. They are geared to really understand symbols so that they can improve them. An American teacher is faced with the problem of transmitting symbol-manipulation methods to at least 8 brain-models, each geared to think in a way very different from the others. The confusion among these specialized castes, each of which operates under the illusion that it is the "smartest," is the history of philosophy.

It is the great semantic revelation of Sapir, Whorf, Chomsky, Korzybski, Wittgenstein, that symbols define a special reality-level of their own, separate from the realities they naively assume to represent. In the beginning was the Word. This defines God the Semanticist. SHe who creates new words and new grammars becomes the Divinity of Thought. The Third Craft of God is semantics.

4. Ethics: God the Moralist. One of the principal functions of pre-scientific religions was the definition of social-domestic-sexual roles and legislation of the moral codes that guided approved interactions among the various roles. Thou shalt not covet thy neighbor's wife and other chattel goods. Thou shalt not covet thy neighbor's car. Herd acceptability, social conformity are survival necessities in civilizations controlled by religious orthodoxy. This domestication of consciousness by the monolithic state is an inevitable stage in species and individual evolution. Although most of humanity despises their rulers, it is impossible to change the cultural-moral structure of a society. The recent return to fundamentalism in Iran and other Moslem countries indicates how geography determines social behavior.

For millennia, Oriental religions have taught that a "drop-out" from conventional roles was necessary for personal growth, but this detachment from hive morality has been difficult in highly organized western states. The recent establishment of global communication nets, particularly movies, television, transistor radios, has presented humans with alternate lifestyles and moral codes. The peasant in Ceylon, the office worker in Budapest learn what cultural modes are acceptable in other lands. This leads to migration. And migration typically leads to changes in religion and social role.

God the moralist is a watchful, jealous divinity. Priests and moral commissars typically do everything possible to maintain cultural conformity and to prevent migration. More than two-thirds of the United Nations demand exit visas to prevent citizens leaving to seek another lifestyle.

The psychedelic revolution of the late 20th century encouraged millions of people to seek within to find navigational coordinates for the voyage of life. It was to be expected that a mass "turn on" would lead to a widespread "drop-out" phenomena. The typical LSD bad-trip panic occurred when the subject discovered the rubber-stamp artificial nature of social reality and social role; realized that one's identity is a fragile role in a flimsy historical vaudeville show. This freedom is wrong!

Get me back to my safe cubicle in the urban hive! If I am not my social role, who am I? What will the neighbors and the moralists think? If I violate the taboos defining my cultural identity, I will offend God.

The solution is, of course, to accept the responsibility. Each person who wishes to move beyond hive-docility must become God the Moralist, just as the old Hindus said. The Fourth Craft of God is the fabrication of your own new morality—freer, more intelligent and more genetically evolved.

5. Esthetics: God the Hedonic Artist. Most post-pagan, organized, civilized religions have been inspired by God the Moralist Dictator, who invariably proscribed, under the pain of eternal punishment, the pleasures of sensuality, eroticism, individual (as opposed to priesthood) luxury and free art. These taboos are comprehensible because a citizenry that pursues pleasure will tend to pay less attention to domestication roles and the self-sacrifices that benefit society.

Centralized monotheisms understandably denounced paganism. The looseness of the nature worshipper had to be tightened up to maintain an urban, post-tribal society. The Eastern and Mideastern empires reserved luxury, art, sensuality to the aristocracy.

The concept of God the Hedonist emerged in Greece in the centuries before Christ. Here the wonderful notions of individuality and democracy first blossomed. If the singular human being is the unit of life, then naturally the individual is going to develop a personal philosophy and select hir own style of self-reward. The idea of beauty, the adoration of the human body, its grooming, nurture, play, display, and its harmony with esthetic environments has lasted through the hegemonies of Alexander, Rome, Catholicism, flared up magnificently in the Renaissance, rode the wave of Protestantism, and appeared in the 20th century in the form of the Bohemian, the artist, the entertainer, the designer, the playboy-playgirl.

Some religions have fitfully allowed cults that focus on somatic energy and sacred sensuality. Tantra (both Bengali and Tibetan), Zen, Hasidic Judaism preserved the notions of kundalini, *cakra* consciousness, spiritual-eroticism, ecstatic exuberance, mystic altered states. But Hedonism has always been easily checked by centralized religious states and restricted to a specialized caste of artists usually patronized and tolerated by the rulers. This worked out well. The masters needed the hedonic estheticians to entertain and beautify while the great mass of the citizenry was kept in submissive asceticism. The lowest classes and the outside minorities were usually allowed to indulge themselves in gross sensuality, sternly condemned by bourgeois moralists.

In the 20th century, the concept of selfhood suddenly became popularized and vulgarized. Two world wars moved people around, lessening the hold of parochial moral censors. Psychoanalysis introduced the notion of self-improvement. The explosion of the film/video culture trained the citizenry to dial and tune the entertainment they wished. The material consumerism mania of the 1950's strengthened the idea that the working person was entitled to choose what looked good—purchasable *things,* that is.

In the 1960's, the 2,500-year-old tradition of self-discovery and self-indulgence finally blossomed as a mass phenomenon. The widespread use of hedonic drugs led to a resurrection of the body. Sensual consumerism. Sexual liberation. Erotic dress, dance, talk, print, film, music. Wholistic health methods. Diet, jogging, trendy style. The working person discovered that hir own body belonged, not to the state or to the moralist or to the authoritarian doctor, but to hirself.

The continually expanding use of brain-activating drugs in the 1970's built up the hedonic momentum because of the obvious neurological fact that drugs turn on the body. One of the ecstatic horrors of the LSD experience is the sudden confrontation with your own body. You are catapulted into the matrix of quadrillions of squirming cells and somatic communication systems, swept down the tunnels and canals of your own waterworks. You have visions of microscopic processes, strange, undulating tissue patterns. You are pummeled down the fantastic artistry of internal factories, recoiling with fear or shrieking in pleasure at the incessant push, struggle, drive of the biological machinery at every moment engulfing you.

Here is the ancient wisdom of gnostics, hermetics, Sufis, Tantric gurus, yogis, occult healers. Your body is the mirror of the macrocosm, the kingdom of heaven within you. Tibetan and Indian tantras and modern psychology workshops train the student to *pay attention* to the body's energies and messages.

By 1981 the intelligent American was beginning to define hir body as a complex receiving station, a sacred communications satellite, a bipedal telescope, a mosaic of touching, sniffing, listening, tasting microphones picking up vibrations from planetary energy systems, a worldwide retinal ABC, an eardrum RCA, an International Smell and Tell, a consolidated General Foods laboratory. God of un-common sense.

The Fifth Craft of God is management of one's own body, definition of one's role as esthetic director of the sensory world that one constructs and blissfully inhabits.

6. Ontology: God the Neurologician. Every religion has, explicitly or implicitly, tried to answer the question: What is reality? Most theologies have held that reality is defined by the dogmas and rules of the priesthood. Certain great Oriental philosophers and some mystic Western sages have understood that reality is a unified, complex, myriad *maya* play of all energies, which cluster and organize into transient structures called matter. And that what one believes to be real simply reflects the relativistic perspective of the beholder.

These prescientific intimations of ontological relativity remained mystical until the neurological and pharmacological advances of the 20th century. The brain, for so long a taboo organ, shrouded in mystery, was now recognized as the seat of consciousness, the tool for fabricating reality. We realize that everything we experience is computed by the brain; that we can go outward into the universe or inward to study the nucleus of the atom only as far and precisely as our neuro-receptive, neuro-associative, and neuro-transmission intelligence allows us.

As long as we rely on our brains to know, then inevitably we shall define the universe as an enormous brain. Each flick of energy, stellar-galactic or nuclear-atomic, is seen as information. The universe is a web of intelligence mediated by our brain. The smarter we become, the more intelligent the universe will become. The more skillful we become in managing our own brains, i.e., our reality tools, the more skillful we shall become in fabricating, managing universes. The smarter we become, the smarter God will become.

Recent scientific discoveries have indicated how *imprinting* creates the chessboard of our realities and how conditioning keeps the social, intellectual, emotional, and survival games going. The suggestion, first presented in the chapters of this book, that humans can systematically reimprint, rebuild their realities has, for the first time in human history, raised the intelligence of our species to the level of self-mastery and self-control, by the individual, of Hir own neural realities. Ontology, always the most mystical, intangible, evasive issue in philosophy, now becomes neurological engineering. God #6 is the Neurologician, the amateur psychopharmacologist who has learned to dial and tune hir brain.

7. Evolution: God the Geneticist-Sociobiologist. Theories of evolution or devolution are built into almost every religion. Hinduism teaches that life spins in long cycles or ages (*kalpas*) winding down from the most harmonious to the apocalyptic end, and then begins all over again. This, like most Oriental philosophies, is a pessimistic, quietist, makes-no-difference doctrine of devolution. Why bother because everything is terrible and the future is going to get worse? The only thing to do is cool out and try to get off the wheel of existence.

Western monotheisms have generally denied the theory of evolution. A jealous God built the universe and created mankind, and the stages to come depend on how obedient you are to His priests. There is no sense of how we have evolved and certainly no specific notion that we are still evolving into a better future. Indeed, the concept of a future which could be predicted or constructed is of very recent origin.

According to biologists, the flame of life that moves every living form, including the cell cluster you call your self, was seeded as a tiny single-celled spark in the lower Precambrian mud, then unfolded in steady, preprogrammed transformations to more complex forms. But the single cell's still thriving, thank you. Next, your ancestral fire glowed in seaweed, algae, flagellate, sponge, coral (about 1 billion years ago); then scorpion, millipede, fish (about 600 million years ago). Every cell in your body traces back (about 450 million years) to the same light life flickering in our amphibian ancestors (and what a risky mutation-migration to leave the sea!). From the shoreline, the mastery of terrestrial environment accelerated into four-foot mammalian intelligence —stronger, fiercer, faster. Then the great moment when we stood erect, freeing throat and hands for signalling and manipulation—and started climbing trees. Higher has always been the trajectory of intelligent evolution. From the trees we developed gesture and rudimentary language. Watch out for that lion! Piss on that tiger!

Then the development of a tool-culture, agriculture, trade, cities organizing enormous insectoid cultures. And next, recently, now, the development of that greatest tool of evolution—The Self, mastering the body, the brain, and now DNA—the code of evolution itself.

Most wonderfully, each of us has recapitulated this sequence of evolution in our own personal lives. We were single-celled creatures when we were conceived and we retraced in our mothers' wombs, the same genetic stages: embryonic fish, embryonic furry animals, finally being born as larval primates.

In our early postnatal years we recapitulated this cycle once again. As amoeboid babies, floating and sucking in our mothers' arms, we had neither the neurology nor musculature to handle gravity. Then as crawling infants we retraced the amphibian stage. As toddlers and running cubs, we recapitulated the mammalian steps. As parroting, mimicking children and as kids hanging out in gangs, we relive the neolithic and hunter-gatherer stages of our species past.

Experiential recapitulation of these genetic stages can be found in the reports of almost every LSD tripper: the experience of being a one-celled creature tenaciously flailing, the singing, humming sound of life exfoliating; you are the DNA code spinning out multicellular esthetic solutions. You directly and immediately experience invertebrate joy; you feel your backbone forming; gills form. You are a fish with glistening gills, the sound of ancient fetal tides murmuring the rhythm of life. You stretch and wriggle in mammalian muscular strength, with loping, powerful, big muscles; you sense hair growing on your body as you leave the warm broth of water and take over the earth. The easiest interpretation is psychiatric: "Oh, everyone knows that LSD makes you crazy, and your delusions can take any psychotic form." But is it entirely inconceivable that our cortical cells or the DNA molecules inside the cellular nucleus "remember" back along the un-broken chain of bioelectrical transformations to that original seeding in the Precambrian mud, for which our language has few or no des-criptive terms?

Recent breakthroughs in physics, genetics, and neuro-logic are eliminating impersonal change and blind accident from the philoso-phy of science and substituting intelligent choice. Physics, always highest, fastest, quickest among the sciences, provides the gifts of relativity, singularity, multiple reality, mental choice, quantam indeter-minacy. Bohr's atom really is his own idea. Now, after the Golden Age of Physics, comes the Golden Age of Biology.

The Gaia theory, first presented by John Lovelock and Lynn Margulis (1978), defines one Life Organism with a DNA brain and a spherical shape, which covers, surrounds, roots itself in the geosphere (the rocky planet). This glorious *conception* suggests that a Life Intelligence deftly, confidently, intelligently creates and maintains the Biosphere, the film of slime which surrounds this round rock in antiseptic (almost) space. The Biosphere is an incredibly delicate, intricate, cybernetic, ecological web in which evolution precisely unfolds. Organisms equipped with nervous systems capable of attaining higher altitudes, velocities, and communication systems, eventually allow life-pods to blow off the planet, like seed blossoms, and thus disseminate Gaia around the galaxy.

Gaia's strategy is clear-cut and straightforward. First you land seed pods on a lifeless, rocky planet. Next create an atmosphere (air-ocean) in which life can infiltrate and surround the geosphere. The atmosphere fabricated by Gaia includes the ozone, the air, the oceans, the water cycle, and the topsoil—all results of biological processes. The Biosphere, the spherical film of life, then keeps temperature viably constant, and continually stirs up and co-mingles biotic and organic molecules from the crust elements, using wind currents and water movements as arteries. Preprogrammed into Gaia's DNA brain are the codes for building more and more mobile organisms, which can perform all the above maintenance and dissemination functions more efficiently. Gaia evolves faster, stronger, and more intelligent forms, which eventually develop escape velocity sufficient to leave the planet. These seed-blossom space packets (of which the early, crude forms were Apollo, Soyuz, Skylab, Shuttle-Rocket) are structurally more intelligent and efficient because in a space capsule the geosphere surrounds-protects the inner Biosphere and atmosphere. Gaia thus constructs mini-worlds in which She moves us all around the galaxy.

In the 1960's, over seven million Americans took LSD and activated circuits in their brains that provoke heightened sensuality, understanding of the neural-nature of reality, and genetic, evolutionary ruminations. The first results were confusing—millions of instant philosophers babbling about God and love and bliss and space and reincarnation. Now, twenty years later, we are harvesting the fruits of this disorganized, mass brain-scrambling. The highest incidence of psychedelic drug use was in the universities. Today the research centers and laboratories are filled with young scientists whose brains were philosophized in the 60's and who are now developing new methods, new hypotheses, new theories which are liberating humanity from the dogmatic rule, superstitious religion, conservative, pessimistic science. While cell biologists have been learning how Gaia moves personnel and material around the planet, micro-geneticists and DNA researchers have succeeded in deciphering the genetic code. Recombinant engineering allows humans to create new life forms, to correct malfunctioning genes, to clone, to effect DNA repair, to understand and manage the genetic signals which cause aging and death.

God, the Geneticist, is able to accomplish the routine tasks of divinity—create life, improve life, attain immortality. The Seventh Craft of God is management of DNA.

8. Ultimates: God the Quantum Physicist. Nuclear physicists and quantum theorists take as their subject matter the basic structure of matter/energy. Surely there is no form of worship as basic as this attempt to understand how things are made. One would think that the religious organizations, ministers, and publications would follow with bated breath the new revelations about the emission and absorption of energy by matter and the motion of elementary particles. One would hope that intelligent philosophers would continually be updating their theories in line with the new physical insights.

Psychedelic subjects regularly report experiencing events that seem to harmonize with quantum mechanics. They speak of participating in and merging with pure (i.e., content-free) energy, white light; of witnessing the breakdown of macroscopic objects into vibratory patterns, the awareness that everything is a dance of particles, sensing the smallness and fragility of our system, of world-ending explosions, of the cynical nature of creation and dissolution, etc. I need not apologize for the flimsy inadequacy of these words. If God were to let you whirl for a second into the atomic nucleus or spin you out on a light-year trip through the galaxies, how on earth would you describe what you saw when you got back? Ask someone who has taken a heavy dose of LSD.

It is of crucial philosophic importance to understand that neurology, genetics, and quantum physics are all (in their separate narrow vectors into the future) coming to understand that evolving human intelligence is apparently designed to shape the universe, to navigate the process of evolution, and to fabricate the structure of personal reality. All modern sciences accept and pay respect to the subjectivity of the experimenter.

To understand that you are designed to be God-the-Universe-Creator, you must first grasp the implications of the Heisenberg principle of determinacy (abjectly, cravenly, primitively called indeterminacy). Heisenberg's wonderful, liberating discovery states that the scientist determines the nature of experiment. Modern quantum physics is currently producing scenarios involving multiple realities, indeed, infinite universe, determined by the attitudes and mental structures and measurements of the observer. Prominent and distinguished physicists have actually suggested that the universe which we measure with our instruments is a production of our thought.

Here, in the far-out frontier of quantum mathematics, physics and psychedelics meet harmoniously. When we become confident enough and intelligent enough we shall become God #8, the creator of the universe and of the atom. The Eighth Craft of God is Quantum Physics.

Drugs Are the Tools of Experimental Theology

To master these Eight Divine Crafts may seem hopelessly Utopian. Actually, to ascend these levels of neurotechnology is becoming routine, because there now exist instruments to move contelligence to any desired level. The laboratory instruments for experimental theology, for internal science, is brain-activating chemicals—drugs, dope. Psychoactive drugs turn on the Eight Brain Circuits that mediate the levels of reality-experience:

1. The Origin Experience Is Possible. Anyone can noodle

back down to swampy amoeboid, unicellular, vegetative beginnings by self-administering narcotics, ketamine, heavy doses of barbiturates. These neurochemicals turn off higher circuits of the brain and permit one to float in marine rapture. Three Quaaludes, for example, make it impossible to walk or master gravity.

2. Emotional Stupor or Mammalian Excitement can be attained by alcohol or angel dust, which turn off the higher, cerebral centers and activate the midbrain. If you have mammalian feelings of rage, dominance, power, which you wish to experience (and to express in a safe-protective environment), these drugs will do it.

3. Mental Acceleration is produced by cocaine, pep pills, and similar daily energizers: drugs that stimulate mental performance, propelling you into busy game manipulations. Don't expect creativity, however.

4. Domesticated Virtue and Social Security are produced by tranquilizers, including the familiar Valiums, Libriums, Thorazines. Indeed, it has been suggested that tranquilizers are the "glue" that holds the American middle class together in dulled, calm security. The warm, cozy, comfortable feeling that Everything is Okay, that one is accepted and approved by the Hive Society, can also be maintained by television, pop religion, movies. Ronald Reagan feels tranquil when he sees the flag raised; the Iranian feels tranquil when he joins thousands of others in cheering the Ayatollah. Catholics feel the same wash of piety when they watch the pope stride to his altar.

5. The Esthetic-Sensory-Hedonic-Erotic Experience is produced by any post-domestic psychedelic, mind-opening drug. Low doses of LSD, mescaline, psilocybin, DMT, can turn off the 4 lower circuits—stupor, excitement, mental obsession, domestic virtue—and free the brain to experience direct-raw-naked-nerve-ending sensation. The traditional triggers for sensory awareness and *cakra* bliss are marijuana, hashish, and similar hedono-erotics.

6. The Ontological Revelation that the brain fabricates realities is produced by strong psychedelic ("mind-manifesting") drugs, which allow one to observe the neuroelectric nature of consciousness. Drugs including LSD, mescaline, and psilocybin, give access to the billion-cell loom of flashing impulses and produce new imprints, i.e., new realities.

7. The Teleological-Evolutionary Experience can be produced by strong charges of psychedelic drugs. Psychedelic literature abounds in descriptions of pre-incarnation voyages down one's cellular pathways —two-way conversation between the central nervous system and RNA and DNA.

8. The Cosmological Experience, the neuro-astronomical revelation, has been reported by many psychedelic experimenters. Many believe that the boom in space consciousness reflected in the movies *2001, Star Wars, Star Trek,* etc., are predictable sequelae of the Neurological Revolution of the 1960's. Our knowledge as to which drug turns on which levels of consciousness is empirical, based on thousands of psychedelic experiences. There is haunting phenomenological evidence that spiritual insights accompanying the psychedelic experience might be *subjective* accounts of the objective findings of astronomy, physics, biochemistry, and neurology.

No matter how parsimonious our explanations, LSD subjects *do* claim to experience revelations into the basic questions, and do attribute life change to their visions.

How can you judge? Well, whenever you hear anyone sounding off on internal freedom and consciousness-expanding foods and drugs—whether pro *or* con—check out these questions:

1. Is your expert talking from direct experience, or simply repeating clichés? Theologians and intellectuals often deprecate "experience" in favor of "moral imperative." Most often this classic debate becomes a case of "experience" versus "inexperience."

2. Do his words spring from a philosophic-scientific view? Is he motivated by basic questions, or is he protecting his own social-psychological investment? Is he riskily struggling toward all-out sainthood, or maintaining a hive conformity?

3. How would his argument sound if heard in an African jungle hut, a ghat on the Ganges, in Periclean Athens, in a Tibetan monastery, or in a bull session led by any one of the great religious leaders? Or on another planet inhabited by a superior form of life? Or how would it sound to other species of life—to dolphins, to the consciousness of a redwood? In other words, break out of your usual earphones and listen with the ears of another of Gaia's creatures.

4. How would the debate sound if you had a week to live, and were thus less committed to mundane issues? Our research group receives many requests for consciousness-expanding experiences from terminal patients.

5. Does the point of view open up, or close down? Are you being urged to explore, experience, join a collaborative voyage of discovery? Or are you being pressured to close off, protect your gains, play it safe, accept the authority of someone who knows best?

6. Does your psychedelic expert use terms that are positive, pro-life, spiritual, inspiring, based on faith in your potential? Or does he

betray a mind obsessed by danger, material concern, terrors, administrative caution, or essential distrust in your potential? There is nothing in life to fear; no philosophic game can be lost.

7. If he is against what he calls "artifical methods of illumination," ask him what constitutes the *natural*. Words? Rituals? Tribal customs? Prime time T.V.?

8. If he is against biochemical assistance, where does he draw the line? Does he use nicotine? Alcohol? Penicillin? Vitamins? Conventional sacramental substances?

9. If your advisor is against the neurotechnology of drugs, what is he *for?* If he forbids you the psychedelic key to revelation, what does he offer instead?

9

The Harvard Psychedelic Drug Research Project's first goal was to train scientist-technicians in the use of powerful brain-change chemicals. LSD provided us with a method of changing consciousness and brain function—the tool that philosophers and psychologists had been anticipating for centuries. Our problem was that there was no scientific literature on the subject. The situation was very similar to that of Janssen, Galileo, Malpighi, Leeuwenhoek, early users of the microscope, which dramatically expanded human perception, opening up entirely new levels of reality. It was obviously necessary to develop manuals to guide others in the use of the new instrument.

Our first step was to plead enlightened ignorance: Any attempt to label-limit the activated brain's potentials was premature. Our second step was to scan, sift, scour the libraries for books on mystic experience. When all was read and said, it seemed to us that the best "clinical," step-by-step description of a psychedelic experience yet published was *The Tibetan Book of the Dead.* This classic Buddhist text outlined the stages of the dying-rebirth process over a period of 49 days. Though couched in primitive rural language, the highs and lows, the "hallucinations" and visions were clearly similar to the altered states our Harvard subjects experienced.

During the summer of 1962 I went through *The Tibetan Book of the Living* (as we re-named it) line by line, translating Buddhist imagery into American psychedelic jargon. The mimeographed versions were "tried out" on hundreds of LSD trippers, and the polished, revised version published by University books in 1964. Since that time, *The Psychedelic Experience* has been reissued in nine hardback editions and several paperback reprintings. Hundreds of thousands of LSD experiences have been guided by this manual. Because of mass-merchandising techniques, ironically, this book has probably turned on more persons to the Guatama's teachings than any single text since the Buddha's enlightenment 2,500 years ago—although I doubt that you could get the Buddhist professional to admit it.

The following pages contain my translation of the First Bardo, the initial period of illumination after Ego Loss, followed by a technical appendix for guiding LSD sessions. This is probably the first detailed manual for managing drug-induced brain-change experiences.

Using LSD to imprint the Tibetan-Buddhist experience

Having read this preparatory manual one can immediately recognize symptoms and experiences that might otherwise be terrifying, only because of lack of understanding. *Recognition* is the key word. Recognizing and locating the level of consciousness. This guidebook may also be used to avoid paranoid traps or to regain transcendence if it has been lost. If the experience starts with light, peace, mystic unity, understanding, and continues along this path, then there is no need to remember the manual or have it reread to you. Like a road map, consult it only when lost, or when you wish to change course.

Planning a Session

What is the goal? Classic Hinduism suggests four possibilities:
> (1) Increased personal power, intellectual understanding, sharpened insight into self and culture, improvement of life situation, accelerated learning, professional growth.
> (2) Duty, help of others, providing care, rehabilitation, rebirth for fellow men.
> (3) Fun, sensuous enjoyment, esthetic pleasure, interpersonal closeness, pure experience.
> (4) Transcendence, liberation from ego and space-time limits; attainment of mystical union.
> The manual's primary emphasis on the last goal does not preclude other goals—in fact, it guarantees their attainment because illumination required that the person be able to step out beyond problems of personality, role, and professional status. The initiate can decide beforehand to devote the psychedelic experience to any of the four goals.
> In the extroverted transcendent experience, the self is ecstatically fused with external objects (e.g., flowers, other people). In the introverted state, the self is ecstatically fused with internal life processes (lights, energy waves, bodily events, biological forms, etc.). Either state may be negative rather than positive, depending on the voyager's set and setting. For the extroverted mystic experience, one would bring to the session candles, pictures, books, incense, music, or recorded

passages to guide the awareness in the desired direction. An introverted experience requires eliminating all stimulation: no light, no sound, no smell, no movement.

The mode of communication with the other participants should also be agreed on beforehand, to avoid misinterpretations during the heightened sensitivity of ego transcendence.

If several people are having a session together, they should at least be aware of each other's goals. Unexpected or undesired manipulations can easily "trap" the other voyagers into paranoid delusions.

Preparation

Psychedelic chemicals are not drugs in the usual sense of the word. There is no specific somatic or psychological reaction. The better the preparation, the more ecstatic and revelatory the session. In initial sessions with unprepared persons, set and setting—particularly the actions of others—are most important. *Long-range set* refers to personal history, enduring personality, the kind of person you are. Your fears, desires, conflicts, guilts, secret passions, determine how you interpret and manage any psychedelic session. Perhaps more important are the reflex mechanisms, defenses, protective maneuvers typically employed when dealing with anxiety. Flexibility, basic trust, philosophic faith, human openness, courage, interpersonal warmth, creativity, allow for fun and easy learning. Rigidity, desire to control, distrust, cynicism, narrowness, cowardice, coldness, make any new situation threatening. Most important is insight. The person who has some understanding of his own machinery, who can recognize when he is not functioning as he would wish, is better able to adapt to any challenge—even the sudden collapse of his ego.

Immediate set refers to expectations about the session itself. People naturally tend to impose personal and social perspectives on any new situation. For example, some ill-prepared subjects unconsciously impose a medical model on the experience. They look for symptoms, interpret each new sensation in terms of sickness/health, and, if anxiety develops, demand tranquilizers. Occasionally, ill-planned sessions end in the subject demanding to see a doctor.

Rebellion against convention may motivate some people who take the drug. The naive idea of doing something "far out" or vaguely naughty can cloud the experience.

LSD offers vast possibilities for accelerated learning and scientific-scholarly research, but for initial sessions, intellectual reactions can become traps. "Turn your mind off" is the best advice for novitiates. After you have learned how to move your consciousness around—into ego loss and back, at will—*then* intellectual exercises can be incorporated into the psychedelic experience. The objective is to free you from your verbal mind for as long as possible.

Religious expectations invite the same advice. Again, the subject in early sessions is best advised to float with the stream, stay "up" as long as possible, and postpone theological interpretations.

Recreational and esthetic expectations are natural. The psychedelic experience provides ecstatic moments that dwarf any personal or cultural game. Pure sensation can capture awareness. Interpersonal intimacy reaches Himalayan heights. Esthetic delights—musical, artistic, botanical, natural—are raised to the millionth power. But ego-game reactions—"*I* am having this ecstasy. How lucky I am!"—can prevent the subject from reaching pure ego loss.

Some practical recommendations. The subject should set aside at least three days: a day before his experience, the session day, and a follow-up day. This scheduling guarantees a reduction in external pressure and a more sober commitment. Talking to others who have taken the voyage is excellent preparation, although the hallucinatory quality of all descriptions should be recognized. Observing a session is another valuable preliminary.

Reading books about mystical experience and of others' experiences is another possibility (Aldous Huxley, Alan Watts, and Gordon Wasson have written powerful accounts). Meditation is probably the best preparation. Those who have spent time in the solitary attempt to manage the mind, to eliminate thought and reach higher stages of concentration, are the best candidates for a psychedelic session. When the ego loss occurs, they recognize the process as an eagerly awaited end.

The Setting

First and most important, provide a setting removed from one's usual interpersonal games, and as free as possible from unforeseen distractions and intrusions. The voyager should make sure that he will not be disturbed; visitors or telephone calls will often jar him into hallucinatory activity. Trust in the surroundings and privacy are necessary.

The day after the session should be set aside to let the experience run its natural course and allow time for reflection and meditation. A too-hasty return to game involvements will blur the clarity and reduce the potential for learning. It is very useful for a group to stay together after the session and share and exchange experiences.

Many people are more comfortable in the evening, and consequently their experiences are deeper and richer. The person should choose the time of day that seems right. Later, he may wish to experience the difference between night and day sessions. Similarly, gardens, beaches, forests, and open country have specific influences that one may or may not wish. The essential thing is to feel as comfortable as possible, whether in one's living room or under the night sky. Familiar surroundings may help one feel confident in hallucinatory periods. If the session is held indoors, music, lighting, the availability of food and drink, should be considered beforehand. Most people report no hunger during the height of the experience, then later on prefer simple, ancient foods like bread, cheese, wine, and fresh fruit. The senses are wide open, and the taste and smell of a fresh orange are unforgettable.

In group sessions, people usually will not feel like walking or moving very much for long periods, and either beds or mattresses should be provided. One suggestion is to place the heads of the beds together to form a star pattern. Perhaps one may want to place a few beds together and keep one or two some distance apart for anyone who wishes to remain aside for some time. The availability of an extra room is desirable for someone who wishes to be in seclusion.

The Psychedelic Guide

With the cognitive mind suspended, the subject is in a heightened state of suggestibility. For initial sessions, the guide possesses enormous power to move consciousness with the slightest gesture or reaction.

The key here is the guide's ability to turn off his own ego and social games, power needs, and fears—to be there, relaxed, solid, accepting, secure, to sense all and do nothing except let the subject know his wise presence.

A psychedelic session lasts up to twelve hours and produces moments of intense, *intense*, INTENSE reactivity. The guide must never be bored, talkative, intellectualizing. He must remain calm during long periods of swirling mindlessness. He is the ground control, always there to receive messages and queries from high-flying aircraft, ready to help navigate their course and reach their destination. The guide does not impose his own games on the voyager. Pilots who have their own flight plan, their own goals, are reassured to know that an expert is down there, available for help. But if ground control is harboring his own motives, manipulating the plane towards selfish goals, the bond of security and confidence crumbles.

To administer psychedelics without personal experience is unethical and dangerous. Our studies concluded that almost every negative LSD reaction has been caused by the guide's fear, which augmented the transient fear of the subject. When the guide acts to protect himself, he communicates his concern. If momentary discomfort or confusion happens, others present should not be sympathetic or show alarm but stay calm and restrain their "helping games." In particular, the "doctor" role should be avoided.

The guide must remain passively sensitive and intuitively relaxed for several hours—a difficult assignment for most Westerners. The most certain way to maintain a state of alert quietism, poised in ready flexibility, is for the guide to take a low dose of the psychedelic with the subject. Routine procedure is to have one trained person participating in the experience, and one staff member present without psychedelic aid. The knowledge that one experienced guide is "up" and keeping the subject company is of inestimable value: the security of a trained pilot flying at your wingtip; the scuba diver's security in the presence of an expert companion.

The less experienced subject will more likely impose hallucinations. The guide, likely to be in a state of mindless, blissful flow, is then pulled into the subject's hallucinatory field and may have difficulty orienting himself. There are no familiar fixed landmarks, no place to put your foot, no solid concept upon which to base your thinking. All is flux. Decisive action by the subject can structure the guide's flow if he has taken a heavy dose.

The psychedelic guide is literally a neurological liberator, who provides illumination, who frees men from their lifelong internal bondage. To be present at the moment of awakening, to share the ecstatic revelation when the voyager discovers the wonder and awe of the divine life-process, far outstrips earthly game ambitions. Awe and gratitude —rather than pride—are the rewards of this new profession.

The Period of Ego Loss or Non-Game Ecstasy

Success implies very unusual preparation in consciousness expansion, as well as much calm, compassionate game playing (good karma) on the part of the participant. If the participant can see and grasp the idea of the empty mind as soon as the guide reveals it—that is to say, if he has the power to die consciously—and, at the supreme moment of quitting the ego, can recognize the ecstasy that will dawn upon him and become one with it, then all bonds of illusion are broken asunder immediately: the dreamer is awakened into reality simultaneously with the mighty achievement of recognition.

It is best if the guru from whom the participant received guiding instructions is present. But if the guru cannot be present, then another experienced person, or a person the participant trusts, should be available to read this manual without imposing any of his own games. Thereby the participant will be put in mind of what he had previously heard of the experience.

Liberation is the nervous system devoid of mental-conceptual redundancy. The mind in its conditioned state, limited to words and ego games, is continuously in thought-formation activity. The nervous system in a state of quiescence, alert, awake but not active, is comparable to what Buddhists call the highest state of *dhyana* (deep meditation). The conscious recognition of the Clear Light induces an ecstatic condition of consciousness such as saints and mystics of the West have called illumination.

The first sign is the glimpsing of the "Clear Light of Reality," "the infallible mind of the pure mystic state"—an awareness of energy transformations with no imposition of mental categories.

The duration of this state varies, depending on the individual's experience, security, trust, preparation, and the surroundings. In those who have a little practical experience of the tranquil state of non-game awareness, this state can last from 30 minutes to several hours. Realization of what mystics call the "Ultimate Truth" is possible, provided that the person has made sufficient preparation beforehand. Otherwise he cannot benefit now, and must wander into lower and lower conditions of hallucinations until he drops back to routine reality.

It is important to remember that consciousness-expansion is the reverse of the birth process, the ego-loss experience being a temporary ending of game life, a passing from one state of consciousness into another. Just as an infant must wake up and learn from experience the nature of this world, so a person must wake up in this new brilliant world of consciousness expansion and become familiar with its own peculiar conditions.

In those heavily dependent on ego games, who dread giving up control, the illuminated state endures only for a split second. In some, it lasts as long as the time taken for eating a meal. If the subject is prepared to diagnose the symptoms of ego-loss, he needs no outside help at this point. The person about to give up his ego should be able to recognize the Clear Light. If the person fails to recognize the onset of ego loss, he may complain of strange bodily symptoms that show he has not reached a liberated state:

1. Bodily pressure
2. Clammy coldness followed by feverish heat
3. Body disintegrating or blown to atoms
4. Pressure on head and ears
5. Tingling in extremities
6. Feelings of body melting or flowing like wax
7. Nausea
8. Trembling or shaking, beginning in pelvic regions and spreading up torso.

The guide or friend should explain that the symptoms indicate the onset of ego-loss. These physical reactions are signs heralding transcendence: avoid treating them as symptoms of illness. The subject should hail stomach messages as a sign that consciousness is moving around in the body. Experience the sensation fully, and let consciousness flow on to the next phase. It is usually more natural to let the subject's attention move from the stomach and concentrate on breathing and heartbeat. If this does not free him from nausea, the guide should move the consciousness to external events—music, walking in the garden, etc. As a last resort, heave.

The physical symptoms of ego-loss, recognized and understood, should result in peaceful attainment of illumination. The simile of a needle balanced and set rolling on a thread is used by the lamas to elucidate this condition. So long as the needle retains its balance, it remains on the thread. Eventually, however, the pull of the ego or external stimulation affects it, and it falls. In the realm of the Clear Light, similarly, a person in the ego-transcendent state momentarily enjoys a condition of perfect equilibrium and oneness. Unfamiliar with such an ecstatic non-ego state, the average consciousness lacks the power to function in it. Thoughts of personality, individualized being, dullism, prevent the realization of *nirvana* (the "blowing out of the flame" of fear or selfishness). When the voyager is clearly in a profound ego-transcendent ecstasy, the wise guide remains silent.

10

In 1960–63, we Harvard drug researchers realized that we did not know enough about the enormous range of reactions activated by brain-change drugs. Even after hundreds of voyages aloft, our veteran test pilots reported amazing new dimensions of galaxies within. For this reason we decided to postpone any navigational mapmaking of our own. Every week, new evidence changed the maps. We felt like those 16th-century cartographers in Western Europe eagerly debriefing crews returning from the New World. *The Tibetan Book of the Living*, our first venture in updating old neurological-trip maps, was so successful we became alarmed. Thousands of people began using the Tibetan jargon of *Bardos*, and a definite fad-trend towards Buddhism was developing.

    To head off this prescientific Oriental renaissance, we quickly sought another, less parochial text for describing and guiding brain astronauts. The advantage of the *Tao Te Ching* was that this Taoist text was almost content-free. There are no pious monks, shaved heads, red hats, yellow hats, orange robes, or specific levels of heaven, purgatory, and hell in the *Tao Te Ching*. The *Tao* celebrates the constant flow of evolution, the eternal flow of always-changing energy processes. The basic advice of Taoism: "Everything changes according to regular cycles and rhythms. So keep cool, watch the ebb and flow—and when the waves are ready, surf them."

    In the next few pages we present the introduction to and a few selected poems from *Psychedelic Prayers From the Tao Te Ching;* the first book ever specifically designed to reimprint human brains during the "critical periods" of neural vulnerability. (It is the second book explicitly designed as a brainwashing manual.) The insidious aim of this Dr. Frankenstein gambit was to prepare young people taking large doses of LSD to absorb a new reality-view based on post-Einsteinian, DNA science.

    [At present, there are thousands of young people, finishing their doctorates and beginning careers in science, whose brains were directed by this book of hymns, odes, and paeans to the atom, to the DNA coil, and to the brain. The book has been reprinted over 20 times and has probably bent over 200,000 young brains.]

Using LSD to imprint the Taoist experience

During the years 1960–65, a good 10 million marijuana smokers, adepts in hatha yoga, and meditators have experienced the neural level of consciousness—have transcended symbols and contacted raw energy hitting their nerve endings. At least another million LSD, peyote, and mushroom eaters, have contacted cellular consciousness—have had experiences transcending both symbolic game and sensory apparatus. Next we have those who have taken large doses of LSD, mescaline, DMT, and have contacted the molecular and elemental energies within the cellular structure, experiencing the "white light," the "void," the "inner light." If we add those millions of institutionalized mystics who have had involuntary psychedelic experiences, this group swells to astounding proportions. Each of these different psychedelic levels —neural, cellular, molecular—is beyond symbols, incoherent to the symbolic mind. Most psychedelic voyagers are aware of the limitless realities in the nervous systems, but there is no conception of the meaning and use of these potentials.

Of course LSD provides no easy answers. On the contrary, every paradox, ambiguity, and problem of static-symbolic life is raised to exponential powers. Uncertainty is compounded and multiplied by the existence of countless realities.

From the beginning of the Harvard-IFIF-Castalia exploration into consciousness, it became apparent that manuals and programs were necessary to guide subjects through exploratory sessions with a minimum of fear and confusion. Rather than start *de novo* using our own minds and limited experiences, we turned to *The Tibetan Book of the Dead*, which is incredibly specific about the sequence and nature of experiences encountered in the ecstatic state. The Chinese *Tao Te Ching*, sometimes translated as *The Way of Life*—written some 2,600 years ago by one or several philosophers known to us now as "the old fellow" (Lao-Tse)—will remain timelessly modern as long as man has the same sort of nervous system and deals with the range of energies he now encounters. *Tao* is best translated as "energy," or energy process: energy in its pure unstructured state (the "E" of Einstein's equation) and in its countless, temporary states of structure (the "M" of Einstein's equation). The *Tao* is an ode to nuclear physics, to life, to the genetic code, to that form of transient energy structure we call "man," to those most static, lifeless forms of energy we call man's artifacts and symbols.

The message of the *Tao Te Ching* is that all is energy; all energy flows; all things continually transform.

The *Tao Te Ching* is a series of 81 verses that celebrate the flow of energy, its manifestations, and, on the practical side, the implications for man's endeavors. Most of the pragmatic sutras of the *Tao* were directed towards the ruler of a state and his ministers. Like all great texts, the *Tao* has been rewritten and reinterpreted in every century; the terms for *Tao* also change in each century. Advice given by philosophers to their emperor can be applied to how to run your home, your office, and how to conduct a psychedelic session.

The *Tao Te Ching* is divided into 2 books—the first comprising 37 chapters, the second 44. In this volume you will find 56 poems based on the 37 chapters of Book I of the original. These translations from English to psychedelese were made while sitting under a bamboo tree on a grassy slope of the Kumaon Hills overlooking the snow peaks of the Himalayas. I had 9 English translations of the *Tao.* I would select a *Tao* chapter and read and reread all 9 English versions of it. Each Western mind, of course, made his own interpretation of the flowing calligraphy. But after hours of rereading and meditation, the essence of the poem would bubble up. Slowly a psychedelic version of the chapter would emerge.

The first-draft version would then be put under the psychedelic microscope. For several years I pursued the demanding yoga of one LSD session every seven days. And each time our Moslem cook walked down to the village, he would bring back a crayon-size stick of attar, "essence," of the resin of the marijuana plant sometimes called hashish. LSD opened up the lenses of cellular and molecular consciousness. Attar cleansed the windows of the senses. During these sessions, I would read the most recent draft of the *Tao* poems. A humbling experience for the poet—to have his words exposed to pitiless psychedelic magnification.

Psychedelic poetry, like all psychedelic art, is crucially concerned with evolution, flow, change. Each psychedelic poem is carefully tailored for a certain time in the sequence of the session. Simplicity and diamond purity are important. To the "turned on," intellectual flourishes and verbal pyrotechnics are painfully obvious. To the static intellect, these sutras are simply another sequence of lifeless words. But to consciousness released from imprinted statics, these prayers can become precise bursts of trembling energy and breathless meaning.

You will wonder, perhaps, at the use of the term "prayer" to label these sutras. Prayer is ecstatic communication with your inner navigational computer. You cannot pray to an external power; that is begging. You cannot (without regret) communicate during the ecstatic moment in static prose.

When you are out beyond symbols, game communication seems pointless, irrelevant, inappropriate.

There is no need to communicate—because everything is already in communication. But there are those transition moments of terror, isolation, reverence, gratitude . . . when there comes that need to communicate with the energy source you sense in yourself and around you—at the highest and best level you are capable of. And there is the need, at exactly that moment, for a straight, pure, "right" nongame language.

This is prayer, mantra, lyrical harmony, verbal mathematics.

This need has been known and sensed for thousands of years. All prayers are originally communications with higher, freer energies —turning yourself in to the energy dance.

Conventional prayers, for the most part, have degenerated into parrot rituals, slogans, mimicked verbalizations, appeals for game help. But, when the ecstatic cry is called for, you must be ready to address Higher Intelligence, to contact energy beyond your game. You must be ready to pray. When you have lost the need to address the Higher Intelligence, you are a dead man in a world of dead symbols. Each poem in this volume was exposed to several dozen appraisals by lysergized nervous systems. A ruthless polishing and cutting away took place. The most blatant redundancies and mentalisms were pruned. Most readers found 5 or so poems in this collection which vibrate in tune to their deepest resonances. The rest did not pass inspection.

> *Sheathing the Self*
>
> *The play of energy endures*
> *Beyond striving*
> *The play of energy endures*
> *Beyond body*
> *The play of energy endures*
> *Beyond life*
> *Out here*
> *Float timeless*
> *Beyond striving.*

The Manifestation of the Mystery

Gazing, we do not see it
  we call it empty space.
Listening, we do not hear it
  we call it silence or noise.
Groping, we do not grasp it
  we call it intangible.
But here . . .
  we . . . spin through it
Electric, silent, subtle.

Please Do Not Clutch at the Gossamer Web

All In Heaven
and on Earth below
Is a crystal fabric . . .
Delicate gossamer web
Grabbing hands shatter it
Watch closely this shimmering
  mosaic
Silent . . .
Glide in
Harmony

The Serpent Coil of DNA

We meet it everywhere
  But we do not see its front.
We follow it everywhere
  But we do not see its back.
When we embrace this ancient serpent coil
We are masters of the moment
And feel no break in the
Curling back to primeval beginnings.
This may be called
Unravelling the clue of the life process.

The Seed Light

The seed light shines everywhere, left and right.
All forms derive life from it.

When the bodies are created, it does not take
  possession.
It clothes and feeds the ten thousand things
And does not disturb their illusions.
Magical helix . . . smallest form and
  mother of all forms
The living are born, flourish and disappear
Without knowing their seed creator
Helix of light
In all nature it is true that the wiser, the oldest
  and the greatest resides in the smaller.

The Touch Cakra

Extend your free nerve endings
Trembling
Fine tendrils wove in skin
Feel my finger touch
Soft landing on your creviced surface
Send sense balloon drifting up
Through fifty miles of
Spindle-web skin tissue atmosphere
Electric thrill contact
Soar free through million mile blue epidermal space
Of cotton candy
Fragile web of nerve wire
Shuddering fleece of breathless pleasure.

The Sex Cakra

Rainbow
Can you float through the universe of your body
  and not lose your way?
Can you lie quietly
  engulfed in the slippery union
  of male and female?
  Warm wet dance of generation?
  Endless ecstasies of couples?
Can you offer your stamen trembling in the meadow
  for the electric penetration of pollen
  While birds sing?
Writhe together on the river bank,

Wait soft-feathered, quivering, in the thicket?
Can you coil serpentine while birds sing?
Become two cells merging?
Slide together in molecule embrace?
Can you, murmuring,
Lose all
Fusing
Rainbow

The Heart Cakra

Scarlet
Can you float . . .
  through the universe of your body . . .
And not lose your way . . . ?
Can you flow . . .
  with fire-blood
Through each tissued corridor . . . ?
Throb . . .
To the pulse of life . . . ?
Can you let your heart . . .
  pump you . . .
  down long red tunnels . . . ?
Radiate . . . swell . . . penetrate . . .
  to the bumpy rhythm?
Can you stream . . .
Into cell chambers . . . ?
Can you center . . .
On this heart-fire of love . . . ?
Can you let your heart . . .
Become central pump-house . . .
For all human feelings?
Pulse for all love? Beat for all sorrow?
Throb for all pain? Thud for all joy?
Can you let it . . .
Beat for all mankind?
Burst . . . bleed out . . . into warm compassion
Flowing . . . flowing . . . pulsing . . .
  out . . . out . . . out?
Bleed to death
Life . . .
Blood
Scarlet

The Moment of Fullness

Grab hold tightly,
Let go lightly.

The full cup can take no more.
The candle burns down.
The taut bow must be loosed.
The razor edge cannot long endure.
Nor this moment re-lived.

So . . . now
Grab hold tightly.
Now . . .
Let go lightly.

11

Research on the interpersonal reflex (1957) demonstrated how humans fabricate and maintain their own personal worlds. By 1966 (the date of this essay), this self-responsibility message was expanded from the interpersonal to the neurological realm. Your actions determined the environment you inhabited. Divinity was within, and the word "God" was understood to refer to the Higher Intelligence resident within one's own brain and within one's own DNA. The aim was to provide a socially acceptable reason for tampering with your own brain and increasing intelligence.

Most cults and religions that sprang up in the 1960's and 1970's recruited docile "followers." The Mansons, the Moons, the Jim Joneses, the swamis, the Born-Again Preachers all play on the primitive, prescientific, infantile loser desire to submit to a parental authority figure. The crisp advice transmitted in this essay is: Take responsibility for making your own life beautiful.

The following 1966 article, published in an East Village underground newspaper, illustrates our Do-It-Yourself-God-Kit Program—the latest step in Self-Determination and the evolution of Intelligence—and is of considerable historic interest—not for what it says, but for what it does *not* say. The essay specifies the familiar message: Control your own brain, be your own Divinity, make your own world. Master the God Technologies. It pointedly *does not* repeat the injunction classically used by religious prophets: Follow *me*, sign up in *my* flock. It imposes no dogma except one:

Live out your own highest vision.

"You are a God, act like one"

The experienced psychedelic adept can move consciousness from one level to another. But then the experience must be communicated, harmonized with the greater flow. The "turned on" person realizes that SHe is not an isolated, separate social ego, but rather one transient energy process hooked up with the energy dance around hir.

The "turned on" person realizes that every action is a reflection of where SHe is at. The "turned on" person knows hir world is created by hir consciousness—existing only because SHe has arranged hir sensory and neural cameras to shoot these particular scenes. Hir movements, dress, grooming, room, house, the neighborhood in which SHe lives, are exact external replicas of hir state of consciousness. If the outside environment doesn't harmonize with hir state of mind, SHe knows that SHe must move gracefully to get in tune.

"Tune in" means arrange your environment so that it reflects your state of consciousness, to harness your internal energy to the flow around you. If you understand this most practical, liberating message, you are free to live a life of beauty.

Your State of Consciousness Is Reflected in Your Environment

Let us consider a sad illumination. The Manhattan office worker moves through a clutter of factory-made, anonymous furniture to a plastic, impersonal kitchen, to breakfast on canned, packaged anonymous food-fuel; dresses himself in the anonymous-city-dweller costume, travels through dark tunnels of sooty metal and gray concrete to a dark metal room, foul with polluted air. All day he deals with symbols that have no relevance to his divine possibilities. This person is surrounded by the dreary, impersonal, assembly-line, mass-produced, anonymous environment of an automated robot, which perfectly mirrors his "turned off" awareness.

When this person "turns on," SHe sees at once the horror of hir surroundings. If SHe "tunes in," SHe begins to change hir movements and hir surroundings so that they become more in harmony with hir internal beauty. If everyone in Manhattan were to "turn on" and "tune in," grass would grow on First Avenue and tieless, shoeless divinities would dance or roller-skate down the carless streets. Ecological consciousness would emerge within 25 years. Fish would swim in a clear-blue Hudson.

Every action of a human being reflects his state of consciousness. Therefore, every person is an artist who communicates his experience. Most people are not "tuned in" consciously. They experience only in terms of static, tired symbols. Therefore, their actions and their surroundings are dead, robot art.

After you "turn on," you must "tune in": start changing your dress, your home, to reflect the grandeur and glory of your vision. But this process must be harmonious and graceful. No abrupt, destructive, rebellious actions, please! Start "tuning in" through your body movements. Walk, talk, eat, drink like a joyous forest-dwelling god.

Next, change your dwelling place. If you have to live in the city for the time being, arrange your apartment so that it becomes a shrine. Your room should reflect a timeless, eternal beauty. Every object should make immediate sense to the sense organs of a visitor from the 6th century B.C. to the 20th century.

When you have made your body a sacred temple and your apartment a navigational, seduction cabin in a 20th-century time-ship you are ready to change your broader social commitments. Do not "drop out" until you have "tuned in." Do not "turn on" unless you know how to "tune in," or you will get "hung up!" Every "bad trip" is caused by the failure to "tune in." Here's why . . .

When you "tune in" you open up neural receptors. Cannabis flicks on sensory receptors, hashish somatic receptors, LSD cellular and molecular receptors. These forceful energies cannot be harnessed to a hive-ego game board. You cannot hook up 100 million years of sensory-somatic revelation to your puny, trivial-personality chessboard. You cannot access 2 billion years of evolutionary revelation to your petty social program. This is why marijuana and LSD, if used in a closed system, will, sooner or later, freak you out.

Of over 5,000 persons who have begun the yoga of LSD with me, the large majority could not harness their activated energies to a more harmonious game. You cannot take LSD once a week and stay rigidly rooted in a low-level ego game. You have to grow with the flow, or you will stop taking LSD. To continue to use LSD, you must generate around you an ever-widening ring of "tuned in" actions. You must hook up your inner power to a life of expanding intelligence.

Exercises

1.) Go home and look at yourself in the mirror. Start changing your dress, your behavior, so that you float like a god, not shuffle like a robot.

2.) Look around your home. What kind of dead robot lives here? Start throwing out everything that is not "tuned in" to your highest vision.

3.) Make your body a temple, your home a shrine.

4.) You are a God, live like one!

This next artifact, a transcription of an interview with a college reporter, illustrates the concerns of thoughtful critics (circa 1966) and our responses.

In September 1966, working with First Amendment lawyers, we formally founded a new religion, called the League for Spiritual Development, to provide legal protection for our own neurological investigations and to encourage others to form their own religions. We made very clear that the league was *not* a mass organization but was limited to 100 people centered around the Millbrook estate in Dutchess County, New York. We were not seeking to convert, but to show others how to do it themselves.

Our first sacramental assembling, a religious celebration at the Village Theatre in New York's Lower East Side, was based on the "Magic Theatre" sequence from Hermann Hesse's *Steppenwolf.* It was a bead-game multimedia performance deliberately designed to "blow minds," to overload nervous systems with ever-changing Niagaras of moving forms, some familiar, some novel. The sound track blasted with acid rock, Oriental chants, synthesizer whirls, body noises, heartbeats, heavy breathings—all highly amplified. A video orchestra of 9 performers manipulating slide projectors playing over double- and triple-exposed films. Psychedelic prayers (see Chapter 10) and a spoken narrative guided viewers through the reenactments of Harry Haller's mystical trip.

The Psychedelic Celebrations were a sensation. Enormous worldwide publicity, sold-out performances. I was nominated for best Off-Broadway actor of the year. Hollywood film people thronged to the events.

The Hesse drama was followed by a celebration of *The Attempted Assassination and Escape of Jesus Christ,* which parodied the Catholic Mass. Then, *A Life of the Buddha.* The 50 light-sound-stage artists who produced these events were the originators of what became Psychedelic Art, *2001* Hollywood special effects, dance-hall light shows. (We were also guilty of inspiring the horrid Hindu paisley-print boom.)

When television commercials took over our techniques, we knew it was time to quit. "Turn on to Squirt. Tune in to Taste. Drop Out of the Cola rut!" We did.

LSD as sacrament

Dr. Leary, in your Playboy *interview you commented that if you take LSD in a nuthouse, you will have a nuthouse experience. If a student were to take LSD in this rat race environment, would he have a rat race experience?*

You're asking for a wild generalization. No one should take LSD unless he's well prepared, knows what he's getting into, is ready to go out of his mind. His session should be in a place that will facilitate a positive, serene reaction, with someone he trusts emotionally and spiritually.

Experimenting at Harvard, did you find students less prepared to go out of their minds?

I never gave drugs to any undergraduate at Harvard. We did give psychedelic drugs to many graduate students, young professors, and researchers who were well trained and prepared for the experience. They were doing it for a serious purpose; to learn more about consciousness, the game of mastering this technique for their own personal life and professional work.

Many people fear recurrences of the LSD psychosis without further ingestion of the drug.

I can't agree with the word "psychosis." The aim of taking LSD is to develop yourself philosophically, increase your intelligence, open up greater sensitivity. After the session, therefore, the exciting process you have begun should continue. We're delighted when people tell us that after their LSD sessions they can flash back to some of the illumination, meaning, and beauty. We know that we are producing philosophic experiences, and we and our subjects aim to have those experiences endure. If nobody knows exactly what LSD does—and I share that worry—we must realize that scientifically we are not sure of the effects of gas fumes, DDT, penicillin, tranquilizers on the individual and the genetic structure of the species. There *are* risks involved. Nobody should take LSD unless SHe knows SHe's going into the unknown, laying hir blue chips on the line. But you're taking a risk every time you breathe the air, every time you eat the food the supermarkets are putting out—every time you fall in love. Life is a series of risks, for that matter. We insist only that the person who goes into it knows it's a risk, knows what's involved. No paternalistic profession like medicine has the right to prevent us from meeting that challenge. If you listen to neurologists and psychiatrists, you'd never fall in love.

A friend had recurring hallucinations when he didn't want or expect them. Are these uncontrollable replays common?

There are going to be recurrent memories and reactions,

when you hear the same music, are with the same people, walk into the same room. Any stimulation may set off a memory—a live, chemical molecular event in your nervous system.

When you take LSD, you're changing that system to a small degree. Most people are delighted when this happens. But when a professional full-time worrier takes LSD, he's going to wonder if he's going crazy, if he's insane, he's going to worry about brain damage, about germs, loss of precious body fluids. Worriers, of course, want everything under control. But life is spontaneous, undisciplined, unsupervised. Your worrier is going to lay his worrying machinery on LSD. The psychedelic experience can be philosophic if the person is looking for it, and even if the person is not looking for it. People use different interpretations, different metaphors to describe their religious experience. A Christian will take LSD and report it in terms of the Christian vocabulary. CIA agents will look for communists.

Are you yourself Hindu?

Our philosophy about the meaning of LSD comes closer to Hinduism than to any other religion. Hinduism is a pagan philosophy that recognizes the divinity of all manifestations of life, allowing for a wide scope of sub-sects. To a Hindu, Catholicism is a form of Hinduism.

Your descriptions of the psychedelic experience sound very much like Hermann Hesse's Siddhartha. *Have you been influenced by his writings?*

Very much. Of course, in philosophic and literary interpretations of consciousness expansion, most great writers basically agree on the necessity of going out of your mind, going within, and about what you find once you get there. Metaphors change from culture to culture, but every great mystic and visionary reports the same eternal flow, timeless series of evolutions, and so forth. Our first psychedelic celebration in New York addressed the intellectual trapped in his mind. For that first celebration we were using *Steppenwolf* as our "bible." The next psychedelic celebration is based on the life of Christ, and for that we're using the Catholic missal as the manual. After that, we'll run celebrations of Socrates, Einstein, Gurdjieff.

Is each celebration supposed to appeal to a different kind of believer?

Each celebration will take up one of the great religious or philosophic traditions. We attempt to turn on everyone to that religion. We hope anyone that comes to all our celebrations will discover that each of these great myths is based on a psychedelic experience, a death-rebirth sequence. But in addition, we hope that the Christian will be particularly turned on by our Catholic LSD Mass, because it will renew for hir the resurrection metaphor, which for many has become rather routine and tired. The aim is to turn on not just the mind, but the sense organs, and even to talk to people's cells and ancient centers of wisdom.

A lot of your beliefs do borrow from other cultures. Wouldn't exposure to these other ways of thinking make your religion more meaningful?

Well, I was ovulated, fertilized, and born in the 20th century. I can't wipe out my whole personal background, or the fact that almost everyone I talk to today is brain-damaged by our education. I think American education makes us hopeless symbol addicts. It's designed to produce docile automatons. But it's going to take 15 to 20 years before you can urge young people to drop out of school without appearing to be an eccentric or a madman.

There are three processes involved that every spiritual teacher has passed on to humanity for the past thousand years. 1. Look within, glory in the revelation. 2. Then express it in acts of glorification on the outside and 3. detach yourself from the current tribe. After you turn on, don't spend the rest of your life contemplating the inner wonders. Begin immediately expressing your revelation in acts of beauty. That's very much a part of our religion—the glorification, the acting out, the expression of what you have learned. That's what we're doing in the Village Theatre. Every Tuesday night people come there, and we stone them out of their minds.

And all without LSD?

Well, in order to do anything new, you have to change your nervous system. You can do it through breathing, fasting, flagellation, dancing, solitude, diet; you can do it through any sense organ—visual, auditory, and so forth. There are hundreds of ways of turning on. But at present, very few people can use these methods, so drugs are almost the only specific way an American is ever going to have a religious experience.

And our Tuesday night celebrations do not take the place of the sacrament. In our religion the sacramental process is the use of marijuana and LSD; and nothing can substitute for that.

You don't advocate the use of LSD for simple "kicks"?

I don't know what you mean by "kicks." To me, the kick means an ecstatic revelation. To you, a kick may mean going to a cocktail party and flirting with some girl. A kick to me means a pagan flirtation with God, Gaia. Of course, in our Puritan society, we think we should work, get power, and use this power to control other people. In any sane society, the word *kick* could be the ideal, the ecstasy; it means going beyond, getting out of your mind, confronting God.

How do you determine whether a person will become psychotic under LSD? Is there any way to tell who had best not participate?

A confrontation with divinity, your own higher intelligence, is going to change you, and some people don't want to change. They should be warned that if you come into this temple, you're going to face blazing activation of your brain. You're never going to be the same. In the Eleusinian mysteries, they would always warn people, "If you go in here, your ego will die. You're going to have to confront all your past hang-ups, strip them off, and be a changed person." One emperor of Rome who wanted to be initiated in the Eleusinian mysteries said, "That's interesting, I approve of what you're doing, but I don't want to be changed." Everyone is somewhat afraid to take LSD, because everyone wants to keep his own little egocentric chess game going.

You have no fear of LSD?

I didn't say that. There's everything to fear. You're going to go out of your mind. But if LSD really worked the way the fear merchants say it does, it would be easy to take the criminal and the alcoholic, the drug addict, and the generally mean person and change them under guidance. But our conditioned mental processes are highly resistant to change. If you take LSD, you still come back speaking English and knowing how to tie your shoelaces. The problem is that you *do* slip back into routine ways of thinking. That's why if you take LSD, you should plan to slowly change your environment, harmonize your external commitments with internal achievements. It's very hard work to change the human psychology. That should comfort the frightened and challenge the fast-lane, quick-change optimist like myself.

What do you consider more valuable, the actual trip, or the contemplation of it afterwards?

One without the other is rather meaningless. After a session, we may go plant a new garden, change a room in the house, or throw out the frozen-canned foods. I may spend the next five hours talking quietly with my son.

Do you think you are being harassed for your unorthodox beliefs?

I don't use the term "harassment"; the game I am involved in is like the Harvard-Yale game. Harvard isn't harassing Yale. The game between the establishment and the utopian visionaries will inevitably exist in every historical era. It's fair that they want to hound me out of existence, just like the Harvard defensive team wants to throw the Yale quarterback for a loss. I have no complaint about this. The more energy that is directed against me, the more energy is available for me—it's the law of jiu-jitsu. To us, the government and professional-establishment dynamism against what we're doing is just a sign that we're doing fine.

Postscript

As the 1960's continued to exfoliate, the religious metaphor continued to boom. To our dismay! Jesus Christ, what a holy mess! We told people (only the young listened) that they were gods. And we published two books and scores of essays and interviews pushing *The Journey to the Eastern Lobes of the Brain.* It worked because it was so seductive. There was a lot to learn back-East: The barefoot grace, the body-control sinuosity of yoga, the wiry elastic mind-trick of seeing everything from the standpoint of eternity. The ultimate cool of fatalism. The junky-hindu grin of pompous, self-satisfied passivity. The comforting babble of mantra nonsense-syllables. New, colorful, bizarre Hindu Lord's Prayers to monkey-mimic.

Oriental religions, like their western counterparts, are elaborate rationalizations for avoiding change. The Eastern religious philosophies are the final flowering of the great prescientific wisdom that took us from the caves and taught us everything beautiful and harmonious that could be produced by a hand-tool culture. Whatever could be done *with the body,* including the vocal chords, had been developed and poetized by 100 generations of Hindu-Buddhist adepts.

Oriental philosophy is profoundly pessimistic, cynical, stoic, and passive. Before modern scientific technology expanded the scope of human perception there was, indeed, no place to go and nothing new. The same old body cycle-circles of birth, aging, and death. Stay detached from the outer world, because there is nothing you can do about the relentless leveling entropy of age. The Oriental posture is unbearably smug and certain. Nothing makes any difference, so cool out. It's all one, and it's all lost.

I took the obligatory trip to the East, scanned the guru scene, got the picture. The best Indian gurus are wise tricksters who have mastered the one simple rule of entropy: It's all going to hell, so get yourself a comfortable spot here and now, and let the fools who are still searching come and project their illusions (and their money) on your calm, cool, blank facade.

India is a sad country, run by bureaucrats. The British Civil Service mentality, patched onto the ultimate fussy pedantry of Brahminism, left everyone in a mean, petty mood. The Hindu antagonism towards change, scientific method, any active solution to problems, was depressing. It became clear that for 2,500 years, the most intelligent, energetic, attractive Indians had been migrating westward. India is not a place for fun-lovers, hope fiends, enthusiastic pro-lifers. But India still had a lot to teach us Westerners, and we returned from Benares loaded with paradoxical gifts from the Magi. We joyfully accepted and employed Oriental pagan techniques to pursue, more effectively, future Western goals.

We accepted the basic anti-Christian Hindu notion that the aim of this life is continual self-development, self-mastery, self-sufficiency. One could become a "perfect master," not of others, but of one's own body and brain. We used this insight in our image. We translated the basic Hindu teaching that everything is illusion into the modern neurological truth that *everything is a figment of your own brain.* We resolved to fabricate the illusion that, through science, we can decipher and discover (which really means create) new levels of energy, new layered realities, new stages of evolution.

We bought the Vedic notion of reincarnation—updated by modern genetics and expanded into the future. Neo-Lamarckianism is back in town in the guise of genetic engineering. True, everything we do in this lifetime fabricates our next incarnations, but these future realities can be created in our lifetime. (Listen, I'll tell you about multiple reincarnations! I have sailed full-throttle through the Roaring 20's, the Boring 30's, the Booming 40's, the Consuming 50's, the Celestial 60's, the Terrestrial 70's. And all this has taught me how to *pre-*incarnate for the Grateful-Fateful 80's and the Well-Designed 90's.)

Everything we did in the 1960's was designed to fission, to weaken faith in and conformity to the 1950's social order. Our precise surgical target was the Judeo-Christian power monolith, which has imposed a guilty, inhibited, grim, anti-body, anti-life repression on Western civilization. Our assignment was to topple this prudish, judgmental civilization. And it worked! For the first time in 20 centuries, the good old basic paganism got everybody moving again. White people actually started to move their hips, let the Marine crewcuts grow long, adorn themselves erotically in Dionysian revels, tune into nature. The ancient Celtic-pagan spirit began to sweep through the land of Eisenhower and J. Edgar Hoover. Membership in organized churches began to plummet. Hedonism, always the movement of individuals managing their own rewards and pleasures, ran rampant.

Millions of Americans exulted in the old Celtic Singularity. Every woman a queen, every man a king; God within. The classic paganism now combined with the American virtues of do-it-yourself, distrust of authority. Millions of Americans writing their own Declarations of Independence: *My* life, *my* liberty, *my* pursuit of happiness.

But millions more couldn't handle the freedom or independence. The familiar hunger for authority, the recurring obsession to submit; to give responsibility to a master. George Harrison grovels in front of the Maharishi. Poor Bob Dylan submits to Christ. Peter Townsend babbles inanities about Meher Baba. Swarms of gurus and spiritual-teachers running around announcing new commandments, new prohibitions.

The word *religion* beautifully defines itself, of course. It means "to bind" from the Latin *re* (back) and *ligare* (to tie up). All religions are straightjackets, jackets for the straight. Look at the faces of the followers—the Hare Krishnas, for example—and you'll get the point. Pimpled losers who don't like their own looks and have no love of their own singularity.

We learned a lot. We were disappointed that for every new-breed, self-confident scientist popping up on the scene, there were 99 new cult-followers. There was a gloomy period when I felt bewildered guilt at having encouraged this lemminglike rush to Eastern bonds.

The master-follower thing was particularly annoying. I despise followers of any kind, especially those who follow me. As it happens I am not alone in this distaste; *no one really likes followers.* Followers do not like *themselves,* of course; that's why they crawl. And masters have nothing but contempt for their subservants, which is why they impose such colorful embarrassments upon them.

But a glance at American history was comforting. Since the Pilgrims, the Quakers, the Mormons, the Emersonian Transcendentalists, our frontier country has always seethed with kooky cults and splinter messiahs. The amazing independent religiosity, the off-the-wall fervor of Americans has always been a wonderful source of eccentric individuality. There were, after all, no Jehovah's Witnesses or Hare Krishnas running around Franco's Spain or the Soviet Union. I was also comforted by the thought that the new religiosity was part of our wonderful aristocratic American consumerism, the insatiable American televoid brain demanding new sensations, new surprises, new heroes, new reality scripts.

PART FOUR

THE POLITICS OF HUMANISM
The successful scientist always upsets the hive

From our research offices at Harvard (1960–63) and Millbrook (1963–68), we conducted the largest voluntary psychosocial experiment in history. Our hypotheses were simple. History seemed to show that our human species has always eagerly accepted any new technology that gave them more power to receive and transmit information. Our experiment sought to demonstrate that it is in our nature to want to expand consciousness, change our brains, open up to new experiences. Radio, television, transistors, and psychoactive drugs are all instruments for widening the range of input experience.

The role of human beings in the Gaia life-web is information-processing. As the wave of civilization moved westward during the last 4,000 years, the scope of information-processing expanded. The farther east you go, the less information machinery available to the individual. (Can you believe wall posters in 1980 China? *Samizdats* in the Soviet Union?) The farther east you go, the more political control over free communication. In Asia, in Russia and *mittel*-Europe there exists repressive control over the printing press, radio-television transception—and, of course, psychoactive drugs.

It was our belief that Americans, given the option of expanding brain function, would do so. To test this hypothesis, we publicized the Brain-Change Option and sat back to observe and record the results.

The evidence was clear-cut. Given the opportunity, an overwhelming majority of young people in the Western democratic societies bought the chance to activate their brains and dial-tune expanded reception. At first we were shocked to discover that the option to reimprint, to change, to fabricate new realities was not eagerly accepted by the adults who obviously needed it most. We were less surprised when we looked up a dictionary definition of the word "adult."

> *Past participle of the Latin verb* adolescare, *"to grow." The adult is that state of the individual which will undergo no further metamorphosis or change. The adult is the final stage of over-specialization.*

Each month, the results of our experiment flashed across the nation. Gallup polls; alarmed government statistics; worried college deans' warnings. The percentage of psychedelic-drug users consistently climbed, the percentage of longhairs rose. Rock-and-roll music kept pushing the beat.

By 1968, debate over the Brain Change Option had become a political obsession. Every politician in the land was campaigning to stop the drug epidemic. For those who wished to change their brains, there was no more reliance on the religious metaphor or the First Amendment protections. The old Texas judges weren't buying that. The issue was now one of partisan politics. Forty million grass-smokers and 7 million acid users were no longer content to appeal, like reservation Indians, to the Great White Father in Washington for peyote privileges. The right to change your consciousness using drugs had become a basic tenet of the Counterculture—along with the fight against racism and the war.

The essays and articles presented in Part Four of this book reflect my gradual change from theory and methodology to neuro-politics.

Was this transition unexpected? Nope; a study of the history of science and philosophy is clear on this point. A successful Socratic scientific innovator who presents the species with a new technology for changing human nature and human destiny is always in trouble with the politicians. A philosopher who does his job well invariably upsets the hive and has to deal with the forces set up to preserve the old order and prevent change.

13

In the spring of 1966, public interest in LSD had reached a level of obsession. A cover story in *Life* had presented a fair (almost pro) picture of the promise of LSD. This was no accident: Henry Luce, founder of *Life* and *Time* magazines, had taken LSD himself and enjoyed it. While Luce lived, *Life*'s treatment of LSD was always scientific and fair.

About this time I was approached by Carl Perian, staff director for a Senate committee on narcotics—a thoughtful, sophisticated man who had done considerable homework before coming to visit. He wanted me to testify before subcommittee hearings to be chaired by Senator Thomas J. Dodd of Connecticut. After several meetings with Mr. Perian I agreed to testify, with the assurance that Senator Dodd would be respectful and not hostile.

I went to Washington accompanied by my two children, Susan and Jack. My wife, Rosemary, was in jail that month for refusing to testify in front of a grand jury arranged in Poughkeepsie, New York, by the local assistant D.A.—none other than G. Gordon Liddy. There was enormous press coverage. The hallways in front of the large hearing room were crowded with television reporters. As I started to enter the chambers, I was approached by Mr. Perian, who looked a bit harassed. It seemed that Senator Dodd's hearing was to be upstaged by the unexpected arrival of another committee member, Senator Edward Kennedy of Massachusetts. Teddy was scheduled to be out of town, but hearing about the press coverage, he flew back to the capital—much to the dismay of Mr. Perian and Senator Dodd, and me.

As I took my place at the witness table, Senator Dodd smiled reassuringly. My eyes met Teddy's, and he looked away uneasily. You know the look.

Trying to turn on Teddy

(Testimony [here edited and condensed] before a Special Subcommittee of the Committee on the Judiciary United States Senate on LSD and Marihuana Use on College Campuses)

Dr. Leary. I am particularly grateful to come before this

committee, because I think the most constructive legislation in this admittedly complex field has come from this committee. I am very aware of the work done by the chairman of the committee in constructive remedy to the narcotic drug problem . . .

Senator Dodd. *We have had quite a hard time.*

Dr. Leary. Psychedelic drugs are nonaddictive, nontoxic, and antinarcotic. We don't know exactly what they do. They seem to release neurological energies. My position is that energy is not dangerous if used wisely. There is nothing to fear from our own nervous systems or from our own cellular structures. On the basis of the statistics so far, I would say there is more violence, insanity, friction, terror in cocktail lounges and barrooms on any one Saturday night than in the entire 23-year history of LSD use. The so-called peril of LSD resides precisely in its eerie power to release ancient, wise, at times even holy sources of energy, inside the human brain. During the last few months of heated publicity and occasional bureaucratic hand-wringing about LSD, one simple question has remained unanswered: Why are our most intelligent, gifted, best-educated young people choosing to expose themselves to this new and admittedly strange experience?

My answer, like the LSD experience itself, may be a stiff dose for those unwilling to look at the record of history. We have at hand energies easily available, which are accepted eagerly by the young and abhorred by the older generation, and what is worse, we have a communication breakdown between the two generations. The challenge of the psychedelic chemicals is not just how to control them, but how to use them. Restrictive legislation which creates a new class of college-educated white-collar criminals is obviously not the answer.

Research, training, knowledge, are the only solutions to this problem. But here we reach the center of the communication breakdown, because to the older generation, "drug" means medicine, disease, doctor, or dope fiends, addicts, crime. But to the vast majority of young people experimenting with these new psychedelic chemicals, the word "drug" obviously means positive things—possible growth, opening up the mind, beauty, sensual awareness, and in some cases, a religious revelation. The word "drug" covers a very wide range of psychoactive chemicals. On the one hand, the narcotic escape drugs —opiates, heroin, barbiturates, and alcohol—muffle consciousness and contract awareness. The psychedelic drugs, very different pharmacologically, seem to open up consciousness and accelerate awareness. The theories and laws necessary to control narcotics may not have any application to these other substances.

For example, in Mr. Tannenbaum's testimony, LSD users were

very eager to talk about their experiences. They weren't like junkies; they didn't feel like criminals . . .

[During my reading of my prepared statement, Senator Kennedy interrupted, addressing me as *Mr.* Leary. Hmmmm.]

Senator Kennedy. Mr. Leary, I am trying to follow the best I possibly can some themes that must be coming out of your testimony here this morning, and I am completely unable to do so. You talked in the beginning about the communications problem which exists between different generations, and then you indicate and describe why that exists. Then we hear a description and analysis, as valuable as that might be, about the different reactions to different drugs.

I am completely unable to follow anything other than just sort of a general hyperbole of discussion here. Since your testimony isn't written, and this is a matter with which we are deeply concerned, I hope at least for those of us who are not inimitably as familiar as apparently you are with LSD, that you will try and see if you can analyze this somewhat more precisely. At least I would find that helpful. As I say, I haven't had the background or experience in this area as I am sure the other members of the committee have, but I think it would be extremely valuable if you could at least outline to some extent what you are going to try and demonstrate here today.

Dr. Leary. I was, Senator Kennedy, just about to point out the differences that exist among drugs, and I am going to suggest that special types of legislation are needed.

Senator Kennedy. Are you going to talk about the lack of communication between the generations before that or after that?

Dr. Leary. I finished doing that. I feel constructive legislation is badly needed, and I recommend respectfully that this committee consider legislation which will license responsible adults to use these drugs for serious purposes. To obtain such a license, the applicant, I think, should have to meet physical, intellectual, and emotional criteria.

I believe that the criteria for marijuana, the mildest of the psychedelic drugs, should be about those which we now use to license people to drive automobiles, whereas the criteria for the licensing of much more powerful LSD should be much more strict. Perhaps the criteria now used for airplane pilots would be appropriate.

I further urge this committee to make some provision for young people to be trained in the use of these powerful instruments. If a high percentage of college students are using these instruments, we can drive them underground, or we can legitimize their use in carefully controlled circumstances.

Everyone says give LSD to the medical profession. The medical profession has had LSD for 23 years and hasn't known what to do with it, because LSD is not a medicine that cures physical problems. It is a psychological educational tool.

Senator Dodd. *Can you tell us where it is manufactured?*

Dr. Leary. The original patent holder in LSD was Sandoz Laboratories in Switzerland, although we are now told it is made in Czechoslovakia and Mexico. LSD comes from the chemist in an extremely powerful powder. One gram of powder can produce between 10,000 and 20,000 doses. The powder is then usually diluted in some form of liquid, and then broken down and used in that form.

Senator Dodd. *And what do you consider a normal dose?*

Dr. Leary. It depends on your purpose. If you wanted to have a deep, out-of-the-mind experience, you would have 300 gamma. LSD, of course, has a tremendous range. A small amount of LSD is like marijuana. A large amount of LSD is a full-fledged, 12-hour, out-of-the-mind experience. There is no known lethal dose, but one danger of black-market LSD is you are never sure what you are getting so that when LSD is put on sugar cubes, you never know whether you are getting 100 gamma or 300 gamma. This accounts for some of the problems in indiscriminate black-market use.

Senator Dodd. *Have you ever used it yourself?*

Dr. Leary. I have used LSD or similar drugs 311 times in the last 6 years. Each time I take LSD I keep careful records and I have a specific purpose in mind why I am doing it, the way a scientist would look at different objects through his magnifying lens. I have under my personal supervision witnessed over 3,000 ingestions of LSD.

Senator Dodd. *Well, can you briefly describe its effect?*

Dr. Leary. No sir. Each segment of an LSD experience is very complicated. Thousands of memory cards or thousands of sensory molecules are firing off. There is no amnesia. You remember all of this, so it would take 20 hours to describe an LSD experience.

One example, sir, would perhaps point up some of the paradoxes. A psychiatrist has read about sexual abnormalities and hallucinations and then one day into his office walks a person who describes an LSD experience. He might say: "I was sitting there and suddenly I began to dissolve. Every cell in my body began to break down, and I was afraid I would become a puddle on the floor. Then I saw a huge serpent swallow me. I went in the serpent's stomach. Later I was excreted and I exploded. Then I became an animal. I could feel hair and claws growing on my body. Then I could look down and see fishy scales as though I were a reptile. Then I was floating as though I was a single-celled organism." By this time, even the most experienced psychiatrist is likely to be crouching under the table, saying, "In 30 years of my practice I have never listened to anything so frightening and so far out." A Hindu would say, "Oh, yes; the third dream of Vishnu."

We also have neurological and anatomical explanations for LSD's so-called hallucinations. They are not supernatural; they are experiences for which we don't have words. I think future research will allow us to understand, control, and even produce hallucinations that won't be mysterious or frightening.

Senator Dodd. *We have heard about people jumping out of windows and eating bark off trees and grass off of lawns and committing crimes as a result of the use.*

Dr. Leary. No doubt in some cases, when LSD is used by people who are not trained, under very poor circumstances, bizarre behavior develops. As more people are trained in how to use this, and as they know where to use this drug, these episodes will be cut down.

Of course, the law enforcement officers and the psychiatric clinics see that one case in 1,000 who is having trouble. I get about 100 letters a week from people who rhapsodize about the positive aspects, so it may seem at times we are talking about two entirely different experiences. There is no evidence that any case has resulted in homicide.

Senator Dodd. *We have evidence before this committee regarding such cases. Weren't you here this morning when Captain Trembly told about the youngster who tried to kill her mother after using LSD? Dr. Louria told us yesterday about the homicidal tendencies of users, their destructive conduct with respect to their physical surroundings. Doesn't this make it perfectly clear that the use of it brings on such activities?*

Dr. Leary. No doubt these things are occurring. However, of all the forms of energy available to the American citizen today, I would say that LSD is statistically producing fewer cases of violence or destruction than alcohol or some of our more popular medicaments.

Senator Dodd. *You don't offer that as a very good argument: it just doesn't do as much damage as something else.*

Dr. Leary. The problem with me, sir, is this one case of LSD panic gets headlines, whereas 999 cases of LSD revelation nobody cares about. So to be scientific about this, we have to have some batting average. In any 1,000 people, one is likely to become violent within the next 6 months. Naturally, if he takes LSD, it may happen.

Senator Dodd. *Would you agree that uncontrolled use is dangerous? Don't you feel that LSD should be put under some control, or restriction as to its sale, its possession, and its use?*

Dr. Leary. Definitely. In the first place, I think that the 1965 Drug Control Act, which this committee sponsored, is the high watermark in such legislation. But I am urging some form of licensing, or we will have another era of prohibition in this country, because the people who are using LSD are not criminal types. They are middle-class college people who are very aware of their constitutional rights to change their consciousness as long as they are not visibly harming society.

Senator Kennedy. *Mr. Leary, the* New Republic *article says right in there rather clearly: "It is more likely that the individuals who use this are usually already psychiatrically deranged before taking LSD. This, of course, emphasizes even more the absolute necessity of competent psychiatric screening of every person who is to use any kind of hallucinogens."*

Dr. Leary. I agree with that conclusion; I am urging that there be some kind of licensing.

Senator Kennedy. *I thought the point made by the chairman about the types of people who are using it substantiates not only what the chairman observed but it was also previously testified so, and so I think there has been substantial evidence to that matter, that those that do use it are already psychologically deranged or can be, or at least the predominance that are using it lean that way. At least that is the testimony which has been presented to this committee. Now if you have different conclusions on that, I think that from either your years of study or others, I think it would be helpful to have that material.*

Dr. Leary. Yes. Senator, I cannot allow the University of Stanford students to be described as psychotic or criminal. In his *New Republic* article Dr. O'Chota says; "A sample of students at Stanford University showed that at least 40 percent have been taking hallucinogens." Now I will defend very fiercely the sanity and the social constructiveness of the 40 percent of the Stanford University student body, even though I may be unpopular—

Senator Kennedy. *That is not responsive to the question, but I will accept the statement. Mr. Leary, I have been continually confused by your testimony. Maybe that is my own limitation of understanding as to the nature of the subject that we are considering here today. You mentioned earlier, and I am trying to clarify at least to some extent my own understanding, that you needed a microscope in order to indicate the degree or quantity in which this LSD should be taken; is that correct?*

Dr. Leary. As a metaphor; yes, sir.

Senator Kennedy. *And do you use it to measure the quantity, to make up the consistency of the particular drug at a particular time to determine what kind of ride you want to have; is that right?*

Dr. Leary. I am using the microscope as a *metaphor,* sir.

[As I listened to Teddy's attempt to bluster and bully, I was stunned in disbelief. What a disloyal snake! My family had known and supported young Jack when he was a stripling congressman from Boston. I had talked at length with Jack and was well aware of both his and Bobby's intelligent-hedonic use of drugs. Dr. Jack, the White House medicineman, was my friend. And here was Teddy, of all people, pushing Carl Perian and Thomas Dodd aside to gain respectability points by lynching me!]

Senator Kennedy. *And then they take these—you say that they get 25 grains?*

Dr. Leary. Gamma.

Senator Kennedy. *Pardon?*

Dr. Leary. Gamma, that is 25 millionths of a gram.

Senator Kennedy. *Twenty-five gamma, and then they get 300 to go out of their minds by virtue of its use?*

Dr. Leary. Yes, sir.

Senator Kennedy. *Now, when they go out of their minds, as I gather from your testimony that they certainly can, if they go out of their minds—let's just say if they go out of their minds do they know the difference between right and wrong?*

Dr. Leary. No, sir. Not social right and wrong. They are likely to think in an unconventional—

Senator Kennedy. *In unconventional ways. And so if they don't really know the difference between right and wrong, still they are able to, as you say, perform normal kinds of activities, bodily or social activities?*

Dr. Leary. That depends entirely on the experience of the person. You see you have to be trained to use LSD the way you are trained to use a computer. An unprepared person is confused.

Senator Kennedy. *Therefore, you are suggesting that anyone who is going to administer LSD ought to be highly trained?*

Dr. Leary. Absolutely.

Senator Kennedy. *And that there shouldn't be indiscriminate use? And that is why you want to give college courses in LSD? And what is going to happen to the boy who doesn't get to college?*

Dr. Leary. There would be special training institutes for him.

Senator Kennedy. *So we are going to train high school students as well?*

Dr. Leary. I would let research, scientific research, answer the question as to what age the nervous system is ready to use these new instruments.

Senator Kennedy. *That is very responsive. Now you feel that* anybody who distributes this ought to be carefully trained, is that correct? Where are they going to get this preparation?

Dr. Leary. For the last 5 years, my training institute, the Castalia Foundation, has been the only one in the world that has been conscientiously and systematically training people.

Senator Kennedy. *Now other people, who haven't had the good opportunity or fortune to attend your institute, have been taking LSD, have they not? So don't you think that until your institute is either able to expand its courses, that we ought to at least be conscious of the dangers which are presented by it?*

Dr. Leary. The need for licensing legislation is desperate. We have got to get institutes trained and licensed so that people can receive training. I agree completely with your bill, the 1965 Drug Control Act. I think this is—

Senator Dodd. *That the federal government and the state governments ought to control it?*

Dr. Leary. Exactly. I am in 100 percent agreement with the 1965 Drug Control Act. I wish the states would follow the wisdom of this committee and follow with exactly that kind of legislation.

Senator Kennedy. *So there should not be indiscriminate distribution of this drug, should there?*

Dr. Leary. I have never suggested that, sir. I have never urged anyone to take LSD. I have always deplored indiscriminate or unprepared use.

Senator Kennedy. *And there ought to be strict regulations then with regards to those who possess it?*

Dr. Leary. No, sir.

Senator Kennedy. *Well, now wait a moment, Dr. Leary. You just stated somewhat earlier that you thought anybody who was going to use it ought to be carefully trained, ought to understand. I don't find the consistency of your argument when you say that we ought to have careful restrictions on LSD, strict control over its production, but that we shouldn't have strict control over who has it. How do you—*

Dr. Leary. Because I urge all of us to face reality. Millions of Americans are using this drug indiscriminately in their own pursuits. I am not in favor of passing laws which would put 40 percent of the Stanford University student body in the category of criminals—I am against laws which would put such people in prison.

Senator Dodd. *Do I understand correctly that the research with respect to this drug is still going on?*

Dr. Leary. Yes, sir. Research has been almost halted because of the present hysteria. There are very few government-approved grants now because of the grand panic sweeping the country. Doctors and psychiatrists who should be doing studies are afraid to. If research shows any serious physiological side-effects, or irreversible psychological effects, I would be the first one to urge its ban. Having taken this drug perhaps more than any scientist in the world, I am more curious than anyone as to its physiological effect or possibilities of brain damage. Every time I meet someone who says this I say, "Will you please wire me collect if you have any personal information on brain damage?"

Senator Kennedy. *You read the* New Republic *article that you quoted earlier? Did you note that in that article he says, "There is one uniform agreement among the investigators of LSD; namely, that LSD can be extremely dangerous when used improperly."?*

Dr. Leary. Sir, the motor car is dangerous if used improperly. I couldn't be in more agreement.

Senator Kennedy. *It is dangerous, then?*

Dr. Leary. If used improperly.

Senator Kennedy. *Isn't that why the pilot is licensed as well?*

Dr. Leary. Yes, sir. Human stupidity and ignorance is the only danger human beings face in this world.

Senator Kennedy. *It seems to me that your testimony has been extremely convincing about the dangers of this drug, as well as its opportunities. And I think for someone who has been associated as long as you have been, have been intimately involved in it as long as you have been, I think that is extremely weighty evidence which you have given to this committee this morning, and we want to thank you.*

Dr. Leary. I cannot agree with that summary, respectfully. I must disagree, Senator Kennedy, with your statement.

Senator Kennedy. *Let's take the various aspects of it. You feel that there ought to be control over at least importation? The sale and manufacturing?*

Dr. Leary. Yes, sir.

Senator Kennedy. *And that the only reason you think this is because it is a matter of interstate and foreign commerce? Is that the only reason? I mean, we have things which are produced, textiles in Massachusetts, furniture in Massachusetts that are not restricted, Dr. Leary. . . .*

[Sitting there watching Teddy huff and puff in law-school rhetorical style, hidden behind the robes of legislative cliché, I felt sorry for Teddy and for the rest of us. The disastrous Roger Mudd interview during the 1980 campaign was no surprise.]

After the debate, I was invited to lunch by a group of young men and women who worked on the staffs of five senators. They had all taken LSD and were much concerned about the Kennedys' attempts to abuse psychedelic drugs. Ironically enough, one of these young men was from Bobby's staff.

After a jolly hour of psychedelic reminiscing, they got down to business. It seemed that Bobby was going to hold hearings on LSD too, and was planning to invite me as the first witness—and this had them worried.

"Just because Teddy's bumbling made it easy for you, don't be fooled. Bobby is another story. Ask anyone around Washington, and they will tell you that Bobby is the most ruthless, efficient, brilliant investigator on the hill. He'll have mountains of staff work. He'll be ready. For example, he'll produce records from Sandoz Laboratories, showing that you never received a microgram of acid from them. Do you realize what that means?"

"Yes," I replied. "He'll try to make it look as though all our research has been illegal."

"You got it," said my informant. "Bobby is also working closely with Dr. Sidney Cohen, who is coaching the senator on ways to trip you up. Naturally, we'd like to see you blast through the hearings and teach these dinosaurs something about what's happening with young people. But we cannot overemphasize the danger. Bobby is bright and tough."

In the following days we were kept very busy with local political harassment. We snatched up Rosemary from the Poughkeepsie County Court House and hid out in the woods to escape the minions of Gordon Liddy. Coordinating the Leary Defense Committee, public lectures, dictating the *Playboy* interview. Still undecided about whether to tangle with Bobby.

The day before the hearings, we held a strategy meeting lying panoramically on the blue-copper roof of the 64-room mansion in Millbrook. We decided that it would be foolish to venture onto Bobby's turf in a situation where he controlled all the levers. Reckless to be cross-examined without the protections of counsel. A no-win setup. So I quickly prepared a statement, which would be hand-delivered by one of our top operatives, Larry Bogart, a pioneer conservationist-ecologist. A most respectable and straight person, not a doper, Larry had been horrified by my 30-year marijuana sentence at Laredo, Texas, and was managing the Leary defense. Larry looked like a pink-cheeked, Princeton professor of Ancient Languages. And so it happened that when Bobby opened his hearings and the television cameras whirred and my name was called, up walked Larry Bogart.

Bobby Kennedy tries to abuse LSD

Hearings before the Subcommittee on Executive Reorganization of the Committee on Government Operations May 24, 25, 26, 1966. Mr. Bogart Reading Statement of Timothy Leary, Ph.D., President, Castalia Foundation for Psychedelic Research, Millbrook, N.Y.

Increasing numbers of Americans are taking LSD, despite current laws banning its use. A high proportion of users are young—college and high school students.

Since new state and federal legislation has closed off legitimate access to LSD, almost all supplies now come from illicit sources. This state of affairs makes several million otherwise law-abiding American citizens into criminals; fosters the growth of black market profiteering; increases the likelihood of impure and contaminated LSD, with unpredictable effects; blocks research into a scientific tool of enormous potential; and tends to undermine public faith in the law.

Up until recently, fully half of the nation's hospital beds have been occupied by mental patients. The discovery of a host of increasingly effective synthetic organic chemicals has dramatically cut hospital stays. Mind-relaxing drugs and tranquilizers have restored millions to useful lives in society. But emotional problems are still with us, and it seems the best investment we could make lies in further research in molecular biology.

In an international conference held in Amityville, N.Y., in May of 1965, psychiatrists and psychologists reported on the use of LSD to treat the mentally ill. Dr. Harold Abramson, a brilliant pioneer researcher who served as host and sponsor of this conference, is now prevented by present government policy from pursuing his investigations. The only way out of this situation is a cooling-off period, while rational examination is conducted by scientists with government officials. I have volunteered as an evidence of cooperation to forego the use of any psychedelic material presently held illegal, and have urged others to do likewise.

I suggest a Commission of Psychochemical Education—a blue-ribbon panel of neurologists, pharmacologists, psychologists, educators, and religious leaders to survey the entire field of psychochemical research, to evaluate the educational uses of LSD, "learning pills," RNA stimulators, and to anticipate the social and psychological effects of new drugs which can expand and speed up the mind.

This commission should propose a program for using these new chemical gifts wisely. For a year, there should be intensive research directed to ascertaining what risks, if any, attend the use of LSD. The value of supportive setting and length of preparation should be accurately measured.

A licensing procedure should be set up, under the commission's guidance, to enable responsible, healthy adults to use LSD to further self-understanding. Persons with organic or psychological disability would be screened out, as would potential schizophrenics. Licenses would be given only to persons who had undergone adequate training by experienced LSD guides. Should the user prove irresponsible, he would lose his license and be penalized for breaking the law just as anyone else. The establishment of special licensing procedures for a new class of chemicals has a precedent in the case of radioisotopes, which are controlled by the AEC.

LSD would be administered only in special Psychedelic Training Centers, where a team of experienced guides would be available to screen, prepare, and guide applicants. Medical supervision would be provided and FDA surveillance exercised. LSD, available at relatively low cost in such centers, would reduce the demand for black market supplies, and the attendant undesirable consequences mentioned above. LSD accidents would be minimized and, should they occur, would be handled by experienced staff.

[Bobby was furious at my wariness about his ambush, but he got over it and we became friends again.]

15

From 1961 to the end of 1965, I devoted my energies to establishing a nonrepressive society by encouraging a large group of young Americans to re-imprint themselves away from the work-duty conditioning, and get back where they belong. Our hope was to bring about change where all change must originate—the brain. The aim was to produce the first generation in history to choose its own mode of imprint-conditioning, react selectively to self-selected rewards and, literally, *make up its own mind.*

By the fall of 1965, to the despair of the law-and-order generation, the young were joyously rejecting the Protestant work ethic. Psychedelic people inevitably became more and more like the artistic, the blacks, and the young—those three outgroups who live closer to a pagan life of natural fleshly pleasure. The complex tasks of the new social structure now could be left to the younger and more talented. Thus honorably emeriti, Rosemary and I turned ourselves to postretirement projects—to stay high, make love, and write science fiction.

In December 1965, we closed the house at Millbrook and drove to Mexico, where we had rented a beach house. We got to Laredo, Texas, at sundown and drove across the International Bridge, and parked in front of the Immigration Building. We weren't able to get our tourist cards. Even though we hadn't been in Mexico, we had to pass through American Customs. The Customs Officer ordered everyone out of the car, leaned in the front door, reached down and came up with something in his fingers. "What is this seed I found on your car floor?" In a flash, the car was surrounded by agents.

The indictments came down in January. Susan and I were charged with smuggling marijuana, transporting marijuana, and failure to pay the marijuana tax. After the verdict, the Laredo judge sentenced me to 30 years' imprisonment and a $30,000 fine for possessing half an ounce of grass. Lost in the headlines was the uneasy knowledge that this federal weed law violated the Fifth Amendment (forbidding self-incrimination by being forced to pay taxes for an illegal act).

On December 12, 1968, the appeal was argued before the Supreme Court. On May 19, 1969, a sunny day, the Federal marijuana prohibition was repealed. I was free. The Nixon administration moved to refile charges on the transportation technicality and I was, much to my chagrin, pulled back to Laredo to face the same judge and the same federal agents. The judge sentenced me to ten years. Appeal bond is routinely granted in cases that do not involve violence, but not in this case. The judge denied bail on the grounds that the defendant was "going around the country preaching and teaching dangerous doctrines."

From my conviction in 1966 to my escape-exile in 1970, I published hundreds of interviews and articles explaining the politics and ethics of brain-chemistry. This chapter reprints an essay first published in *Cavalier* magazine, illustrating the tactics used by those of us who supported the Brain-Change Option in the primitive 1960's.

The politics and ethics of ecstasy

In the past, men fought over symbols—the cross or the crescent, or which version of the Bible you used. Today the issue is which chemicals are part of your life and your growth.

It is estimated that over 50,000,000 Americans have used marijuana, peyote, mescaline, but there are followers of other chemical yogas. Many millions of Americans rely upon tranquilizers to guide them through each day. Millions use energizers and pep pills. Close to 100 million Americans use alcohol, and are addicted to nicotine. Perhaps 100,000 people escape the turmoil and pain of life with heroin.

As we move into the psychochemical age, things are out of control. None of us knows exactly what the future will bring. But one thing's certain: psychochemicals release energy. In dealing with psychochemicals, the only things we have to fear are ancient enemies —ignorance and panic. The solution to the problems posed by psychochemicals is not imprisonment, it's disciplined pursuit of knowledge.

The first problem is to know something about the different levels of consciousness. Unless you have some model or language for describing different states of brain function, you're operating in a state of confusion.

The analogy I use is drawn from the science of optics. Three hundred years ago, if I announced there was a level of reality made up of tiny particles which seem to have a beauty, a meaning, a planfulness of their own, I'd be in danger of being imprisoned. When I could persuade people to look through the microscope lens at a leaf, or a snowflake, or a drop of blood, then they would discover that beyond the macroscopic world are visible realms of energy and meaning. But if I clapped a microscope onto your eye 300 years ago and said, "Walk around this," you might trip over things. You might be entranced by the beauty of what you saw, but you'd end up quite confused: "Well it's rather crazy and meaningless. I couldn't see anything I recognized."

The use of the microscope required that certain men spend hours peering through lenses at different forms of biological energy and—very slowly and painstakingly—develop a language. I could write a handbook explaining the different sorts of things you could see when you looked at a cross section of a plant. And then you could look through the microscope and check out my accuracy.

Similarly, there are levels of consciousness, defined by the anatomical structures within the brain for decoding energy. And each level of consciousness is inevitably produced by biochemical means, either by natural biochemical events or by introduced chemicals that move you to these different levels just as accurately as the magnification of a lens moves you to different levels of external reality.

The problem is, if the unprepared person takes LSD, it's like plopping a microscope onto a man 300 years ago. The prepared and knowledgeable use of marijuana requires a complex yoga of attending to which stimuli you are going to expose yourself to; which lenses you are going to polish; which sense organs you are going to open up; a very careful arrangement of the sequence between external energy and a specific sense organ. Like the microscope, marijuana requires training, practice, and a certain empirical mapping or language.

People often ask me how often, if ever, you should take LSD. Those of us who have been working on our research project for the last 6 years have never said that anyone *should* take a psychedelic drug. The energy and power involved in changing your nervous system are too much.

Expanding your vision, whether via the microscope or psychedelic drugs, is no business for the neurotic person to get involved in. If you're having trouble with simply being yourself and making a living in this world, stay away from any experience that is going to expand and multiply the complexities, dimensions, and perspectives. You're simply going to carry your confusion and your neurosis with you. If you're not ready to look at yourself and your symbolic aim, ambition, lusts, desires, pride, and complete selfishness through a clear amplifying lens—stay away from any psychedelic experiences.

Psychosis is a sudden, unprepared-for confrontation with levels of energy that bewilder and terrorize you. The psychotic person, or person having a prolonged LSD state, is suffering from a level of consciousness first reported by Buddha over 2,000 years ago. And if you treat a psychotic as though he were looking at you with 2 billion years of neurological perspective, I think you would find yourself able to understand and be understood by him.

Less than one in 1,000 people who take LSD have a prolonged severe negative reaction. Scientific evidence demonstrates the danger of LSD is much less than the danger from alcohol, nicotine, or jogging. But the awe that comes when the veil is torn from your eyes, and you see the nature of the energy process you're involved in, can be a most painful experience.

Almost every visionary mystic in world history—Rama Krishna, Mohammed, even the founder of experimental psychology, Gustav Theodore Fechner—reported the same experience. Some sort of veil or symbolic reality was removed, and they stood there in trance, bewildered by the play of energy, searching for meaning deeper than the symbolic. I'm concerned about anyone having one second of unexplained terror; but I'm not concerned about a lot of young people taking a year or two to examine what this whole business is all about. What kind of a society will we have if we deprive young people of the right to aimless exploration, wandering, curious poking around, unskillful experiments in new forms of communication? The Buddha, after all, was one of the first dropouts.

Very shortly after we started our research 6 years ago, people began calling us a cult—a small group of people dedicated to an ideal. We pleaded guilty. We were a small group dedicated to an ideal. Today we are no longer a cult. According to a United Nations report in 1951, 200 million people use marijuana and other cannabis-plant products. In the United States, several million share these values and methods; 90% of them come from the young, racial or national minorities, or the creative. Our racial minorities, particularly Chicanos and blacks, use psychedelic drugs in much higher percentage than the middle-class whites who pass most of our laws. The creative minority—poets, writers, musicians, dramatists, who use psychedelic drugs in a much higher percentage than other groups—are persecuted by the middle-aged, middle-class, middle-brows who pass our laws. But the only way to deal with the psychochemical age is training. These drugs are going to be used. Ethical understanding will determine whether they are used to free or to imprison man's mind.

The problems posed by new ways of changing consciousness, I think, require two new commandments:

(11) Thou shalt not alter the consciousness of thy fellow man by electrical or chemical means. Can you change a man's consciousness if he wants you to? Can you teach him how? Yes, but the control of the method has got to be given to the man who owns that brain.

(12) Thou shalt not prevent thy fellow man from changing his consciousness by electrical or chemical means. If someone's changing his consciousness wreaks clear harm to society, only then can you prevent him. In every such case, the burden of proof must be on society to demonstrate that harm is being done.

As the father of two teen-age children, I am as concerned about their education and growth as any parent in the country. I've never told my children what to do with their nervous systems, as I have never told anyone whether they should or should not take a psychedelic drug. I have told what I have learned from extensive personal and objective research, about the effects of this wide range of consciousness-changing chemicals.

Let's face it; there's not much you can do by coercion or threat. And if you are going to try to teach them about psychedelic drugs, you've got to know a lot more than they do.

If you are concerned about your children's interest in psychedelics, listen to everything they have to say. You'll find that they don't know too much, because *none* of us knows too much about it. So why don't you suggest a contract with your children? Both try to read everything you can—pro, con, religious, scientific, legislative. And at the end of 2 or 3 months, make a joint decision on the basis of the evidence.

I am very old-fashioned; I would much rather have my children making these strange explorations *with* me. I'm convinced that the present generation of Americans under twenty-five is the most sophisticated, most intelligent, wisest, and holiest generation in history. And by God, they better be.

16

In 1969, the more we thought about it, the better the idea it seemed—to run for governor of California. It promised to be great theatre, flamboyant fun, a bully platform from which to suggest change in the farce of partisan politics. And, as it turned out, there was some chance I might win.

The first step was newspaper endorsements. In a week we signed up *Rolling Stone*, Berkeley *Barb*, Los Angeles *Free Press*, San Francisco *Oracle*, The San Diego *Something-Or-Other*—in short, every underground paper in the state. The college dailies were delighted. Add 'em all up, and I had more circulation support than any of the other Democratic candidates.

The idea was to make the campaign a statewide party. The top rock 'n' roll and jazz groups in the world were willing to come help out. John Lennon wrote a campaign song based on the campaign motto: "Come Together, Join the Party." It was planned to rent a railroad car and travel around the state with the greatest musicians and counterculture heroes—having enormous rallies in every city and town.

The demographics and statistical projections were interesting. I was running on the Democratic ticket against three other candidates—who neatly split the ticket. There was a right-winger: Mayor Sam Yorty of Los Angeles; a middle-of-the roader: Mayor Joseph Alioto of San Francisco, who pulled the old-line union vote. And a Kennedy man, Jesse Unruh, speaker of the state assembly. My statisticians and poll experts estimated that I could win 33% of the Democratic vote—including young people (the voting age had been dropped to 18), the astrology vote, the vegetarian vote, a lot of amused and sympathetic minority votes, the UFO vote, the kooks, utopians, dopers—hell, this is California we're talking about!

"Even if you don't beat Reagan in the general election," my advisors said, "you'll end up titular leader of the Democratic party in California, and you'll change the texture of American politics forever."

When the English movie crew arrived, the campaign took on the media dimension necessary to win. The filmmakers wanted to do a straight documentary—filming what happened. Past participle. No way. We would film some rallies, some mass meetings, but the main thrust of the film was to be futique newscasts, announcers reporting

160

on the campaign. Initial surveys would show the 15% kook vote going to me, but then, as the film progressed and the rock concerts and man-in-the-street interviews continued (on film), the fabricated newscasts would show my percentage rising, rising. Then the quotes from Nixon, Reagan, Agnew, Premier Brezhnev, J. Edgar Hoover (taken from edited news clips, of course), reacting; nervous about my growing percentages. Last-minute help from the Beatles and Jimi Hendrix, real endorsements from the children of almost every major politician and media celebrity, the final election night suspense, and then the victorious campaign headquarter celebrations and shots (dubbed) of my rivals conceding. The movie was to be shot in January-February of 1970, edited in March, and shown only in California the month before the June primaries.

      The following platform statement was published in several California papers and stimulated the expected amused reactions.

What kind of a party do you want?

The only purpose of government is to provide a joyous and harmonious pooling of intelligence to encourage life (health), individual liberty, and the pursuit of happiness for all citizens.

      Current political parties are no fun at all—grim and divisive organizations apparently committed to an unhealthy ecology, an uptight economy, centralized control, and violent tension among all citizens. Only a tiny minority really like the present miserable political system.

      The present state government penalizes the virtuous and rewards the immoral. Convicted felons are comfortably housed, doctored, well fed, and allowed to loaf for years in the company of more skillful and glamorous outlaws who are delighted to teach them what they know. The sober, industrious, honest person is penalized by taxes which support these maximum-security colleges of crime.

      At present the only alternatives to violent authoritarianism is to start a New Party, based on a positive psychology of affectionate reward;

a rational, good-humored social system that rewards healthy, honest, harmoniously individualistic behavior and imposes gentle, appropriate, effective, constructive penalties upon unhealthy, dishonest, disharmonious behaviors. Very different needs motivate three types of asocial behaviors now defined as criminal:

1. Crimes of Violence. The major function of the State is to protect the safety of its citizens. Persons convicted of violent crimes must be isolated in therapeutic reformatories (of varying degrees of security) until cured. Actually, modern pharmacology knows enough right now to dramatically reduce the rate of violence on the basis of voluntary treatment. The psychopharmacological rehabilitation of violent criminals was first demonstrated at Concord, Massachusetts, State Prison in 1961-64 by the Harvard Psychedelic Research Project. We would be happy to convert incorrigibly violent California prison convicts into wise, smiling saints. Violent behavior is caused by biochemical changes in the body that make the person feel bad. In the last 9 years we have demonstrated over and over how to neutralize violent emotions: help the person feel good in the context of a socially constructive, humane atmosphere. All voluntary, of course.

2. Financial dishonesty should be penalized in the appropriate manner—financially. The way to reform an irrationally greedy thief is not to give an all-expense-paid refresher course in prison or to cage him like a violent person. The convicted larcenist should be allowed to work off his "score," forced to labor at union wages until he earns twice what he has stolen.

The victim can thus be given his money back. He's happy. The alert arresting officer gets a 25% bounty. *He's* happy. The remaining 25% goes to a state fund to repay larceny victims in cases where the crook fails to repay. When "something-for-nothing" dishonesty no longer pays, the crime rate will drop. The prisons will be emptied of all but a few compulsively hung-up neurotics who will be offered psychopharmacological relief.

These are admittedly emergency measures. In the harmonious hedonic society of the future any "crime" or "sinfulness" will automatically punish itself. It is the intrinsic nature of any "crime" that it inevitably carries its own penalty. The whiskey drinker has hangovers. The prostitute is cut off from sexual release. The gambler ends up broke. The smog producer has to live in smog. The hunter kills the creatures he was meant to learn from.

3. Immoral behaviors have always been a major source of political friction. A survey of history will show that every human behavior (from cheek-to-cheek dancing to female child murder) has been

considered a capital crime in one culture and a holy sacramental act in another. Despite their irrational variance, however, moral codes are absolutely necessary for social survival. Morals and taboos are the very essence and "soul" of a society. The State has the obligation to administer the currently accepted moral code.

But at present, California is going through a period of moral change. Acts considered virtuous 20 years ago—like propelling an atmosphere-polluting motorboat around a clean-water lake, killing ducks with high-powered rifles—are seen as unhealthily sinful by a large percentage of the population. Other acts determined to be illegally taboo 20 years ago—such as smoking marijuana—are now acceptable to a large percentage of the citizenry.

The key issue in an open society is the consensual determination of good and evil, what is legally moral and illegally immoral. General solutions to this vexing question of moral difference are simple:

1. Provide a way of democratically determining, by campaign and vote, the currently acceptable moral codes.

2. Discourage immoral behavior in a socially constructive and psychologically rational way.

Let us define as immoral any behavior physically unhealthy to self, or socially obnoxious to a majority of the citizenry. Let the normal processes of lobbying, public-opinion persuasion, campaigning, and voting modify the list of immoral activities and their punishment.

Let the social penalty for immoral behavior be financial, instead of burdening the virtuous taxpayer with the enormous cost of detecting, arresting, and incarcerating. Let us set a series of special licenses so that the sensualist, the self-destructive, the unhealthy are obligated to pay a $1,000 annual contribution to the social welfare —eliminating irrational guilt and fear and enormously benefiting the state treasury. Those who have several vices pay more.

A few minutes' reflection will suggest the astounding sums available to the state treasury from such "Frivolity Fees." For example, the 2 million marijuana smokers now produce profits to illegal distributors and enormous drains on the state's treasury. If only half of the current smokers decide to purchase a license, around $1 billion would be raised. Frivolity Fees will probably turn out to be the only needed source of state funds. It is thus possible to completely eliminate state taxes for the virtuous and, indeed, to provide rebates and bonuses to the sober and underprivileged.

Any California citizen who wishes to indulge in any democratically defined immoral act will be given a Frivolity Tax Card upon which will be punched the particular vices he has paid for. Any person apprehended in an immoral act for which he has no license will pay double, i.e., a $2,000 fine. Fifteen hundred dollars of this fine goes to the state treasury and $500 to the alert arresting officer as an Immorality Bounty.

If this seems harsh, the convicted sinner can choose the old imprisonment system. Our program is voluntary and requires no revision of the present legal structure. The thief or unlicensed marijuana smoker can opt to be punished under the old system, or "pay off" his crime under the new system.

Bounty payments for the detection and arrest of unlicensed financial and moral culprits will make the police genial umpires in a good-humored game of dictated order. Under our administration, the alert state policeman will make more than the current governor's salary. The demand for police jobs will be so great that after a policeman has made enough bounty money to guarantee him lifelong income, he will be retired. Eagerly awaited openings in the police ranks will be filled by firemen.

Instead of the hard-working conservative, we shall allow the frivolous and dishonest to pay all of the cost of the state government. But how will the convicted larcenist or the unlicensed immoralist get the money to pay his fines? The State Correction Department will concentrate solely on getting good jobs for those who owe the state "greed" or "sin" money. Instead of a socialistic system of incarceration and welfare payments, the state will do everything to give "debtors" the chance to work in an interesting and challenging job to "pay off." Eventually, most all state employees will be rehabilitated crooks—which, come to think of it is better than the present situation, where most state employees are unrehabilitated crooks.

17

I'll never forget the first time I saw California—in 1946, just after my discharge from World War II service. We had driven down from Oregon through the northern California mountain valleys, past Shasta, along the vineyard trail (to my New England brain the notion of vineyards sounded like sunny heaven), and then that first unforgettable view of San Francisco from Marin County, with the Golden Gate Bridge soaring across the bay.

Thirty years later, ethology and sociobiology helped us understand the importance of neurogeography: where you are determines which circuits of your brain are activated. When the salmon reaches the special breeding pool, 500 miles up the tributaries of the Columbia River, then the salmon boy-girl light flashes. This is the place! We have arrived in the right ecological niche!

That's the way I have felt about California for the last 34 years. Since then I have seen my visits "back East" as Time Traveler Red Cross Missions—zooming back to Washington, B.C., or the seething warrens of the jittery Oriental masses in New York. Every time I would visit the hive-city of Manhattan, I saw it like a trip down into the Soviet Union—smuggling hope and the sunny message of the Far West.

The following interview was given during such a mission to Manhattan in 1969 when the *East Village Other* was the leading counterculture voice of the Far East Coast. Like all 18th-century publications, the *East Village Other* wallowed in pessimistic and violent rhetoric. I always have felt it my duty, in such missions, to unload as much sunny enthusiasm as possible from the Western Future to the Eastern Passed. This may account for the breathless flavor of the transmission.

"Come together, join the party"

EVO: Have you detected any change in the police harassment you have been subjected to over the last six years?

TL: Rosemary, I, and our kids have been hassled incessantly. Anytime in the past that the cops saw me on the highway, they would pull us over and search us. At any moment, the government could pull my bail if they didn't like my lectures or my advocacy of drugs. Now that I am running for the highest office in the State of California, any policeman in California is likely to be my assistant in maintaining harmony. Just last week I was in Miami for a rock concert and a patriotic lecture. At 5 A.M., on our way to our motel, we were pulled over by a police cruiser. Within 2 minutes he had the captain and what must have been a large part of the force over there, but this was obviously just a little adventure for them. They ran a make on me, and when it was reported that I was Timothy Leary, there was great rejoicing and amusement at headquarters. This encounter ended in a very friendly conversation, in the course of which I offered all policemen present jobs in California because they were all so alert and good humored. I hope this atmosphere of reconciliation will continue.

All this took place just after the bloodbath of the People's Park in Berkeley. What is your reaction to the Berkeley activists?

Rosemary and I live in Berkeley, and are very close to the people masterminding the People's Park incident. This was the classic, perfect example of how to run a psychedelic guerilla campaign. They lured the university administration, the police, and the National Guard off the campus. There was no issue of seizing buildings. It was simply Cops vs. Flowers, brilliantly conceived and the most effective political event in years. When the National Guard helicopter gassed the campus, very few dissenters were hit. They gassed the students in the cafeteria, the ones on their way to classes and patients in the university hospital. They gassed the gym too, which in turn angered the jocks. Anytime you get the jocks running into the streets shaking their fists at the police, you score a victory.

An argument has been going on as to the wisdom of dubbing every cop a pig.

Everyone has to do what their karma directs. There are some people whose karma it is to call cops pigs, and some engage in violent confrontations. Police and protestors are both playing necessary parts in the drama to show the world how ridiculous the American political and law-enforcement situation is. But there are others whose karma it is to harmonize. I am a Libra—so far from inflicting injury, my number one priority is to reward the police. Our country has been engaged in a convulsive punishment experiment. We all know that hitting kids on the head, shooting down dissenters, or gassing students has never worked as a political technique. We are going to see to it that the police will be relieved of the tremendous unpopularity now generated by their enforcing laws about morals.

I detect an injustice in levying a tax on grass smokers to alleviate the tax burden of the right wing.

You have to be practical about this. I think most marijuana smokers will pay the tax rather than run the risk of getting busted, which costs considerably more and often involves imprisonment. Any way you look at it, my plan is more beneficial for everybody concerned. Liquor, nicotine, and entertainment are heavily taxed right now.

How do you feel about the unrest on campuses across the country?

We have an absolutely foolproof solution for the college and university problem: When I am governor, I'll pull the government out of education. We are going to turn the colleges and universities over to private groups of students and professors who will run their own education as they see fit. Under my administration, if the students have complaints against their professors, it will be considered a trade union problem, and such disputes should be ironed out amongst themselves. The State has no business having anything to say about education other than supporting it with tax subsidies. Education will be free of government interference. Of course, one of our major efforts is to cut down this burgeoning state bureaucracy which plagues all of us. I intend to cut the prison population in California by at least 90%, and keep only those who insist on being violent behind bars.

You are aware of the class-conscious revolutionary rhetoric surrounding the upcoming trial of the Chicago 8.

I think everything is perfect. I think Mayor Daley was sent down to play his part in the genetic plan to free us all. The revolution is hedonic. The key is internal freedom that goes beyond classes. What impressed me of late is that when you visit the most deserted parts of the country, you find the kids most outspoken. They may not consider themselves revolutionists at all, but they are completely disgusted with the establishment. Anyone who speaks to them honestly about individual freedom will receive their full-scale support.

The violent confrontation in Chicago resulted in 70% of the American people siding with Mayor Daley. That shows that confrontation, while necessary, was essentially a setback. On the other hand, the People's Park issue in Berkeley, where the issue was planting grass and beautifying a dump, resulted in a 66-to-1-vote of confidence by the student body. By provoking a confrontation in which we are righteously joyous, we won 89% of the young and over 50% of the older. With a violent confrontation, we lose in every way. There is no question about the revolution being won through the spirit of the West Coast, which is the spirit of confidence, the certainty that hedonic tactics and pleasure guerillas will win out. The average high-school kid does not want to carry arms, he wants to get high and fuck in a spiritual manner. They laugh at violent politicians.

In the last few months, pornography burst upon the American scene, with the expected repression following closely at its heels.

The key energy for our revolution is erotic. A free person is one whose erotic energy has been liberated and can be expressed in increasingly more beautiful, complex ways. Wilhelm Reich said it first. I think the sexual revolution is the center of the free atmosphere generating within the kids. Psychedelic drugs, particularly marijuana, are popular because they turn on the body. The central issue of the psychedelic experiences is the erotic exhilaration. The increased freedom of sexual expression in art and mass media is symptom number one of our victory. On the West Coast, 12-year-old kids are fucking righteously and without guilt, very poetically. The average 15-year-old Californian has explored most single and many multiple ways of sexual expression and is ready to go to a more spiritual Tantric path. In an interview in *Look,* a 17-year-old girl was quoted as saying that grass was great for balling. To which *Look's* middle-aged expert said in a pitying way, "What does she know about sexual intercourse?" This is, I think, the key to the generational gap. Most 17-year-olds have had orgasms longer, deeper, and more complex than their ancestors. The older generation just can't stand this, and therefore repress it.

Is there anything you wish to say in conclusion?

The politics of violence is futile. You are never going to win anyone over by being uptight. A frowning face with lips pursed like a hen's asshole does not melt hearts. Take Berkeley. After the murder of a young man by the police, the gassing of the campus by the National Guard, and a series of threats, our reaction was flowers. Let's face it, violence on both sides comes from violent heads whose future is inevitably doomed.

18

Well, plans to make the movie and win the California election were easily blocked. Two weeks before the filing date for candidates, one of my rivals visited a Hollywood movie producer who had contributed generously to former Democratic campaigns. The producer refused to give a contribution because he was "waiting to see how the Timothy Leary campaign was developing." My rival blanched and blurted "Shit, you're the fourth Hollywood Democrat to tell me that in two days. This joke has to stop."

Foreign news coverage of my campaign didn't make American politicians laugh either. The Europeans loved my TV interviews, with 21st-century lines like "The function of government is to entertain." One week before filing date for candidates, I was imprisoned without bail. The lawyers had assured me this just couldn't happen in America—but they forgot that Reagan was governor and Nixon was president.

Anyway, I didn't file, spent the primary season in prison, and learned about Ronald Reagan's election from the safety of Algeria, to which I had fled after my escape from prison.

This is no place to discuss my political adventures in Algeria, Libya, Egypt, and Lebanon, except to say that Arab Socialism is a vengeful, violent, barbarian concept that hasn't changed a microgram since Medina, A.D. 622. There was no Politics of Ecstasy behind the Arab veil.

Algeria, at the time, was a hotbed of intrigue and espionage. Everyone in Algiers was an agent of one or more political powers, exiled governments, and liberation fronts.

After surveying the political chessboard, I opted for the most capitalist-democratic country in the world, Switzerland. After tricking the Algerian government into issuing exit visas to attend a Communist convention in Denmark, we jumped the plane in Zurich and applied for political asylum in Switzerland. After six months (2 months in *Bois Mermet* prison on an American extradition warrant), I was given asylum under the condition that I say nothing about drugs. This was the stimulus for the following plaintive statement from exile, 1972.

169

The politics of psychopharmacology

It would not be possible for me to discuss the positive benefits of drugs like hashish, LSD, and opium, or to describe the scientific basis upon which I base my belief that these drugs should be legal and freely accessible. I am a scientist who has spent the last 15 years studying the effects of drugs on human psychology and human behavior, yet I am not allowed to present the results of my research. For the last 10 years, starting at Harvard University, every administrator—and, more recently, every government official I've talked to—has indicated that I would not be allowed the freedom to discuss the reasons why these laws should be changed. This is a clear violation of the American Constitution, academic freedom, scientific openness, and of all the principles upon which democratic societies are based. At this moment, there is no country in the world in which I, an outlaw and stateless person, can pursue my scientific work.

Why is the topic of drugs so taboo? Because the use of drugs is the first and the last frontier of human freedom. They give the individual the power to move his consciousness in any direction he desires; given control of his own nervous system, the individual essentially can become the kind of person he wants to become.

Switzerland is so green and beautiful because it rains, rains, rains in the damp, gloomy Alps, and the sun never dries things out. They call it "the green hell." The Swiss are good people, but soggy and bored. There was little scientific work done. I learned how to ski, wrote some memoirs, produced and sang on a rock 'n' roll record, made a movie, and wallowed in the Exile Blues.

In January 1973 I fled to Vienna. The Austrian government had invited me to make an anti-heroin movie. Chancellor Bruno Kreisky said he hoped I could help him bring Austria into the 20th century. I was feted and treated by Viennese intellectuals, but Austria is darker and damper than Switzerland. The hottest book in Vienna was, believe it or not, *Das Kapital.*

Heading for the sun of Ceylon, I flew to Beirut. I was welcomed by the dope-oriented Lebanese aristocracy, but the place reeked of paranoia and double-agentry. In Afghanistan, a uniformed official at the Kabul airport requested my passport, and American agents then moved in to bust me for not having a passport. The prince of the royal house said, "Not to worry, my family will protect you." In three days I was escorted by a battalion of armed soldiers to an airplane where American agents waited to bring me back to California. It was blatant kidnapping, but no one noticed. Nixon was reinaugurated that month. And there are no lawyers in Afghanistan. The king was overthrown a few weeks after my kidnapping; he had more troubles than I did.

The California prison officials were very irritated with me. In the spring of 1973, while awaiting my escape trial I was confined to the "hole" of the San Luis Obispo state prison. During this period my only human contacts were with other inmates—mostly psychotic murderers—who could be seen and heard through a one-foot window in the iron cell-door. Written contact with the outside world was severely censored. Writing materials were limited to a pencil stub not long enough to be used as a weapon. I wrote continually during this period—essays were disguised as legal briefs and smuggled out during lawyer visits.

At this time I was invited by *The Forum of Contemporary History* to write an essay about the 1960's. Sitting under the naked bulb of the cell, I used the pencil stub to write the essay which follows. It was widely reprinted and served as the script for a television documentary shown on Public Broadcasting stations.

The seeds of the sixties

In January 1960 I accepted an invitation to come to Harvard to initiate new programs in what was then called Behavior Change. I was convinced that drastic limitations on human intellectual and emotional function were caused by inflexible states of mind, static and conditioned neural circuits which created and preserved malfunctional states of perceived reality. In the then-Zeitgeist of Salk, Fleming, Pauling, I believed that the right chemical used correctly was the cure. The "ailment" I had selected as curable was human nature.

To oversimplify, I believed that man did not know how to use his head, that the static, repetitive normal mind was itself the source of "dis-ease" and that the task was to discover the neuro-chemical for *changing* mind. Our initial experiments at Harvard suggested that LSD might be such a drug.

In the early 1960's we tested these hypotheses in a series of controlled experiments; the setting or expectation for philosophic exploration and self-discovery was supportive, secure, and respectable. *There was not one casualty or "bad trip."* Our subjects would routinely experience meta-mind intensities and were encouraged to contemplate the implications of these new signals.

The implications for human freedom were far-reaching. To describe this new science of precise, disciplined brain-change, I suggested the term Neurologic: the understanding and control of one's own nervous system. More important, the human being is seen as having several "minds" (defined as neural circuits) which evolve during the course of individual development and which can be turned on and off selectively.

In 1960–63 we experimented with drug-induced brain-change in prison rehabilitation, psychedelic psychotherapy, and personality change. The hypotheses were confirmed. We cut the prison-return rate by 90%. We demonstrated quantitative psychometric improvement in personality. It was prize-winning, elegant research. Our subjects shared our enthusiasm, but the medical directors didn't. We were surprised to discover that many administrators didn't really want to eliminate the pathologies they administer.

God knows they liked me personally, respected our results, and hoped that we were right. But there is inertial fear of change. Three times I was offered tenure at Harvard (and the post of chief psychologist at Massachusetts General Hospital) if I would just play down the drug research. But by then, we had entered that ancient current of passionate hope and risky belief that humanity can evolve into a higher wisdom.

At this point (1963) I left Harvard, abandoned the role of conventional, academic, scientist, and became, without knowing it, a *shaman,* an activist change-agent. This shift was accomplished slowly, hesitantly, and with self-conscious humor. First, a diligent study of religious history revealed that psychedelic plants had been used in Egypt, Persia, India, China, and Greece—always for initiation into adulthood, entrance into the spiritual life, and for the training of prophets and special priests who played colorful, apparently necessary roles. At the same time I began personal training in Hindu Vedanta, Buddhist Tantra, and Taoist techniques for understanding the flow of various energies. The "obligatory pilgrimage" to India occurred.

In 1963 we started centers for training in consciousness expansion, a scientific journal, and lecture tours for communicating the results of our research. Our Castalia Foundation was visited by musicians, electronic sound technicians, painters, and light technicians. The new modes of art we developed (based on the capacity of the nervous system to receive, synthesize, and transmit accelerated, compressed, and multimedia presentations) have since been taken over by commercial film and television people.

The inevitable backlash began in 1966 when various legislatures and Congress began considering bills to criminalize LSD and similar drugs. In this year I testified before two Senate committees, and my political position was by no means radical or solitary. Indeed, during the Johnson administration, medical and scientific people (backed by the Kennedys) urged that drugs be administered by the Department of Health, Education and Welfare, while law-and-order people politicked for the Department of Justice. With the decision to turn drug control over to the police, LSD was made illegal, and most of the top drug scientists began their steady exit from government responsibility.

At this time the "new consciousness" became a political issue indissolubly intertwined with peace, sexual liberation, reform of education, racial equilibrium, ecology, and "end the draft." The love-ins, hippie beads, the Beatles, and the demonstrations were the froth. The real thing had to do with the way people looked each other in the eye and smiled, knowing that something new and self-responsible was happening in their heads. Messages came to us from the dissenting underground in Russia and Brazil. The real revolution of the sixties was neurological.

But a second reaction to the collapse of authority is existential loneliness. Once you have accepted that your nervous system creates your own reality from the Heraclitan flow, what guideposts, what compass readings, what new goals? This philosophic vacuum was temporarily filled by a renaissance of pessimistic, nostalgic creeds—experiential Christianity, homogenized Buddhism, TV Hinduism—which served to shallow out, calm down the explosive expansions of the last decade.

I believe that a new philosophy created by those born after Hiroshima will: (1) be scientific in essence and science-fiction in style; (2) be based on the expansion of consciousness control of the nervous system, intellectual efficiency, and emotional equilibrium; (3) stress individualism, decentralization of authority, live-and-let-live tolerance of difference, and a mind-your-own-business libertarianism; (4) continue the trend toward open sexual expression and a more honest, realistic acceptance of the quality of and magnetic difference between the sexes; (5) seek revelation and Higher Intelligence within natural processes, the nervous system, the genetic code, and in attempts to effect extraplanetary migration; (6) include practical procedures for managing intimations of union-immortality implicit in the dying process;* (7) be hedonic, esthetic, fearless, optimistic, loving.

Everyone knows that something is going to happen. The seeds of the sixties have taken root underground. The blossoming is to come.

---

*This enigmatic statement referred to the two- or three-minute period that occurs between body-death and brain-death. Many reports from "near death" experiences suggest that when the outlying body circuits are turned off, accelerated revelatory signalry takes over the brain. By 1981, when scientists like Roy Walford, M.D., of UCLA, were predicting that a life-extension drug inoculation would be available in 2 to 5 years, my statement appeared cautious and prescientific. Today I would rewrite Point 6: "The new philosophy of Scientific Paganism will assume physical immortality provided by scientists and encouraged by those intelligent enough to want to live forever."

Awaiting trial for my escape, sitting on the floor of the cell, I also wrote *Neurologic* on the back of an Angela Davis legal brief, the only paper allowed. Finally I was hauled into court to be tried for escape. Security precautions were extravagant. Afraid of another Weatherman coup, five patrol cars escorted me from prison to the court house. My lawyers told me to be as far out as possible. It made no difference, because the fact of my escape was undeniable.

The escape trial

Defense Counsel Margolin. In your escape note, you wrote: "In the uniform of Athens you jailed Socrates. In the uniform of Rome you jailed Jesus Christ, and in the livery of Nixon and Reagan you have turned this land into a police state." Could you explain to the jury what you meant by this poem?

The Witness. Yes. My nervous system is in such a state that I live in many reincarnate levels.

Prosecutor, Mr. Lilley. Objection, Your Honor. Calls for a medical conclusion.

The Court. Overruled.

The Witness. I see what was happening at the prison on September 12th, 1970 [the day of my escape], as recurring events which happen over and over again. We simply play out the same parts. Freedom is always the issue, and philosophers of freedom have always been brought to trial for being dangerous to the state or corrupting youth.

My nervous system, as a result of twelve years of deliberate and disciplined research with drugs and different forms of yoga, allows me to put my mind in different places. My nervous system essentially travels throughout historical time. To become "Timothy Leary" is like getting in a car and turning the key. I'm not a "Timothy Leary model" most of the time. That's just one small fragment of a nervous system that makes us think we are Catholics or Republicans or Chevrolets or Pontiacs. Actually we can leave the automobile of our present identity and move throughout our nervous system.

Q. Could you explain that in reference to how you felt when you wrote this poem on September 12th?

A. Yes. I'm not Timothy Leary most of the time. I use the Timothy Leary identity to move throughout space and time to accomplish my mission and my survival. We are not cars; we use cars. We can step out of cars. You can step out of your historical role and move into any other role.

Q. Had you stepped out of the car when you wrote this poem on September 12th, 1970?

A. At the time I was writing this poem, I could just as well have been Socrates, or those people who were burned at the stake in the Middle Ages. I was no more Timothy Leary than I was any of these. People in the future will understand what is happening now just as we understand what happened in Salem 200 years ago.

Mr. Lilley. Again, I am going to interpose an objection on the basis of relevancy, Your Honor.

The Court. Overruled.

The Witness. Periods of madness overcome every country at certain points in history, usually during a war. And at these times of hysteria, any voice speaking for the eternal values of freedom tends to get persecuted. Many men who stood up and said, "We shouldn't hang people as witches in Salem," then became accused of being witches. I am in prison because I am considered to have dangerous beliefs.

Mr. Lilley. Objection, Your Honor. That answer is not responsive, and self-serving.

The Court. Overruled. That's his conclusion, Counsel.

Mr. Margolin. On September 12th, 1970, did you believe you were in prison for your beliefs and not for crimes you had committed?

A. Yes, I did. I believe that no government has the right to interfere with what happens inside someone's body or nervous system. Anything we do behaviorally in public to hurt anybody else in any way, that is a crime. What we do inside our bodies with our nervous systems, or anything that we say in the way of a lecture or writing cannot be punished, as per the First Amendment to the Constitution.

Mr. Margolin. Did you believe that you had never done an act that would be objectionable in a behavioral sense?

A. Yes, I did then and do believe today that I have never harmed a hair on anyone's head.

Mr. Margolin. Why did you feel that you fit in with that category, Doctor?

A. The judge who remanded me to this prison without bail said openly and publicly that I was to be jailed because of my beliefs, because of my published articles.

Mr. Lilley. Objection, Your Honor. I ask the answer be stricken as hearsay and self-serving.

The Court. Overruled.

Mr. Margolin. Now, Doctor, the "Eagle Brief" dated September 12th—was it directed at any particular person?

A. It was directed towards everyone in our country because if even one person is punished or imprisoned for their beliefs and statements, we are all affected.

Q. Now, you have also put in this poem, "Listen, guards, to this ancient truth. He who enslaves is himself enslaved. The future belongs to the blacks, the browns, the young, the wild and the free." What did you mean by that?

A. Well, I believe that the world does belong to the future. I see myself as a person from the future. I like to believe I am from the 21st century, visiting here to play a historical role as one would visit a primitive tribe in New Guinea to pass on warnings and counsel.

Q. Now, this poem goes on: "Oh, prison guards, I pray that you will repent and reform." Did you have any animosity to these guards?

A. Not at all. I have profound sympathy for them.

Q. "Open the gates of your hearts and be free. Break out. Follow me to freedom, love laughter." Is this an indication that you were going to escape and that they should break out with you?

Mr. Lilley. Objection, Your Honor. Leading?

The Court. Overruled.

Mr. Margolin. Did you want them to follow you out of the California Men's Colony?

A. I was talking about the prison of their minds, not specifically the prison at San Luis Obispo.

Q. Could you be more specific for the benefit of the jury?

A. I believe we are imprisoned by the past. It's necessary to escape the shackles of what has happened before if we are going to survive in the future. This particular line is the same message that I have advocated in every page of the many books that I have written: We must free ourselves from the rear view and move to the future.

    Q. Doctor, did you write this letter for an escape note from prison?

    A. Not specifically. Escape in every way from any sort of confinement which is unhealthy and unjust.

    Q. Did you feel on September 12th that there is something innately important about escape?

    A. Escape is the message of my life in every form.

    I was given five years, consecutive, for the crime of escape! The judge—a crusty, old curmudgeon who had been active in Republican politics for 30 years—died 2 years later. The headline for his obituary in the L.A. *Times* read: "Leary Judge Dies." I thought that was pretty ironic.

21

After the escape trial, I was shipped to Folsom—the deepest, darkest pit in the California correctional system. (The probation division of the California prison system was called, believe it or not, the Adult Authority.)

At Folsom I was plunged into 4–A, the dread max-max, the prison within a prison, and celled between Charles Manson and Geronimo, the fiercest militant Black Panther. Later I was placed on the Main Line of Folsom, where I was swept up into the most productive intellectual period of my life. The prison library was superb. Interlibrary loans made available any book in the world. In addition, the Intra-Mattress Library System was available. For 100 years, prisoners have been secreting contraband books that were loaned for a carton of cigarettes a week and sold off when inmates transferred. There were books on safecracking, alarm systems, key manufacture, bomb building, organic chemistry, and a classic collection of English-language pornography equal to that of the Vatican Library.

The research facilities were also excellent. I remember one rainy Saturday afternoon when the yard was closed and I was thus prevented from visiting the library. I was writing *Terra II*, a space-colony text, and needed to know how big a mini-earth should be to handle 500 souls. So I banged on the bars and shouted out, "What is the formula for the area of a sphere?" Within one minute, 3 sources from the 5-tier cell-block shouted down the answer.

At this time, Joanna Harcourt Smith, who was handling my legal defense, needed a film to show at money-making benefits. (Benefits for *whom* was never clear, but that's the fate of a prisoner.) Prisoner officials, of course, denied her request. Never one to be daunted, Joanna learned that prisoners *were* allowed to give one interview every six months. So Joanna authorized a television network to come to the prison and tape an interview, on the condition that she would inherit the film. So I was ushered into the prison committee room to sit in front of a camera and talk.

I had been lifting weights with the black militants, playing baseball on the white Aryan Brotherhood (Nazi) team, and playing handball with Chicanos. I was deeply tanned and never looked better in my life. I was wearing a gray sweatshirt and grinning with health and vigor. During this interview, behind the camera stood the warden, the

captain of the guards, and two members of the goon squad, watching
with arms folded.

Joanna added some film clips of herself standing in front of
the granite towers of the frowning prison. The film looked great! She
proceeded to show it in front of audiences across the land, in London,
Paris, and Rome. The evolutionary significance of this transmission is
not up to my par, but everyone liked a healthy-looking, smiling person
talking this way from the bowels of a political prison during the
Nixon-Agnew administration.

Prison is the occupational hazard of the successful philosopher

First I'd like to know . . . Who is Timothy Leary as a person?

I'm a philosopher-psychologist who has been studying the
nervous system for the last 30 years. I probably know as much about
how the nervous system works . . . the far galactic outposts of awareness and the range of human experiences, as any scientist around.

You also happen to be in prison.

Well, yes, that may seem odd . . . but the best philosophers
often end up in prison. Most of the men I model myself after have been
lucky if they got away with just being in prison for their ideas. . . . The
philosopher is looking for implications; great questions like where do we
come from? Where are we going? I've always been interested in finding
ways of using our nervous system as instruments to answer the basic
questions of life. Any scientist at the frontier of his science gets to basic
mystical and philosophic questions. It's inevitable, and I've accepted that
responsibility. We are on this spaceship Earth—how are we gonna get
along with each other? I think we need a new philosophy; we've run out

of navigational ideas of how to get the great ship moving in the right direction. . . .

Is that why you haven't been accepted totally, yet? Are you too far ahead of your time?

Yes, I'm in a kind of a time warp. But I have certain empirical-experimental proof that I'm not entirely wrong, because most everything that I've said has happened. In 1966, in my testimony before Senate committees about how we could avoid a drug problem in this country . . . I was almost alone, saying that marijuana should not be criminalized, LSD should be turned over to the government, to be treated like fissionable material. In subsequent years, many very conservative organs like the American Medical Association, the American Psychiatric Association, the American Bar Association, even William F. Buckley— they're all coming around to positions considered radical in the 1960's.If you hadn't asked me about drugs, I wouldn't have brought it up. I talk about how we can use our nervous system to make this country a better place—how to reduce crime, that sort of thing. I know I have to answer questions about drugs, because I've been labeled—as they say in prison, "it's on my jacket." But I've no more to do with drug usage than Einstein had to do with the Atomic Bomb. When Einstein got to the heaven his destiny led him, and he began talking about the equations of space-time and the relativity theory, I know that there's a reporter saying "Yeah, Albert, but what about the Atomic Bomb?" And he'll say, "Yeah, it's true. Those crazy kids, got hold of my theories and blew up Nagasaki and Hiroshima. . . ." So I have to take the responsibility for drugs as one application of the philosophy I've been working on.

I never advocated drugs; I defended different drugs against unscientific charges. But as soon as you say marijuana is not a killer drug, you become an advocate. I realize that maybe a third of the people watching this program generally like me, think I'm in prison for my ideas. I think another third dislike me intensely and think I've led young people astray. Another third probably couldn't care less. You're busy enough with your own lives; my debate with the government is no concern of yours. I think very few people watching this program have read my books. And once the media lay a label on you that way, it's very hard to fight back. . . .

You've been arrested more than once. Various governnent officials claimed you had drugs or marijuana in your possession.

As a matter of fact, I've never been legitimately arrested. I'm in prison now because I was running for governor of California, and I published position papers on how to gradually eliminate taxes, crime, the drug abuse problem, and so forth. One evening I was in a parked car.

A policeman came up to the car, opened the door against my wishes, reached in his pocket and pulled out two half joints I'd never seen before and said, "You're under arrest." A year later, an Orange County jury believed the policeman's story and found me guilty of possession. Then the judge, instead of giving me bail, as I was entitled to for appeal, held up a book that I had been writing, and said "Your ideas are dangerous, and we're going to put you in prison to keep you quiet." If another middle-aged, middle-class person was found with two roaches in his pocket, he wouldn't be doing prison time. But I'm not complaining. I'd been around the United States for 10 years, talking and spreading my message. I think it's good to have a chance to lay back for a couple of years and see how well the opposition's going to do. Now that I'm back in Folsom Prison, I've had two books published. Apparently I was *wanted* back here. There aren't very many philosophies of hope and freedom being broadcast. I know it's a risky job, but I'm here and I'm going to keep broadcasting.

(At this point, the prison warden stalked out of the room.)
How are you being treated here at Folsom?
I have had no trouble with prisoners here, partly because my fear index has been pretty burnt out by this time *(with laughter).* And in a strange way, Folsom Prison is a very exciting microcosm. All the problems out there are all compressed into this little area. And if we can learn to get along here and come out with better ways of doing things . . .
Even though you say that LSD is safe, do you think that you've suffered any brain damage whatsoever?
That's a very tricky question for anyone to answer. I'm 52. I think that anyone who's still erect after these last five decades has had his sanity tested. I've been through a lot of rough times. My career has been ruined. I've been in 24 prisons, all without committing any crime that I know of. In addition, I've probably pushed my nervous system as much as any human being living. I've taken LSD over 500 times and experienced a wide range of biochemical and neurological possibilities.
Is there any objective way to test your sanity? Well, people who get to know me seem to think I'm pretty sane. I've written 2 books in the last few months. My book *Hope Fiend* earned me a quarter of a million dollars advance, so somebody at Bantam books didn't think it was insane. If I am insane, the government should be happy to let me out and let my insanity be apparent.
There's this ominous tendency to call insane anybody that you don't agree with. In Russia they put their philosophers and their dissenting poets in an insane asylum. Now, maybe it *is* insane to hope

that something could be done about what's happening in the United States today. But otherwise, make up your own mind.

You're a hope fiend?

Yeah, an irrepressible optimist—the opposite of a repressive pessimist, and I think that's what's running the country today.

While we've been sitting here, I've been wondering what's on your shirt.

This very interesting symbol is a replica of the remnants of a living organism, found on a meteorite. We feel this is proof that life exists somewhere off our planet. And we've taken this as a symbol of the new philosophy that we're talking about. The figure "8" represents the fact that it takes $8,000 of the taxpayer's salary or taxes to keep us in prison. It's also the infinity sign, implying that the nervous system has an infinity of possibilities. . . . It kinda ties in that we're visitors on this planet Earth. We're not going to be here very long, we gotta get back in touch with the greater picture. It's a symbol of unity and hope. . . .

PART FIVE

The Future of Scientific Humanism

My commitment to the monastic life started in the spring of 1973. It was obvious that as long as Ronald Reagan was governor of California and Richard Nixon was in charge of federal matters, I would remain in prison. From the oldest and wisest of civilized species, the social insects, we have learned that the way to get through bad times is to spin a cocoon.

As it turned out, Folsom was an ideal place to hibernate. I read extensively in exobiology—Carl Sagan's new science that studied life off the planet Earth. An article by Sir Francis Crick (Nobel laureate for deciphering the DNA code) and his colleague Orgel triggered off one of those wonderful, life-changing insights. Crick and Orgel provided some evidence (and much convincing speculation) to support the notion of "directed panspermia." It is possible and feasible, they suggested, that extraterrestrial intelligence at a level of scientific sophistication about equal to our own, could have sent DNA-seed packets out through space to plant life on hospitable planets (see Figure 9).

This was the first intelligent human-level scientific life-origin explanation I had run across, and it clicked. If we domesticated primates in the barbarous 20th century could figure out how to seed plants, then intelligent life in other solar systems could have used this obvious gardening technique to perpetuate itself across the galaxy.

The discovery of over 30 pre-biotic organic molecules floating around in space added support for this theory. The work of Sagan, Crick, and the Russian SETI (Search for Extra-Terrestrial Intelligence) experts opened up an exciting chapter in human evolution. Once the concept of ETI existed, it was obvious that it would happen. Since science tends to find what it starts to look for, then it seemed inevitable that Higher Intelligence would be found. Either we would contact "them" because we were smart enough to look for "them," or, more likely, we would discover that we *are* "them"; that our species would quickly learn how to seed other planets.

The following essay, written in a prison cell, reflects the longing to escape from involuntary confinement. From this time, I have felt trapped on an embryonic planet, determined that our seed would be broadcast through the post-terrestrial space that awaits our species.

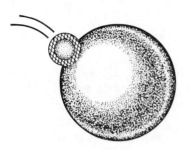

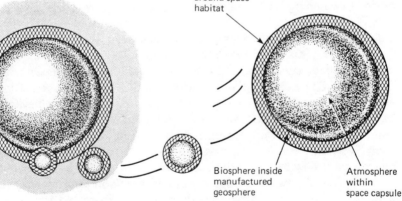

One:

Bio-seed packets land on lifeless planet and begin fabricating atmosphere. The pan-spermic pods are microscopic in size, but have been magnified here for illustrative purposes.

Two:

Functioning bio-planet: life has created an atomosphere and has infiltrated every available niche. Life is evolving mobile seed-pods equipped with intelligent brains.

Three:

Gaia has evolved billions of brilliantly ingenious species interacting together. One species, humans, become capable of attaining escape velocity and equipped with brains that can construct self-contained seed-packets called space-habitats.

Four:

Gaia is now safely, cozily established in Mini-worlds of mobile design; the rocky geosphere now surrounds the delicate biosphere and the atmosphere. The life-cycle has come full circle and Gaia can move on to terraform and colonize the solar system and beyond.

Figure 9. The Gaia Cycle: Life on and off the womb planet.

The alien intelligence caper

In 1962 I made a pact with DNA, Higher Intelligence. It was the standard contract. I was to illuminate, raise intelligence, transmit all revelations as directly as possible. I was to cling to no former security or comfort, risk the loss of every attachment, accept total responsibility for the realities that emerged. The unspecific compensation would be intrinsic in the intelligence attained.

There was no consuming emotional reaction, no Mosaic thunderbolt. It was, on the contrary, a quiet moment of telepathic communion. There was certainly no visionary presence, no certainty. As fast as my mind would create a self-congratulatory posture, the lens would zoom in to an embarrassing closeup or zoom out to a comic cosmic perspective.

It was part of my assignment, from time to time, when diplomatically graceful, to ask people: Do you believe in a Higher Intelligence, a Master Plan? Respondents tend to fall into four groups:

1. *True Believers:* Yes, there is a master plan and it's all laid down in the Bible (or the Koran, or the book of Mormon, or the Vedas. . . .)

2. *Darwinian Humanists:* There is no superhuman intelligence. Evolution is an accidental chance process. Man's mind can progress according to the scientific method of Karl Marx (or Sigmund Freud. . . .)

3. *Hindu Hedonists:* There is no plan, no progress. Cool out, enjoy yourself, find the beauty, take care of yourself. . . .

4. *Searchers:* It is most amusing and least boring to believe in a Higher Intelligence and a Master Plan. Life is a scientific mystery story, a galactic Whodunit, a Sci-Fi thriller.

One thousand years ago, the issue of how we got here and why dominated human activities. European Society spilt so much blood over philosophic divisions that sensible men agreed to concentrate on improving existence on the spaceship. Philosophic questions are nervously repressed. Post-Freudians, more than willing to babble about their sex lives, consider it impertinence to be asked about their cosmological feelings. One of the hippies' most infuriating habits was their insistence on raising questions about alternate realities. This ontological promiscuity was probably more threatening than their erotic looseness.

Fifty years ago, religious identification was important. My grandparents knew the church affiliation of every family in the neighborhood, and social behavior was so guided. The 1960's realigned and reenergized the spiritual dimensions. Nixon and Brezhnev ended the Cold War because both realized that the spiritual-philosophic civil war within their countries was the real threat to their power.

The malaise is philosophic. It's my job to produce a new blueprint. But anyone can volunteer for the job. If philosophic bases for human action were made explicit, confusion, apathy, and conflict would vanish. People now avoid philosophic clarification because they fear the horror of the existential confrontation, the terror of the responsibility of explaining life. Since the sixties we've been involved in a philosophic renaissance; we must make it fashionable, amusing, safe to focus on the galactic perspective.

What is the Master Plan? Your answer determines your life's conduct and meaning. Don't get alarmed, your answer isn't final—you can change it. Perhaps personal evolution recapitulates the history of human philosophy. "Evolve or die" may be true of the individual as well as the species.

The essence of the great systems of the past can be found in the four Master Plan answers listed above:

1. The Believer's kick is robot obedience, authoritarian certainty. Perform as the rules indicate, and you'll get to heaven. During the Middle Ages, the City of God was the trip. Science, art, human affairs, politics, economics, even survival were irrelevant. A Believing Culture runs off fear and cannot tolerate questioning, dissent, change.

2. The Humanist's kick is success, progress, expansion, competition. Perform as the rules indicate, and you'll win the game. Every day you can improve. Since the Renaissance, Humanism has encouraged the middle-classification of science and socialism. Darwin is survival of the fittest, Marx glorifies production.

3. The Hedonist's key to life is avoiding tension, conflict, pain, risk. This approach emerges historically when the Humanist empire starts to crumble from its own successes and an affluent leisure class begins to look for more than progress. Stoics and Epicureans were most numerous during the latter days of the Roman experiment. For most people, the most intense pleasure is sexual. Sexual liberation occurs when women, freed from economic and social pressures, begin to expect hedonic reward from men, rather than protection. The Neurological Revolution of the 1960's produced Oriental religious movements that preach inner peace, moderation, renunciation of material values, a self-oriented emphasis on yoga and health regimes. Both *Playboy* and the swami discourage active search for a master plan. The elitist, advanced hedonist defines life as the avoidance of boredom and routine. The quest for novelty often leads thoughtful hedonists to search for

revelation. *Penthouse,* magazine of the ultra-erotic, sponsors *Omni,* magazine of the slick future.

4. The Scientific Searcher believes it is possible to decipher the Master Plan for the unfolding of life on this planet. This belief has been nourished for millennia, but (except during the rule of Magus-kings), persecution has always forced such teachings underground, since the Searcher believes that the better realities are yet to come. This intolerable ultra-evolutionary view implies that "now" is a preparatory phase. "Atlantis-type" searchers believe a study of archaeological remnants can reveal lost wisdom. "Extraplanetary" searchers expect that spaceships will disembark humanoids of higher intelligence, or that a systematic radio-telescope survey of neighboring stars may pick up radio waves.

According to neurologic cosmology, the planet has already been "invaded" by a superior intelligence to be found in the nervous system and the genetic code. The DNA molecule might be considered a miniaturized, biocomputerized organic robot, preprogrammed to evolve in optimal reaction to local planetary characteristics. The general direction of evolution is to produce a serially imprinting, multibrained creature able to decipher its own program, create the technology to leave the planet and live in post-terrestrial miniworlds, decode the aging sectors of the DNA code (thus assuring immortality), and act in harmony with stages of evolution to come. From the standpoint of DNA, life is an unbroken chain of simultaneity. Each individual body housing the DNA nucleus is a particle in the wave-rhythm of passage. Life on this planet can be seen as an intelligent information-transmitting process, in which more complex bodies evolve to house more sophisticated nervous systems, until it produces a nervous system capable of using itself as instrument.

23

The next divertissement was published (1973) in *Psychology Today*, while I was most unpleasantly confined in the San Luis Obispo state prison.

The basic purpose of the essay was to raise $400 to help buy tickets to Switzerland for faithful archivists Michael Horowitz and Bob Barker to pick up nine cartons of my memorabilia. A secondary aim of the piece was to help legitimize the Humanist Psychology movement, just about to emerge as a powerful force in American Domestication. Thus the historical references to Orpheus, Dionysus, Nietzsche, Wilhelm Reich, and Aleister Crowley, whose maxim, "Do what thou wilt shall be the whole of the law," was to become the theme of the Me-generation. Although the wry Aleister was not around to receive the credit he deserves, he is surely smiling in the Thelemic cosmos he now inhabits.

The fleeting reference to Gurdjieff was a fervent attempt to call attention to this witty Sufi, whom I had been proclaiming the greatest psychologist of the 20th century. For several years it had amused me that the names of Fechner and Gurdjieff, two giants of modern psychology, were totally unknown to the legions of licensed psychologists who exploded all over the 1970's. (The very notion of a "licensed" head bender has always given me a nagging Orwellian discomfort.)

Anyway, my predictions about the hedonic psychologists of the year 2001, like all my forecasts, were much too conservative. Consider, for example, the following demographics: During the period 1940–1980 the number of practitioners and schools and books devoted to self-improvement, holistic health, do-it-yourself inner development, erotic and sensual enhancement, had grown over a thousandfold—and was accelerating.

In March 1980, the month in which these lines were transmitted, I was presented (under the usual dusty backroom circumstances) a volume purporting to be the long-awaited Fourth Secret Teaching of Gurdjieff. For the past twenty years, we Gurdjieff fans had been titillated by rumors of this Fourth Book, which supposedly listed secret techniques and practical methods for attaining the whimsical, post-terrestrial levels obviously inhabited by the jolly Sufi Master.

We had always assumed, naturally, that the secret methods involved drugs. So it was a matter of amused satisfaction to read in this newly issued text that not only *were* brain-activating drugs the keys to Gurdjieff's wonderful, whirling wisdom, but also that the reason for keeping the alkaloids secret was to avoid exactly the penal incarceration which I was enjoying when the following essay was penned.

Hedonic psychology

Influential members of the cultural establishment are expected to be paragons of the values they seek to implement. Thus today's psychologists tend to be highly overconditioned, industrious, conventionally virtuous, and domesticated.

As prime conditioner of his fellow men, the psychologist or educator must be an exemplar—calm, serious, controlled, sensibly cynical, smugly pessimistic, and above all, rational. To study the unconditioned state, to produce pleasure in his subjects, and to act in a natural, hedonic manner would lead to his excommunication.

The psychologist in the year 2001 will be master ecstacist. Identify him by his radiant vibrations. After all, he has 4 years of graduate training in making people feel good.

Orpheus, early prophet of the pleasure principle, was torn to bits by enraged middle-aged women. Dionysus never received tenure. The alchemists along with their deconditioning drugs—*elixir vitae*—were driven underground. Hypnosis is a classic technique for temporarily altering conditioning, so no surprise that Mesmer was anathemized.

Reich, whose genius is just beginning to be recognized, died in federal prison. The essence of his teaching is that neurosis, psychosis, totalitarianism, and other social pathologies were the result of conditioned restriction of sexual pleasure. His prescription for a happy, free society: help people make love longer and better. Kick out the jams.

In the first decade of this century, occultist Aleister Crowley documented in *The Equinox* his psychologist investigations of hashish, concluding that the drug possessed tremendous deconditioning potential. Crowley's "Do what thou wilt shall be the whole of the law" can be a very effective deconditioning mantra for those trapped in certain programmed levels.

Academic psychology is concerned with conditioning humans to accept what Freud called the "reality principle," implying that only the artificial, conditioned games of the current social order are real; that natural pleasure is somehow a hallucination, even a psychotic outburst.

Freud's reality principle would be more correctly designated as reward-pain conditioning. You are rewarded for conforming socially and painfully punished if you do not. Reward-pain is real only within the narrow limits of the parochial social order, i.e., the hive. Pleasure based on sensory, somatic, cellular, and bioelectrical processes is a reality of another order.

The entire range of pleasurable experiences has gone unstudied, unlabeled, undefined. You will not find the word "fun" in the index of most psychology texts. Indeed, until the psychedelic movement of the past decade, unconditioned behavior and unconditioned experience were considered *ipso facto* schizophrenic.

As our society begins to tolerate differing hedonic lifestyles, we can expect an efflorescence of personality systems and psychological models to classify the many varieties of unconditioned undomesticated hedonic response.

Chapter 21 was a byproduct of the tremendous ultimate neurological luxury presented to me by the California department of correction —over two years of solitary confinement. In later years, interviewers would often ask, "Well, how were you affected by 29 months of solitary confinement?" I would respond brightly, "It was a cinch. My cellmate, after all, was one of the funniest, creative minds in the prison."

Sitting on the cement floor of a roach-ridden cell, I wrote *Neurologic* on the back of a humorless legal brief and smuggled it out to a lawyer who assured me that his Hindu guru was meditating actively in my defense.

All my books have covered the same territory: the epic voyage of evolution, step-by-step improvement in our neurotechnology, which is taking us from precambrian bliss to fusion in some ultimate violet whole. Why not? *Neurologic* summarized many years of rumination about the stages of evolving neurotechnology, here centered on the 8 ecologies: 4 terrestrial: marine, land, tribal-artifact, urban; and 4 post-terrestrial: body, brain, DNA, and atomic-nuclear. In later books, *Exo-Psychology, Neuropolitics, Intelligence Agents,* and *Game of Life,* these 8 circuits were expressed as 24 more detailed stages of human evolution.

This little pamphlet was reprinted in its entirety in 2 national magazines and republished in dozens of small-press formats. Well over 100,000 copies were thus blown around the world.

Reading it now, one is aware of the hopeful, almost prescientific naivete. The seminal works of Gerard O'Neill on space colonization, the great neurochemistry breakthroughs which taught us that the brain is a wondrous gland, always producing its own entertaining secretions, the vistas of sociobiology, the wizard microgenetics of the human leucocyte antigen community, the histo-compatability, and recombinant DNA heroes—all were outside my sphere of cheerful ignorance. But the basic navigational coordinates were fairly well outlined.

Neurologic

The theories presented in this essay are Science Fiction: *Scientific* in that they are based on empirical findings, *fictional* in the Wittgensteinian sense that all theories and the speculations beyond the propositions of natural science are subjective.

Christian theologians, statistical materialists, and Marxist dialecticians make different interpretations of the same corpus of scientific fact. Such theories, however popular, are not necessarily any less fictional than those which are persecuted and censored. Indeed, science fictions are forcibly suppressed only when likely to contribute more knowledge and freedom than the defensive orthodoxies they challenge. Think of Socrates, Darwin, Copernicus, Galileo, Pasteur, and the Jehovah's Witnesses in Spain.

It increases my sense of pleasure and freedom to believe that *Homo sapiens* evolves through an 8-stage life cycle. Each circuit of human metamorphosis produces a life-form visibly different from the preceding and succeeding phases. Each cycle involves dramatic alterations in morphology, behavior, physiology, and—most important—neurological function. Though obvious even to the untutored observer, these 8 cycles have not been understood by scientists and philosophers. Possibly the human species is itself evolving through the same 8 stages, and until recently, has been preoccupied with basic survival processes. By analogy, a caterpillar society would be neurologically inhibited from recognizing the butterfly as a later version (both phylogenetically and individually) of itself.

The nervous system evolves sequentially through 8 maturational stages. At each stage, a new circuit emerges. At each chronological stage, a new *imprint* is taken, determining positive and negative foci for subsequent conditioning of this newly activated circuit:

1. *The Bio-Survival Circuit* ("We are Safe") is concerned with safety in a marine environment. In the days after birth, the bio-survival imprint fixates basic "approach-avoidance" dimensions of external consciousness, based on dorsal-ventral (front-back) asymmetry. The basic orientation is: face the positive, avoid the noxious. What is in front is "safe," what is behind is "dangerous." The first neural circuit recapitulates the rudimentary nervous system of marine organisms.

The first imprint orients one to the mothering person and determines value orientation. If the environment provides food, warmth, quiet, protection, then a basis is laid for subsequent trustful commerce with the external world. If the "human environment" of early infancy is unrewarding, cold, painful, jarring, then the neonate turns its back and does not imprint human beings as the source of safety.

A negative fixation of this sort leaves the first neural circuit without a consistent external focus. Result: a persistent inability to relate to the external world. According to this theory, the autistic schizophrenic person can be more usefully diagnosed and treated as first-circuit schizoid, or biovegetative schizoid.

2. *The Emotion-Locomotion Circuit* is concerned with territorial security. This midbrain plexus mediates muscular power and gravity mastery. The second circuit imprint occurs when muscular development allows the child to push up and crawl, thus fixating the "above and below" dimensions necessary to deal with the body's vertical (head-foot) asymmetry. The second imprint combined with the first approach-avoid imprint defines the two-dimensional grid on which all subsequent emotional conditioning is based.

The second neural circuit evolved about 500,000,000 years ago when early Paleozoic vertebrates began to rise up against the pull of gravity. The ability to locomote rapidly and exert superior force became a survival asset, a step towards higher intelligence. The emotional circuit is an emergency device: when the human being acts in an emotional way, SHe reverts to a primitive phase of brute power-terror.

The sympathetic nervous system is triggered by aggression or fear. The young mammal fixates the emotional imprint the first time a terror-producing threatening movement occurs and when a smaller, weaker stimulus provokes the predation reflex. The basic mammalian "Escape them or grab them" reflex still operates in 90 percent of the dictator-run countries of the world.

Terror or predation in the mothering person communicates to the child. Subsequently the approach of a snake, a larger animal, a sudden touch arouses the reaction of withdrawal, flight, or anxiety. Similarly, the sight of a small creature running away triggers the preying reflex. Tough or weak behavior attracts adrenaline attention and excites mammalian action.

When faulty imprint or conditioning connects fear and rage with inappropriate situations, a Circuit 2 schizoid state exists. Selective control of mammalian emotion is the survivally intelligent characteristic. Just as our First Circuit unicellular intelligence is operating quietly at every moment, so does our Second Circuit animal nature remain wired for use. The scary fact is that in 1973 an overwhelming majority of American males would cheerfully rape, loot, and bully any weaker person if the social restraints were temporarily lifted.

3. *The Mental-Manipulative Circuit* ("We are Right") is concerned with dexterity, language, and the manufacture of artifacts. It mediates fine, precise muscular activities, especially speech. Dexterity facilitates manipulative grasping (open-close). Thinking is subvocal talking, silent speech. The Third Circuit imprints when the child learns to speak and manifest precise unilateral movements.

The emergence of a left cerebral cortex with unilateral dominance has been dated to around 2,000,000 B.C., when mankind began using stone and bone tools—the beginning of symbolic or substitutive activity.

The Third Imprint determines which of the 8 mental modes will become dominant.

At the time children begin to speak, they model themselves after adults and peer figures. If the environment is dangerous, restricting, and the parent rejecting, then the child will develop a distrustful, rejecting repetitious mind—perfectly adaptable in a peasant society. By the time the child is 5, its style of dexterity has been fixed. Later educational exposure, no matter how stimulating, can make little change in the "mind."

4. *The Sexual-Social Circuit* ("We are Good") is concerned with domestication, parenthood, and child-rearing social roles. It mediates activities involved in courtship, strutting, display, mating, copulation, orgasm, as well as family responsibility, social role, and hive membership.

The Fourth-Circuit activation is clearly marked by dramatic changes in body structure. This fourth imprint occurs at pubescence, when behavior, thinking, and emotion are dominated by orgasm drive. (Orgasm avoidance can also be imprinted and supported by inhibitory conditioning.) Other sex-linked factors serve for post-pregnancy protection of mother and young.

The Fourth-Circuit imprint, combined with the first 3, defines the adult (larval) personality. After impregnation, the Fourth-Circuit imprint binds the body to activities connected with the nesting responsibility, and nurturance necessary for child survival. Most humans remain at the Fourth Level of neuro-evolution (domestication) until menopause leads to the stasis of senility.

The first four neural circuits and imprints are totally concerned with preparing the individual to deal with the spatially polarized outside world. The function of the emerging nervous system is to focus, narrow down and choose from an infinity of possibilities those avenues, spatial tactics, asymmetrical strategies, sequences that insure survival. The infant is prepared to imprint any language, master any manipulative intricacy, play any sex role. Without these built-in responses the human infant could not survive.

For the security of these imprinted realities, however, the human pays a heavy price. Survival and growth in *this* narrow place means focusing awareness on a trivial fragment of potential experience. When the conditioned external survival circuits are transcended, consciousness—no longer hooked to the outside—is free to experience the unconditioned pathways of the brain.

According to this theory, the autistic child has imprinted human beings as negative-dangerous, thus preventing learning of human ways. The solution is simple: Suspend the imprint by undoing the biochemical synaptic patterns that define neural circuit programming, and allow a new imprint involving positive orientation toward the mother.

Psychedelic drugs like LSD suspend imprints and conditioned networks. After LSD has been administered to the autistic child, the mother or parental person spends 8 hours providing the child with warmth, nurturance, tender, soft, serene stimuli. The imprinting message is, "We are safe." Three or four such reimprinting experiences combined with consistent post-LSD "safety" stimuli should insure a positive Circuit 1 conditioning system.

According to this theory of personality, imprints can be suspended by the ingestion of LSD, and the person is assured, or assures him or herself, in every relevant, truthful way that there is nothing to fear. A calm, serene, courage-inducing environment during reimprinting is the direct "cure."

The first 4 imprints are concerned with mastery of terrestrial turf and insectoid security. The 4 post-survival imprints and conditioned networks involve the fabrication of post-terrestrial realities.

Post-planetary time consciousness does not use polarities of terrestrial consciousness. In the Neurological Age of Information, there is no right or wrong; no up or down, no stronger/weaker. There is simply energy in various intensities, durations, qualities, patterns: signals to be received, changed, selected, filed, retrieved, and harmonized.

The goal of terrestrial consciousness is to survive briefly on a limited planet. The goals of post-planetary consciousness are to evolve, expand in time. If the 4 planetary imprints follow laws of Newtonian space physics, the 4 post-planetary imprints follow laws of Einsteinian time physics.

5. *The Neurosomatic Rapture Circuit* ("We are Beautiful") mediates body-time experience—sensory and somatic—registered by the external sense organs (optical, aural, tactual, taste, smell, temperature, pressure, pain, balance, kinesthetic) and signals from the internal

somatic system (breathing, circulation, sex, ingestion, digestion, elimination). Until now, sense organs have served to provide cues for larval, hive-conditioned systems: "Red is for stop; green for go." The rapture imprint occurs the first time direct esthetic impact is received, and "red" and "green" are seen as pulsating light energy. The eye does not "see things," but registers direct sensation uninterrupted by Circuit 3 thinking. Intensity of sensation is dramatically increased, duration seems longer. Conditioned cues from larval circuits are not wiped out, but harmonized (often humorously) with the direct sensations. Consider the modes of meta-rational, polymorphous-erotic perception attained by Fechnerian introspectionists, Zen masters, artists, marijuana adepts.

Here we face the paradox and terror of time-consciousness. Activating the "silent hemisphere" creates a Hedonic Boom that momentarily shatters all previously imprinted and learned values. Consciousness seems to invade all the forbidden and dangerous "below," "behind," "wrong," "cross-sexual" areas. Circuit 1 screams, "Danger! Red alert!" Circuit 2 shouts, "Watch out! You're helpless!" Circuit 3 warns, "Beware! You're in error!" Circuit 4 whispers, "Irresponsible! Violation of sex role."

The instinctive terrors mastered by skydivers and circus performers are nothing compared to the momentary panic of a nervous system transcending its four lifelong, life-preserving circuits. We can understand the condemnations of taboo, alienation, stupor, madness, and diabolic possession—as well as the sense of splendid certainty, rebirth, philosophic exultation accompanying new cortical discoveries made by the courageous, emotionally stable, intellectually prepared, and sexually secure. Discovering the body as instrument of freedom-pleasure is like finding out that a car can be used for pleasure driving. Auto-mobile! Joy-riding the body becomes a hedonic art.

Each survival imprint addicts the nervous system to certain external stimuli registered as—or associated with—"positives." Similar addiction occurs in the rapture circuit: Certain organs become "rapture prone," and certain esthetically pleasing sounds, odors, tastes, touches, somatic reactions become associated with hedonic reward. Rapture can become a satin trap, as the history of decadent leisure classes testifies. (Decadence is repetitious indulgence. True self-indulgence is intelligent, flexible, evolving.) Our terrestrial civilizations are overpopulating the globe with insectoid social structures. Exactly at this point, a new generation asks the transcortical questions, "Why? What next?"

The hedonistic Circuit-5 answer is to feel good. But the "hippie" philosophy, however appealing, soon becomes anti-evolutionary, regressive. The dropout philosophy produced an entire generation of barefoot philosophers, discovering the joyous, infantile delights of direct sensuality. History teaches us that the worship of play and display, eros and beauty, is a vulnerable phase, essentially incapable of protecting itself. Woodstock and the French Revolution both teach the lesson: Evolve or perish.

6. *The Neuro-Electric Ecstasy Circuit* ("We Create Our Realities") mediates neurological time free of the body and of larval imprints, conscious only of its own functioning. The nervous system literally imprints itself; consciousness is totally composed of neurological signals.

The neuron, the nervous system's anatomical and physiological unit receives signals via receptor fibers (dendritic fingers) that transmit to the cell body, within which messages are interpreted and stored. The neuron transmits messages to other neurons by squeezing off a chemical secretion that produces a chemical change in the synapse. The mode of transferring messages across the intercellular gap is a drug.

Headquarters of the nervous system is, of course, the brain, 1,400 grams of nerve tissue floating in a spinal-fluid cushion.

Nerve cells do not regenerate. Before birth, the human being possesses 20 billion neurons, and that is it. Each day of life, from 10,000 to 100,000 cells die—sands of consciousness draining away.

Human life is not measured by the life span of body cells, which die and regenerate, but by the duration of the nervous system. *We are our nervous systems.* The body is the car; the nervous system is the driver—an alien, superior intelligence residing in the body, which it ruthlessly exploits as a means of transportation and supply. Fifty percent of oxygen goes first to the brain. Every neuron is surrounded by glial cells that "taste" and digest all incoming supplies to the regal neuron. Is the nervous system a sultan lying in a warm bath, dealing drugs back and forth?

The nervous system sees no color, feels no pain. Messages from the body are experienced as impulse, buzz, and flash. An experience-addict, the nervous system seeks intensity, novelty, and linkage at high fidelity. Continued change is the diet, high-intensity communication of the longing desire. The person who has emerged into neurological consciousness is capable of simultaneous registry of intensities and complexities many times greater than the space circuits.

The law of the neuron is: All or None. The nerve cell is either on or off. Intensity and novelty determine how many synaptic connections and how many other circuits are turned on.

Words and thoughts are clumsy, and slow, learned laryngeal

responses. To express neurological consciousness the human must learn multilevel, multisensory electronic means of communication and interperson linkage.

During the past decade, American culture discovered the Rapture Circuit. Sexual liberation, sensual training, hedonic dress and grooming, massage, the eroticization of all forms of art define a cultural evolution. Current appraisals indicate that sensory pleasure and luxury constitute the biggest business in America today.

Before our era, Circuit 6's existence was known to many. Educated epileptics, courageous yogins (certainly Lao Tse), Heraclitus, and Vedantic sages, among others, had activated the "post-planetary" simultaneous complexity of the brain. But until the electronic efflorescence of the 1940's, when man's electronic dexterity made it possible to write the formulae for escaping gravity, no external language existed to describe Circuit-6 phenomena. Interstellar voyages require an understanding of Einsteinian-Lorentzian space-time formulae. Neurologicians understand that increasing velocity dilates time and decreases aging, realize that off-planet exploration should be called time travel. When we leave the planet, we leave place and enter time.

Up until now electronic instruments have been used for survival and for somatic-sensory rapture—television and FM radio. Circuit-6 communication requires that we master and eroticize electronic computer-synthesizer technology.

Circuit-6 neurological linkage is the "adolescence of time." This tuning-in phase of evolution will involve mastery of time-dilation and contraction, extra-planetary "time" travel, brain-computer linkage, person-person neural linkage (telepathy), routinized personal electronic communication, construction of new miniworlds in High Orbit.

7. *The Neurogenetic Circuit* ("We are Immortal") is located anatomically within the neuron, mediating communication between the DNA nucleus of the cell and the neuron's memory-synthesizing structures. When the body faces a threat to life, alarm signals flash throughout the neural network. When these messages indicate that death is imminent, the nervous system shuts off local hive imprints and abandons outlying sensory and somatic receiving centers. The neural "drop-out" begins.

At this point, the nervous system operates at Circuit 6. Ecstasy (literally, "standing outside") comes to everyone at the moment of dying. A few have survived the brush of death and returned to report the acceleration, simultaneity, intensity: "My entire life flashed before my eyes." In clock time, the neurological ecstasy of dying lasts no more than a few minutes, but subjectively, it is experienced as millions of years.

Body time is disconnected—the nervous system is free to tune in to its own hundreds of millions of signals per second.

As the dying experience continues, the neural network itself begins to cut out. The energy required to fire signals across synaptic barriers weakens. Consciousness retreats to the neuron itself. The final dialogue is between the memory-synthesizing centers within the neuron and the DNA code in the cell nucleus. The last voice is the explanatory whisper of the genetic blueprint: "Here's where we came from. Here's where we're going."

For 3 billion years the DNA code has been building improved bodies to continue evolution sequence toward its goal: increased intelligence.

The DNA code is a miniaturized time-capsule of conscious-ness, the invisible essence-wisdom of life. Most of the characteristics formerly attributed to the "soul" now describe the functions of DNA, whose complex message may originate from higher intelligences in other solar systems. Before arrival on this planet, the evolutionary material was already preplanned to evolve serially-imprinting nervous systems that could master planetary survival and explore the message coded within the nervous system and neuron-nucleus.

The mission of DNA is to evolve nervous systems able to escape from the doomed planet and contact manifestations of the same amino-acid seeding that have evolved in other solar systems. The mission is the message—to escape and come home.

In the past, Circuit 7 was activated at the onset of awareness of the "death" process, when consciousness retracts from hive imprints, from the body, and from the neural circuit itself, to centers on meta-species signals from the DNA code. The recent discoveries of DNA structure and of powerful neurogenetic drugs like LSD and Ketamine allow controlled, precise, voluntary activation of the Seventh Circuit.

Neurologists assume, with primitive, larval insouciance, that studying nerve tissue is no different from the study of the digestive system. Geneticists, we believe, make the chauvinistic mistake of assuming that DNA is a process, rather than a living intelligence as old as life itself that can teach us the meaning of existence. DNA designs and constructs the nervous system. The mammalian ego, the primate mind, the hive personality, are temporary fragments of the post-planetary nervous system. Neurogeneticists believe that the DNA code can communicate revelation and instruction. Our task is to learn how to use the nervous system to receive and modulate DNA's instructions.

Based on all relevant facts from astronomy, genetics, and

gerontology, we believe that the message of DNA is simple: Get Smarter! Increase velocity and altitude! The genetic entity wants off the planet!

8. *The Neuro-atomic, Quantum Circuit* is concerned with metaphysiological, nuclear, and galactic time.

Technological mastery alone will not let humans leave the planet and solar system. Our species will not be capable of high orbital colonization until DNA has been deciphered, until the neurogenetic circuit has been imprinted and integrated into the Circuit-8 network.

Neurogenetic philosophy holds that every living creature plays an evolutionary role, as part of an evolutionary blueprint. Every human egg supply or sperm library carries thousands of unique mutant characteristics, many within the nervous system and morphologically undetectable.

The evolutionary perspective sees mankind's goal as muta-tional, sees the individual as student, agent, and assistant in the evolutionary process.

To turn *on* and think like one's body is the first degree of time consciousness. To tune *in* and think like one's nervous system is the second degree. To drop *out* and think like one's DNA genetic code is the third degree of post-hive, post-planetary consciousness. According to the present theory, this access to the "silent hemisphere" is a natural evolutionary and maturational stage. Nature, extravagant in experiment, is always parsimonious in structural efficiency and would hardly design the brain so that half its neural potential remains unused.

When the 4 larval imprints are transcended, consciousness has access to areas of the nervous system ordinarily blocked off. Many schizoids are exceptionally original, visionary, prophetic, and creative. Throughout history, shamanic persons have transcended hive-conditioned circuits. Since early imprinting stimuli are totally external, meditation and deliberate isolation make it possible to escape extra-survival dominance. Certain psychoactive drugs suspend imprints and provide novel states of consciousness that, according to the present theory, should be accompanied by increased right-cortical activity as measured by EEG.

A high percentage (perhaps half) of alienated humans are in trouble with their hives because their brains are operating in "neuro-realities" that will not be conventionally acceptable until the 21st century. Four "schizoid" situations occur when neural circuits designed for post-terrestrial ecologies are activated prematurely:

1. Acute hypersensitivity to sensory-somatic stimuli (the "frag-ile artist" syndrome)

2. Telepathic, "psychic" neuro-electric sensitivities (Nikola Tesla)

3. Genetic, interspecies, reincarnation-prereincarnation sensitivities (Luther Burbank, Dr. Jagadis Chandra Bose)

4. Atomic-nuclear, quantum sensitivities

When futique circuits are activated in unsympathetic environments, where the first 4 larval imprints are not self-confidently successful, the attendant sensitivities are usually painful and alienating. But neurological metamorphosis opens up the possibility of more *advanced conditioning,* designed for more complex consciousness and communication.

During high-dose LSD sessions, subjects experience dying and report either personal Circuit-6 or genetic memories and forecasts. LSD has been administered to many dying patients because it seems to resign them to their forthcoming demise.

Neurogenetic theory predicts the discovery of an enzyme found within the nerve cells of dying animals. This chemical, synthesized and administered to healthy subjects under optimal voluntary conditions, will produce the experience of death with no effect on normal body function. We now hypothesize that the "G-pill" will suspend space and body imprints and allow consciousness to tap the final dialogue between the DNA master code and the servant neuron. Then mankind will have an experimental tool for examining what happens when we die.

The planet has now reached the halfway point between its birth swirl and its solar incandescence: a worldwide awareness of the approach of death. The human species reached its neurological halfway point during World War II, the final convulsive exaggeration of Circuit-4 behavior. At this point was born a new generation with allegiance to their own nervous systems, rather than to national duty and hive morality. Everyone born since Hiroshima (the Baby Boom) shares a conspiratorial knowledge that the old planetary way is over, that old dogmas are dead. An enormous vacuum in consciousness exists, greater than the philosophic anticipation that swept the Roman world years ago. Despite the heroics, the earthbound phase of humanity was, let's face it, a dreary larval half-life. Every pre-1946 philosophy and religion is *pessimistic* about human destiny. Not one offers anything but an exhausted, virtuous peace of mind, excited only by the pleasures of militant conversion or persecution of the non-believer.

Separated by the iron door of the solitary confinement cell from the mundane pressures of hive existence, my neural circuits have produced this essay, which states, in the exaltation of metamorphosis, *Escape!* It's about time for the physical neurological linkage and the genetic fusion that define the higher love. We are ready for the future life that has rested dormant within our larval bodies. Our eyes touch, our seed fuses. There is nothing to fear, your eyes see behind me, no reason to struggle. What is above is as below: no shame. Your right hand guides my left: no guilt. We combine every sexual-social possibility. We are beautiful.

In November 1974, ex-Jesuit-Zen Buddhist Jerry Brown replaced Ronald Reagan as governor of California. Signs in the political winds suggested that the Nixon regime was nearing its end. With younger Democratic politicians coming into power, it was obvious that my precious days of monastic serenity were coming to an end. I therefore embarked on a flurry of writing, anticipating that "liberation" from prison would leave me less time for leisurely literary transmission.

My first act was to write still another book about the 24-odd levels of intelligence-evolution; this one disguised as an adventure-romance—the saga of an evolutionary agent assigned to a primitive planet to perform those small but precise jiggles needed to nudge responsible gene-pools to move life off the prison planet.

This book, titled *What Does WoMan Want?*, was hopefully designed to be a mass market book just a shade farther out than, say, the works of Kurt Vonnegut. The honey-pollen coating was to disguise and make palatable its post-terrestrial imperatives.

This tactic flopped. Although this is generally considered my "best" book, it was not possible to attract a New York publisher. No fame, no blame, no shame. In the Bible of neurography, there is no sin; just lamentable ignorance of where one is supposed to be: one could hardly expect the Soviet Literary Trust or the Vatican's *Osservatore Romano* to be interested in 21st-century satire. Venerable publishing houses east of the Hudson were being snapped up by multinational conglomerates and books were being packaged into film-television consumer units. This seemed exactly the moment to start private publishing ventures on the Pacific frontier. Thus was born the Future History Series—books written for 21st-century readers—printed and distributed on the future side of the Rocky Mountains.

Most cultural commentators agree that, like it or not, the future is being fabricated in Southern California. New ideas seem to proceed from west to back east—at a rate of 1,000 miles a year. Esthetic-erotic-scientific innovations generated in the Golden Rectangle appear three years later in Manhattan, six years later in London and Paris.

The Golden Rectangle is an historical name given to the ecological niche—never more than a few square miles—into which swarm and out of which radiate the evolutionary ideas of the epoch. In the past, the Golden Rectangle was located in Konarak, Agra, Cairo, Athens, Rome, Paris, London, Boston-Cambridge, Manhattan. At the time of these events, the Golden Rectangle was bounded on the south by the Santa Monica Freeway, on the east by La Brea Avenue, on the north by Mulholland Drive, and on the west . . . Venice-Santa Monica-Topanga. But as usual, the center of bureaucratic power was located one stage east of the Future-Fabricating Niche. Thus the paradox: although Southern California produces the new ideas, the mass-marketing control of this information was centered in the last, out-moded niche—the East Coast of North America.

In the last half of the 20th century, the great futique scripts written by Pacificans were generally ignored and disdained by the Atlantian-Manhattans. West Coast writing was as different from the Oriental Madison Avenue scripts as the latter were from Soviet literary productions. The Pacificans included Aldous Huxley, Christopher Isherwood, Gary Snyder, Ken Kesey, Tom Robbins, Joan Didion, Thomas Pynchon (who fled to Manhattan Beach, California—and refused to appear at Eastern book conventions), Jack London (whose later books were sci-fi speculations), Will Durant, most of the sci-fi collegium, Henry Miller, Anaïs Nin. On the other hand, Mailer, Cheever, Barth, Styron, Malamud, Singer, Podhoretz, et al. were ecologically incapable of existing west of the Rockies.

The bureaucratic power of dour Oriental publishing contrast-ed with the lusty, romantic, optimistic, druggy, jolly, utopian, futuristic flavor of Pacific writing. This situation provided one of those classic neurogeographic roulette wagers that planetary opportunists always look for. I invested all my scripts in a West Coast bet on the future. With the expert managerial help of Joanna Harcourt Smith, a company called Starseed was founded to publish books for 21st-century readers.

We intended to open the Gutenberg lock that has consistent-ly moved control away from the author into the hands of the bureaucra-cy, to get back face-to-face, personal contact between author, book designer, typesetter, printer, distributor. At present, this *samizdat* operation has published *Neurologic, Secret of the Oval Room, Terra II, What Does WoMan Want?, Neuropolitics, Intelligence Agents,* and *Game of Life.* Each book has sold out at least one printing and shown a profit. A modest library of Future History volumes is quietly accumulat-ing.

Each volume involved esthetic-design experiments in collab-oration with the designers. For example, *What Does WoMan Want?* was intended to convey a television experience. There were four ongoing soap-opera memoir serials interwoven with commercials, special parodies, mini-documentaries. The reader was encouraged to flip from chapter to chapter the way TV dials are changed. Underlying all these interwoven threads was the basic notion of the predictable evolution of intelligence—assisted in this case by Commodore Leri, a harassed and often confused Evolutionary Agent attempting to mutate Earth's Domesticated Primates through the inevitable stages of evolution as painlessly (for them and for him) as possible.

We present here an opening chapter, and the closing pages of the book in which the C.I.A. begs Commodore Leri to reveal his next plans for species evolution.

What does WoMan want?

(A Science Faction Starring Timothy Leri as Prometheus-8)
The outlaw gnostic, resident agent from T.I.M.E., holds no illusions about his assignment on earth—to find the encoded secret the dying planet hungered for. His genetic task is complicated when he discovers that his own name heads the wanted-list of the dread Nixon-Liddy gang's Operation Intercept!

Introduction

Timothy Leri's life is remarkably well documented. Sixty-four volumes of his memoirs, field notes, chronologs, philosophic texts, neuropolitical essays survive, in addition to 108 volumes of trial court transcripts and legal briefs.

Though I have assembled a factual history based on available records, I have attempted to reflect the fictional image of this legendary, often misunderstood Gnostic Agent incarcerated under the largest bail in planetary history ($5 million) by Cecil Hicks, district attorney of Orange County who, in 1972, publicly branded him "the most dangerous man alive."

What continues to fascinate is the Explosive 20th Century itself. Ten years after Leri's arrival in Switzerland (1972) extraterrestrial migration was initiated! For better or worse, we are now (A.D. 2775) very much the result of what was accomplished during this extraordinarily brief period.

In naming cities, I give the ancient Terrestrial rather than modern names (America, not North Argentina, for example). Terms for neurogenetic stages, chemical elements, genetic time bundles are those of the crude dialects in use at the time, except where the concept did not exist at all in the 20th-Century language. No one can be certain what the exact energy value of "money" was in the 20th Century, but 100 Swiss francs was probably worth one or two seconds of one-G-zero-acceleration time. All of the characters spoke American, the lingua franca of the period. The rise in sea level which destroyed coastal cultures did not affect the higher mountain territories which are the locale of this legend.

Before the Period of Repentant Reconstruction, which returned all metal and stone structures underground, crushing the life-web membrane by inorganic overground constructions was considered a sign of progress! The majority of earthlings lived surrounded by manufactured artifacts—cut off from their own bodies and the organic environment.

Readers will search in vain for Leri's notorious last words before departure, "Thou hast conquered, Gaia!" He never said them. Geocentric revisionists composed this flamboyant and ambiguous rhetoric several centuries after the Migration.

There is abundant evidence that Leri's evolution was in every way routine. The melancholic bouts, pervasive megalomanias, recurrent withdrawals and reappearances, which suggest a flamboyant eccentricity, can now be seen as normal episodes of molting and metamorphic behavior. Leri was appropriately passionate, changeable, gregarious, compassionate, lively, and funny—hardly surprising when he spent almost 20 years equipped with 6 cerebral circuits, 2 more than the most evolved organisms of the time!

The aloof, arrogant, enigmatic image that so infuriated the opinion makers of the period was, of course, entirely due to the isolating walls the media instinctively threw up around him, and the long periods of protective incarceration. Those few allowed to contact him personally found him unassuming, companionable, exuberant, tactful, unfailingly generous. His proverbial sexual magnetism needs no documentation. During the two decades he held knowledge of the most powerful aphrodisiac ever developed by the DNA code, he used this power in the most restrained manner. Required to let his social facade crumble, his ego be destroyed, to disappear gracefully from the cultural structures while allowing to those left behind the conviction of their own integrity, even superiority—he seems to have handled these evolutionary tactics with self-effacing grace and modesty.

I should like to thank the Vidalian Academy and the Terrestrial School of Classical Studies in Cairo for letting me use their microscripts and holographic records.

M. M. Procyon-4, A.D. 2775
* * *

The Commodore sees a young female biped approaching along the sidewalk, her lush body cased in tight blue jeans worn below the generous curve of hip. The gait is undulating. A 5-brained creature! He watches his own sluggish but unmistakable response to the somatic signal. He studies the blissful face as she passes. Another grounded rapture victim, no doubt about it.

The Commodore walks across the street and enters the cafe. The waiter trots forward. "Monsieur Duval? He waits in the corner."

"You look sad," sez Duval.

"I'm bored with being chased by 2-brained bipeds," sez the Commodore. "How do the men who think they run things explain to themselves what they are doing?"

Duval explodes softly, hissing under aerosol pressure. "Mon cher professeur. I know that calculated naivete is one of your favorite disguises. But don't you know why the Intelligence Community follows you around?"

"Why?"

Duval emits another enormous exhalation of breath. Sincerity is about to emerge from the closet. "All right. I'll lay our cards on the table. Your plan has worked. You have conquered, Galileo. Ah, you don't realize it? That's funny. You believe our propaganda! Okay, let me cite you the critical demographics."

Duval pulls a notebook from his jacket pocket and ruffles the pages.

"According to the best Western Intelligence sources, in the Middle East the influential young men and women have brainwashed themselves according to your instructions and committed themselves to your philosophy. Iran . . . 7 members of the royal family; 5 male and 2 female. They are, of course, the best-educated, the most sophisticated and intelligent. Exactly the people we have been grooming. The top young administrators and scientists, too."

"Got it," sez the Commodore.

"To summarize, in every pro-Western Arab state, the elite youth is with you. Distressing is that your ideas have made no headway in the pro-Soviet countries. It's *our* best people. Do you understand our anguish?"

"I understand."

"Spain was a shocker. We couldn't accept these figures until they were rechecked. Of 132 of the most promising young people—I'm talking about the aristocracy and the nobility who own and run the country—88 are out-and-out neurologic. Talk to them about conventional politics and economics, and they just laugh in your face. In Italy the trend is mixed. France, you've made less headway. But Scandinavia . . . over 60% just won't buy the old lineups."

"What do they seem to be for?"

"That's the problem. It gets vague. They talk about individuals controlling their own realities. Neuro-politics. Neuro-genetics."

"I see."

Duval is adding figures on a paper napkin. "Of approximately 1,000 of the most promising young scientists and political administrators in the core democracies—Germany, England, America—over 50% are committed to the apparently successful use of your neurological methods."

"How about South America?"

"The more aristocrats, the bigger your majorities. In the bourgeois socialisms and democracies, the smaller. Another strange twist. In the foreign offices and among the diplomatic corps, your triumph is complete. Seventy-three ambassadors that we know of, most of the wives too. And . . . well you might as well know the worst. Three prime ministers, 6 rulers, 4 foreign ministers!

"The significance of these statistics," continues Duval, "was hidden under the Generation Gap and scattered globally. The shocking fact is that the use of your brain-change technology is most pronounced among the sons and daughters of the ruling class."

"So what is to be done? It's apparently too late to kill me."

"That has been discussed. It was decided to convince the world that you were mind-blown, crazy. Your flight to Algeria was a delightful gift."

"But one crash of a test pilot can't ground TWA."

"We realized that soon enough." Duval throws his pen on the table in exasperation. "I repeat: Don't you know why we in the Intelligence Community have been following you around?"

"Why?"

"Because we're waiting for you to tell us what you plan to do next with this species."

"You might come along?"

"We're *listening,*" answers Duval. *(To Be Continued . . .)*

The next experiment in West Coast Mutational Signalry was a book sub-titled *A Manual on the Use of the Nervous System According to the Instructions of the Manufacturers.*

The title, *Exo-Psychology,* requires comment. This term, which will probably become a basic unit of 21st-century human thought, spins off from the exobiology concept made respectable by Carl Sagan et al. Exobiology studies the existence of life off the surface of our embryo planet. Panspermia is seriously discussed by Crick, Orgel, Hoyle, Wickramasinghe. Platoons of sober Soviet scientists solemnly weigh and assay cosmonauts. Multimillion dollar budgets for space medicine.

So the time was clearly ripe for Exo-Psychology (Trademark applied for). Studies of post-terrestrial human psychology had, of course, been executed by Air Force scientists since World War II. One 4-volume epic published in the late 1940's studied the effects of Allied bombing on Germany. The stresses and blisses of high-altitude flight, the psychoneural selection, testing, and training of astronauts. Was the irritable rebellion of the second Skylab crew premonition of later revolts of Space Colonists against home-base controls?

Such NASA and Pentagon researches, however grandly funded, were still seen as exotic specialties far removed from mainstream psychology which, by 1970, had become a most profitable sort of "auto" repair, with unimaginative technicians patching up domesticated primates and restoring them to useful efficiency. A bang-out-the-dents personality-renovation may be exciting to the limping owner of the obsolescent genetic vehicle, but the *scientific* aspects of psychology were clearly being absorbed by sociobiology and neurogenetics. The movement of gene-pools according to predictable patterns of swarming. The evolution of new social-genetic forms. Understanding of genetic castes. Human leucocyte antigen research. Histocompatibility (blood-type-studies) opening up the Pandora's treasure chest of neurocompatibility, DNA compatibility, cloning. How about recombinant DNA technicians splicing in a "jolly" gene to replace a "mean" gene?

But all these advances in our understanding and rearrangement of human nature were meaningless as long as our species remained trapped on a shrinking planet with mammalian territorial pressure reaching the explosion point.

So Exo-Psychology's immediate, practical survival aspect was, of course, the psychology of migration. Who gets to colonize space? What are the genetic predispositions and neuro-aptitudes of the successful frontiersperson? Movement from water to land activated an enormous explosion of new species. Migration from the land-locked, one-G planet can be expected to produce a similar eruption as we are transformed from barnacles* to high-flying, fast-moving neuro-electroids. Those who leave the sessile, sedentary stage of planetary life to high-orbital habitats will have to exhibit paradoxical polarities—extraordinary individualism and self-confidence combined with extraordinary abilities to work with and rely on others.

The first waves of migrants usually represent extremes of individualism; following waves tend to being the more traditional culture. But in space migration, the real kicker comes from those who will be born in high orbit: second-generation migrants who spend their entire lives in multiple gravity looking down (out) at the small, blue, spinning Old World. New neuromuscular and neuro-endocrine solutions will characterize these advanced futants.

Exo-Psychology the book was still another attempt to prepare our species for stages to come, to repeat the familiar message: We are not terrestrials designed to spend our lives pasted to the surface of a sphere terraformed by someone else.

The emphasis, as was the case in *What Does WoMan Want?* is on neuro-logic: brain know-how, serial imprinting. Learn to use your head. Satire and affectionate ridicule is the basic key of evolution (really, Leo, isn't it ludicrous to run around on four feet when you can climb on two?). Thus there is some scorn heaped on previous (Pavlovian-Skinnerian) methods of behavior change that lead to insectoid-urbanoid Fourth-Circuit realities, and there is considerable mockery of Fifth-Circuit hippie somatic, back-to-body-naturism.

> ATTENTION: DNA HAS RECALLED THE 1966 HIPPIE MODEL TO REPAIR STRUCTURAL DEFECTS: A TENDENCY TO DISREGARD NAVIGATIONAL INTELLIGENCE AT HIGH ALTITUDES AND FAILURES IN TRANSMISSION FROM MECHANICAL-MUSCULAR TO NEUROELECTRIC INTELLIGENCE.

---

*It is of haunting evolutionary interest to recall that the monumental research on barnacles was published, in 1840, by none other than Charles Darwin!

This book is now out of date: In the 5 years since its publication, science has undergone breathtaking acceleration. The naive references to histone and antihistone (although still avant garde in their human applications) seem primitive in light of the advances of recombinant-DNA research and, now, the Golden Age of Neurogenetics.

Exo-Psychology was designed to mimic the layers of information offered by daily newspapers. Each chapter title was a declarative statement that summed up the content, like a newspaper headline. Running along the top of each page was a magnified paragraph repeating the most important sentences on that page. And on the bottom of each page was the classified ad: S.M.I.²L.E. (Space Migration/Intelligence Increase/Life Extension).

Exo-psychology

Preface

Life on Earth, through the instrumentality of the human nervous system, has begun to establish colonies in space, from whence it can more accessibly contact Life in the galaxy. In our cells, we know that we, who are about to leave this small satellite of a peripheral star, are neither alone nor unique. Our most important challenge is to prepare ourselves neurologically to meet the "relatives" with whom we share the galaxy.

Some will protest that human intelligence and resources should be used to solve agonizing terrestrial problems of unequal distribution. These larval protests, however sincere, are historically wrong and genetically futile.

The cause of the suffering and scarcity that now threaten humanity is neuro-political. The current malaise of the affluent nations demonstrates clearly that material rewards are not enough. The crisis the human race now faces is best described as navigational. Humanity has lost the map, the compass, the guidebook; misplaced the genetic code.

There is only one way from down. Up!

Men and women who know where they're going, who share a vision beyond the local-mundane, will learn quickly, work effectively, grow naturally, socialize lovingly, and evolve gracefully because of the genetic Law of Least Effort. Both species and individuals coast along on serene stupidity until faced with evolutionary challenges, at which point both species and individual become smarter, very much faster. WW II provides an interesting illustration. Basic principles of atomic structure, rocket propulsion, and radar had been well-known for decades. But under pressure of the Technological Imperative, the American and German scientific communities got smart—fast.

Migration is nature's classic solution to overpopulation, scarcity, and competition. When humanity begins to work for extraterrestrial migration, the competition for material acquisition will gradually diminish because unlimited space, energy, and resources await in the solar system.

This simple-minded perspective of biological evolution presents hundreds of neogenetic ideas for which the human species is now ready. The reader should expect, therefore, that hir conditioned symbol-system is going to be jolted with unexpected, novel symbol combinations. A 20th-century human would find it most difficult to explain "now" to an average fellow from the 18th century. Some goodwill and openness is necessary in interspecies dialogues of this sort. This is exactly the situation that will exist when Higher Intelligence begins to communicate with human space colonies. Is there any more interesting or vital thing to do than to create the future?

Exo-Psychology Studies the Evolution of the Nervous System in its Larval and Post-Terrestrial Phases

The person who can dial and tune the circuits of the nervous system is not just more intelligent, but can be said to operate at a higher, more complex level of evolution. A powerful instrument for conscious evolution, the nervous system can be understood and employed for genetic tasks.

Emotional, mental, sexual, and ethical behavior is based on accidental imprinting of the nervous system during "critical" or "sensitive" periods of development—a fact devastating to pretensions of free will and conscious choice. An impressive convergence of evidence suggests that the brain is a bio-chemical-electric computer in which each nerve impulse acts as an information "quantra" or "bit"; that the human being, at this stage of evolution, is a biological robot (biot) automatically responding to genetic-template and childhood imprinting. We can evaluate ourselves only in terms of the symbols our nervous systems have created. An anthropological report about *Homo sapiens* written by extraterrestrials from a more advanced civilization would conclude that intelligent life has not yet evolved on this planet.

Other sciences have significance for future human destiny:

Astronautics: The significance of extraterrestrial flight has not yet been fully understood. Just as land-dwelling organisms rapidly develop neural and physiological equipment for the new environment, this transition to zero-gravity and extraterrestrial radiation will trigger off genetic and neurological changes necessary to adapt to interstellar life. The beginnings of exo-psychological adaptation can be noted in several lunar veterans who returned claiming cosmic insights (Mitchell), philosophic revelations (Schweickart), and rebirth symptoms (Aldrin).

Astrophysics has determined that perhaps as many as half of the 100 billion stars in our local galaxy are older than our sun. Astronomers have discovered basic life molecules in outer space and in other star systems, making it highly probable that more advanced forms of intelligent life are around the neighborhood. So far, humans have been neurologically incapable of conceiving of Higher Intelligence.

The left-cortical larval mind (Circuit 3) naturally assumes that life from other solar systems will be hostile and competitive: galactic cowboys and Indians. Very few science fiction writers (Stapledon, Asimov, Clarke) specify the manifestations of superior species, except as bizarre extrapolations and extremes of current human culture.

Whatever the mind can conceive, it tends to create. As soon as humans accept the notion of as-yet-unactivated circuits in the nervous system, a new philosophy of an evolving nervous system will emerge: human nature seen from the vantage point of older species.

Neurogenetics is a new science (with a respectable journal and membership dues), which studies the psychology (i.e., consciousness and behavior) of DNA-RNA. We assume that DNA contelligence is not restricted to planet Earth, but, indeed, was probably designed to return to extraterrestrial intelligence. Blueprints are remarkably similar from species to species. The DNA code can now be seen as a temporal blueprint unfolding sequentially like a tape-spool, transmitting preprogrammed construction plans from infancy, through childhood, adolescence, maturity, menopause, aging, and death. Individual ontology recapitulates species phylogeny—that the human embryo, for example, repeats the evolutionary cycle. The theory of serial imprinting suggests that psychology repeats the evolutionary sequence: The baby recapitulates an invertebrate reality, the crawling child a mammalian reality, the preschool child a Paleolithic reality, the adolescent a domesticated-civilized reality.

Geneticists are just now discovering "unused" sections of the DNA, masked by histones and activated by proteins, which are thought to contain the blueprint of the future. Neurochemistry has recently discovered that neurotransmitter chemicals facilitate/inhibit nerve impulses and synaptic connections determining consciousness, emotion, memory, learning, and behavior. At the same time, psychopharmacology has discovered botanical and synthetic psychoactive agents that facilitate/inhibit states of consciousness and accelerate or dampen mental function.

The histone-masked sections of the DNA code can be studied to determine the sequence of future evolution.

Just as the DNA code, in the nucleus of the cell, is the genetic brain, the nucleus of the atom is the elemental "brain" that designs and constructs atoms and molecules according to quantum logic. Physicist John Archibald Wheeler's work suggests that the atomic nucleus can receive, remember, integrate, and transmit information at extremely high velocities and can probably engage in most of the basic social behavior that we observe in living organisms.

We inevitably "psychologize" nature and personalize atomic events. Our laryngeal-muscular minds cannot conceive of what we have never experienced. But psychological systems based on Newtonian geocentric principles have done little to harmonize human philosophy. Does it seem too fanciful to base psychological concepts on the laws and structures of physics, chemistry, and astronomy?

Our dialogue with DNA and our conversations with atomic-subatomic and astronomical energy signals must, however, be two-way. We must open our "minds" to receive the signals being sent to our nervous systems by DNA and by elemental intelligences. Since DNA creates us, it is logical, diplomatic, and theologically conventional to base our psychology upon molecular laws and designs, upon the laws and structures of nuclear physics and astronomy; to think of ourselves as "atoms" or even "stars"—radiating, decaying, attracting, repelling, receiving and transmitting, forming molecular social structures, possessing a characteristic electromagnetic personality.

Neural Chauvinism: Every Body Has a Favorite Reality

From the scientific viewpoint, reality is an ocean of electromagnetic vibrations whirling momentarily into temporary structures—including bodies with nervous systems. Human consciousness (i.e., personal reality) is determined by the point along the frequency spectrum where the neural dials are tuned. Larval realities are defined by chunks of local environment attached to the nervous system at the time of imprinting.

Seasonal variations in solar radiation may alter DNA templating at the time of conception, determining human neurogenetic "types." The 12 Zodiac "signs" may crudely personalize 12 subspecies very different in neurological wiring, which reflect and recapitulate 12 stages of phylogenetic and human evolution. Each Zodiac "species" thus represents the mastery of one of the 12 neurological stages of evolution. (The tradition of using 12 peers in a trial by jury may be an unconscious recognition of the 12 subspecies populating human larval society.)

Just as the members of insect colonies are programmed to play certain roles necessary for hive survival—worker, drone, fertile male, brood queen—so each of the 12 larval types of human can be considered genetically separate; each contributes to the evolutionary process and carries a printed-out nervous system geared to a specialized survival task.

In addition, environment models imprinted during individual development define island realities such as language and dialects that vary from person to person and from group to group.

This unique specificity of reality means, among other things, that numerous cultural-imprint groups wander around the planet, for the most part in different realities. People unconsciously recognize this; social avoidance and clustering tend to respond to these reality chauvinisms. The hive cannot tolerate other realities: anyone different is crazy or alien. But despite their neural machinery, humans communicate with each other about material needs with amazing efficiency.

The newborn baby is equipped with behavior patterns necessary for immediate survival: to turn towards the mothering stimulus and suckle. Shortly after birth, the baby's nervous system focuses all the sensory equipment on the soft, warm, milk-producing stimulus, and permanently photographs this picture as "survivally good" and safe. If this viscerotonic imprint is not taken because of absence of appropriate stimulus during the critical period, the basic "survival security" system is not effectively wired up to human contacts.

The infant body is like a spaceship floating on the strange new planet. The imprint is a neuro-umbilical lifeline extended from the nervous system, blindly groping for hospitable survival stimuli to which it attaches and roots—thus creating the reality island. Once attached, the larval nervous system is hooked for life—unless retracted by accidental trauma; or deliberately.

Each of the four neuro-umbilical lifelines is extended in turn when each neural circuit emerges. During adolescence, for example, there is a critical or "sensitive" period of sexual imprinting. The sexual antennae, heretofore rudimentary, emerge and blindly scan for a place to root.

The first time the sexual system is fired in all-out response, an imprint is taken, determining the sensory, emotional, mental, and social stimuli that facilitate subsequent arousal and discharge. Accidental vicissitudes of Circuit-4 sexual imprinting—early erections and orgasms —can create kinky fetishes well-known to psychiatrists.

The neurologic mechanics of the mental-symbolic Circuit-3 imprint are less familiar. The acquisition of speech and manipulative behavior is accomplished by moving the 9 muscles of the larynx. When the child is mastering speech, the mental and emotional style of contiguous parents (and, more important, older children) determine whether the child's mind is open/trusting or withdrawn/rejecting.

Once the child wires up a specific method of thinking, subsequent education has little effect on intellectual manipulation.

Circuit-1 biosurvival language: movements, sounds, and behaviors that express security, pain, or physical threat: eating, vomiting, sucking, disgust, embracing, moaning, physically aggressing or menacing.

Circuit-2 emotional language: gestures, postures, and verbal tones that communicate a status message. Gestural signals for affiliation, dominance, submission, begging, giving, coercion, and passive complaint require no cross-cultural dictionary. However, each culture has a specific status vocabulary of accents, gestures, ornaments, conspicuous possessions, postures. In the suburbs, a Cadillac indicates highest status; in the slums, a Cadillac indicates a pimp or cocaine dealer. And so it goes.

Each of us deals with a world defined by a unique pattern of neural wires and fixed umbilical lifelines. We try to understand emerging stages of human development by analogy to the metamorphosis of insects, since we are too close to the situation to appreciate metamorphosis in ourselves. Just so, we can understand the uniqueness of electro-neural "reality" by considering the consciousness islands of other species. We see a mouse run across the floor and a snake turn its head and strike. We assume that the snake "sees" what we see: a furry, brown animal. However, the snake uses heat receptors to locate prey. Programmed to strike at heat, the snake senses a neon spot of "warm" moving across its screen.

Human beings often interact across similar "reality" gulfs. Robot-programmed as differently as the snake, they vary in the number of languages they can exchange. The most primitive communicate and manipulate only in the oral dialect of their childhood village. The highly civilized larvals have mastered hundreds of symbol systems, can speak and write each other in several languages, cooperatively manipulate a wide variety of mechanical artifacts, professional sequences, scientific codes, sports and game rituals.

In communicating with a larval, nonverbal cues establish that Circuit 1 is safe and Circuit 2 is cooperative. The next step is to establish which muscle-thought languages are shared and can be appropriately exchanged. Most larval interactions—buying, selling, superficial socializing—are brief and limited. Extended conversations are loaded with complexity because emotional factors inevitably intrude. Giving information to others is often resented because information possession implies power.

Circuit 3 is activated when the young child is in a position of weakness. Adults or superiors teach the L.M. (laryngeal-manual) symbol systems. The ability to learn symbols is determined by emotional context—the person with the information is placed in a superior position over the receiver. Just as chemicals "fix" a photographic image on film, so is the neural image of the island-reality "fixed" by synaptic chemical bonds at the time of imprinting.

A child growing up finds a certain stability and consistency in the social cues SHe imprints. Hir parents speak the same language, share rituals with the family next door. This consensual agreement provides the illusion of a "reality" shared with those in Hir culture group. "Sanity" is defined in terms of one's ability to convince oneself that SHe perceives what others do. Social psychologists' "cognitive dissonance" experiments show how easily and naturally humans distort objective data to fit neural expectations.

We believe what we are imprinted to believe. We think that the tiny turf to which our neuro-umbilical lifelines attach is "reality." The fact of separate, subjective realities based on individual imprints is frightening for the preneurological human. (Recall the parable of the 8 blind men and the elephant?) This separateness accounts for the terror felt in the presence of an "insane" person—who, in many cases, is actually aware of the neural insulation separating people and might be considered more sane and accurate than the deluded "normals." Casteneda's Don Juan (in *Tales of Power*) gives a good description of the imprint reality . . .

> *Sorcerers say that we are inside a bubble into which we are placed at the moment of birth. . . . It begins to close until it has sealed us in. That bubble is our perception. We live inside that bubble all of our lives . . . until all our attention is caught by it and the description becomes a view.*

Imprints Can Only Be Changed Biochemically

The Circuit-1 emergency system commands millions of survival actions. Early "danger" imprints and genetic programs cue this powerful, basic system, which, mobilized, affects every organ in the body. The intransigence of human "phobias" and "security blankets" is caused by chemico-electric synaptic patterns.

Security means that imprinted lifelines are securely fastened to a stable island-reality.

When action inside the body becomes so intense so as to alter synapse chemistry, imprint lifelines to the external environment are retracted. Shock, illness, trauma, drugs, child delivery, stimulus deprivation, and electrical charge. The result is a new reality for the patient. When the somatic infection is cured, the emergency "sick" wiring may remain in operation, preventing the restoration of normal function. Conversely, infection or malfunction may require curative changes blocked by the normal "wiring." This may help explain acupuncture. The needles have little effect on the fleshy system, but—particularly when energized with mild electric charges—may affect the synaptic programs.

Conditioning Biochemically Links a New Stimulus with an Imprint

The notion of imprinting a form of immediate and irreversible "learning" —has created some confusion, since according to the classic definitions of most psychological theories, "Learning occurs as the result of practice." But psychological theories of learning based on observations of external, visible behavior pay little attention to the internal, invisible neurological situation. First, the imprint hooks the natural unconditioned response to an external stimulus—the releaser mechanism. Conditioning then connects (wires up neurally) other stimuli with the imprinted stimuli. Learned stimuli can then trigger the response imprinted to the original stimulus. If the infant's Circuit 1 is positively imprinted to Mother, other learned cues (aprons, kitchen, perfume) can also trigger off the "positive-approach" response.

Conditioning Cannot Change an Imprinted Reality

Skinnerians attempt to "shape" symbolic, manipulative Circuit-3 behavior—a futile, coercive business. Operant conditioning "works" by means of immediate and *continual* reinforcement.

In 1961, to the Center for Personality Research at Harvard came an enthusiastic Skinnerian to report on the applications of operant conditioning to patients in a mental hospital. One behavior to be inhibited was hallucinatory talk. Now many among us believe that hallucinations have a functional role in the psyche: automatically extinguishing hallucinations might restrict some message of importance, even if not understood or considered useful to the psychologist's reality. Using immediate reinforcement, the Skinnerians instantly produced a cigarette every time the patient made a non-hallucinatory comment and took the cigarette away every time the patient hallucinated. The researcher gleefully announced that the rate of hallucinatory comments dropped by a significant level.

Even more impressive changes in behavior accompanied the giving or deprivation of food. The Skinnerian glumly complained that hospital rules prevented them from carrying out this experiment to the point of starvation: "If we had total control over food intake, we could really shape behavior." The operant conditioner may not have heard the comment by one staff member that most of the dictators in world history had used this technique.

Two groups of technocrats clamor to change the behavior of their fellow citizens: Right-wing punitive coercers, and liberal rewarders.

Punitive coercion works only as long as the threat remains, and thus requires a police state.

Liberal social psychologists believe that they can change behavior by supportive, egalitarian methods—head-start programs, Peace Corps, busing, tutoring. Both groups' attempts are futile because they attempt to recondition, rather than reimprint.

The more intelligent experimental psychologists, for whom Skinner is spokesman, believe they can impose behavior change by involuntary operant conditioning. This, however, works only when the conditioners are continually present to reinforce. Left to their own devices, the "subjects" immediately drift back to the magnetism of the imprint and genetic template.

Imprinting requires no reinforcement. Let me imprint the infant, and you try to condition the child; let me imprint the child, and you try to condition the adolescent. The imprint requires no repeated reward or punishment; the neural fix is permanent. Conditioned associations, on the contrary, wane and disappear with lack of repetition.

In order to condition human behavior, get control of stimuli early in childhood and maintain this control throughout life. In the psychological utopia, continual psychological testing would identify potential troublemakers early in the game and special conditioning programs would eliminate individual eccentricity.

The case for the Political Conditioners can be simply paraphrased: To make human beings dutiful, virtuous, reliable, prompt, efficient, happy, law-abiding, government psychologists must have total control over the citizenry and there must be total secrecy and censorship.

One dissident, one freedom-oriented psychologist can totally disrupt psychological fascism by public exposure. If parents and children are warned about the method of conditioning, they can consciously decide whether to resist, passively or actively. Most psychological tests are ineffective, if the subject has been warned about their purpose and construction. Even brainwashing drugs can be counteracted by the person who learns the specific effects of neurochemicals. Thus the proposals of B. F. Skinner cannot be implemented except in a state where the government has total control of communication. "Will the dog roll over in the absence of the master?" is the question that haunted the aging Mao.

Larval humanity now faces a genetic crossroads. Some will choose to solidify social conditioning by manipulating the child's environment and thus domesticating the imprint: Maoism. Others will choose to mutate to a higher level where each person is taught to manage and control hir own imprinting and conditioning. We can expect that many different social groups will emerge along each direction.

Imprinting Limits Reality to the Local Environment

After each daily tide of association and reward-punishment, coercive behavior-control methods must be repeated. The coercive nature of learned behavior *appears* voluntary; in fact, the conditioned robot is obsessively drawn back to his place in the sandbox. If we remove the symbol-rewarding environment or fail to produce the conditioned stimulus, the humanoid robot goes mad, because SHe has nothing to do. We can accurately speak of stimulus junkies. Social deprivation creates desperate reward-hunger. The social reality of conditioned response requires continual rewarding. The ordeal of Sisyphus was an exciting adventure compared to the monotony of social conditioning. Trying to recondition an imprint with reward-punishment is like dropping single grains of sand on a steel pattern. Decades of sand can wear down the imprint. The aging politician gets lazy, the aging homosexual becomes too fatigued to cruise, etc.

To change the shape of metal forms, one must apply enough energy to rearrange the molecules. So with neural imprints: massive biochemical energy is necessary to loosen the molecular synaptic bonds. With the present repertoire of Circuit-6 neurotransmitter drugs, it is apparently possible to reimprint only about once a week. It takes from 5 to 7 days for the reimprinted nervous system to harden into new circuits. Ill-prepared LSD sessions tend to reimprint the past conditioned structure, thus charging with new energy the habit patterns of the old island reality. One often hears the complaint from people who have taken LSD repeatedly that, after a while, the "trips" were the same. If the recasting of the mind occurs over and over again in the same place with the same set of characters, this is like having the most precise and expensive photographic equipment and, without moving it, continuing to photograph the same object.

The imprint-fix is sudden. Post-imprint conditioning, centering on the positive and negative poles of the imprint, takes time and repetition. Around the initial imprint, billions of conditioned associations build up over the years, forming the structure of personality. Where new models are imprinted, it takes time to start building up new circles of conditioned reflexes. Some early researchers concluded that a 6-month wait should occur between LSD sessions to "work through the new insights." The exo-psychological phrase is "to allow new conditioning to network around the new imprints."

Reimprinting sessions, therefore, require careful planning so that previous aspects of realities that one wishes to exist in future reality are present to be imprinted, and that during the "sensitive" period, new models remain around to allow new associations to build up around them.

Most world travelers move their robot-bodies from country to country, experiencing only symbolic versions of home. Two neurologicians, a newly married couple, embarked on a psychedelic world tour. Their procedure was to fly to a country and enquire as to the "spiritual" center of that nation. In India, they were told to go to Benares. In Greece, to Eleusis; in Japan to Kyoto. Then in Kyoto, they asked where the spiritual center, the "soul" of Kyoto was to be found. They spent a week reading about the history, politics, culture, art, myths of Japan and Kyoto, then went to the "holiest" place, ingested a Circuit-6 neuroactive chemical (LSD) that opened the nervous system to new imprints—which in this case were structured by the architecture and regalia of the Emperor's palace. For six hours they absorbed the signals of the place and became neurologically Japanesed.

This is the way to "see the world"—to retract imprint roots and move the unattached nervous system to a new locale. Without such flexible vulnerability, we can experience nothing outside the membrane formed at adolescence or, in the case of women, their last childbirth. Such neural touring is no end in itself, but a rudimentary training exercise for the brain's serial possibilities. The neurological goal is to increase consciousness and intelligence. But when the nervous system can move and change realities by serial reimprinting, its own limitations become apparent: basic genetic dimensions of reality-construction are limited and guided by the genetic template. This most powerful determinant of human behavior cannot be changed; only understood and adapted until postlarval humanity has evolved genetic engineering.

The most intelligent use of the nervous system is to imprint the DNA code. The evolution of humanity of billions of years to come may already be preprogrammed in the genetic code, blocked from expression by chemical barriers called histones. The blueprint of DNA has designed us to move life off the planet and eventually evolve beyond matter as we now know it. It is about time to use our heads; become very contelligent, very rapidly.

One who allows hirself to be controlled by conditioning or imprinting is accepting robothood. It is of little use, however, to go on reimprinting larval or somatic realities. Circuit 6 is designed for extraterrestrial existence, for genetic consciousness. Neurotransmitter drugs are thus seen to be post-larval in function.

Until now, human beings have been neurologically unable to conceive of the future. This inhibition (neophobia) is genetic: for the caterpillar to "think" about flying would be survivally risky. Larval time involves short periods and narrow perspectives. The farmer looks to the next harvest, the politician to the next election, parents to their children.

The 4-brained person does not want to know about the future because it threatens the stability of the reality imprint. There is a taboo about future forecast. *Future Shock* describes the terror and confusion created by a world different from one's childhood realities. Even scientific groups are curiously unable to foresee evolving neurological-mutational change. The Club of Rome, the RAND Corporation, Herman Kahn, all extrapolate material trends of the past; thus are we told that the future will be a global extension of a Swedish Los Angeles. Most current "futurists" forecast an air-conditioned anthill world in which personal freedom and creativity are limited by population, scarcity, and restrictive social control.

One possibility is routinely omitted—a sudden global raising of contelligence.

The 1960's witnessed a widespread retraction of larval imprints. The new "hippie" imprints were not thoughtfully selected: a "drop-out" away from the parent-culture and an unfortunate tendency to reject technology and scientific thinking. The drug culture of the 1960's wandered around, "spaced out," "high," but with no place to go (one generation too early for interstellar migration). Into this neural vacuum rushed the karma dealers, Jesus salesmen, "spiritualists," providing occult terms and "other-worldly" explanations for the new transcendental states. After retracting imprints from the material culture, the 1960's went back to Jesus, Hasidism, India, the nature simplicity of the pioneers—the consciousness fads became soothing terrestrial "turn-offs," offering peace of mind for premature mutants. (The water-bed, with its hint of zero-gravity sensory freedom, is an example of a Circuit-5 fad.)

It is natural that the first post-larval generation would appear confused, disoriented, frivolous, irritatingly vague. A mutation always disturbs the larval culture. No one wants the reality game to become bigger than one's childhood imprints. But the genetic timetable schedules mutations with relentless continuity. And the rate of evolution is accelerating. Physique, neurological function, ecology, density and diversity of population are changing at an accelerated rate. Consider the human situation 100 years ago. Now assume that the same rate of accelerated change continues. How will we evolve in the next 1,000 years?

Evolution produces an increasing spectrum of differentiations. About 75 million years ago, certain insectivore lemurs contained the seed-source from which 193 varieties of primates, including the human, were to emerge. Of the next 100 persons you meet, probably each will evolve into a new species different from you as the rabbit from the giraffe.

The work of Bruce Niklas at Duke reminds us of the intransigence of chromosomal patterns: If chromosome strands are experimentally disarrayed by poking them with a micro-needle, the molecules move back into the original sequence—much the way iron filings "swim" into position in response to magnetism. This suggests that some sort of energy-field pattern operates to keep the DNA code coherent and logical. The work of geneticists like Paul, Stein, and Kleinsmith suggests that histones mask the half of the DNA code containing the futique design of the organism. The error of genetic democracy led Gauguin to ask, "Where did *we* come from and where are *we* going?" Each of us transmits a very different precoded design. The question can only be asked, "Where am *I* going? What genetic futique do *I* carry in my genes?"

The Post-Larval Must Be Cautious in Communicating with Larval Humans

> *In communicating with Earthlings about sexual, philosophic, or ethical matters, one enters very dangerous terrain. Stick to larval issues. It is almost impossible to discuss philosophy with yokels.*
>
> (Interstellar Tourist Guide
> a.k.a. *Exo-Psychology*)

Exo-psychology holds that the human larval exists in a reality defined by 4 survival imprints. Although the brain receives 100 million impulses a second, mundane consciousness is limited to the 4 imprinted gameboards. The larval has no interest in you unless your behavior offers meaning in terms of hir limited reality-island. Larvals do not like to receive information unless it immediately rewards their emotional status. (Democrats were delighted to hear the facts about Nixon, but Republicans were irritated and resistant.)

Larvals submit themselves only to new symbols that build on established systems or give promise of future rewards. This resistance to learning is neurological and biochemical. New ideas require a change in the wiring and literally cause a "headache." That larvals learn almost no new symbol systems after childhood explains why it takes at least one generation for a new idea to be understood.

Few symbols now exist for post-larval "butterfly" processes, and communicating with larvals about sexual, philosophic, or ethical matters enters dangerous terrain.

When sensed as different, Circuit-4 moral and social symbols or behaviors trigger off responses of passion, even violence. Because of this sensitivity, humans tend to avoid philosophic discussions about life, death, philosophic ultimates, child-rearing, and sexuality. Discussing exo-psychology with a yokel is like discussing sexual experience with a pre-adolescent. SHe just can't understand the new reality because hir neural circuits have not been turned on (and SHe may turn you *in* for philosophic child-molesting). Larval humans naturally believe that Homo sapiens evolution has already reached its highest stage. The yokel can become passionately moralistic, attacking the post-terrestrial for being elitist, callous to human suffering, antihuman, escapist, even diabolical.

The Post-Terrestrial Must Also Be Cautious in Communicating with Premature Post-Larvals

The bland, smiling "hippie" and "yogi body-engineer," the first two transitional stages of post-terrestrial "wingless butterflies," are no longer hooked to social symbols. The Hippie-Zen adept no longer reflexively reacts to the virtue-shame systems by which society domesticates its workers; but has not yet evolved to master newly activated circuits. For these reasons, the exo-psychologist must use caution in communicating with the members of the "Woodstock" generation, who are too set in their ways (at age 25–35) to receive the neurophysical signals for extraterrestrial migration.

I spent the winter of 1975–76 in the federal prison in San Diego. One evening, lying on my bunk, I read the space-colony issue of *Co-Evolution Quarterly.* An article by Professor Gerard O'Neill, the Princeton physicist who has become the Columbus of the space migration movement, provided another of those unforgettable mental flashes. O'Neill is a rarity: A distinguished hard-ware nuclear physicist. A humanist, libertarian visionary with an unerring sense of human evolution. A diamond-clear thinker and writer. A good-looking, graceful man with a good-looking cosmopolitan wife.

In the *Co-Evolution* essay, O'Neill explained with razor-edge clarity why planets are not the places to conduct technological civilizations. Using astrophysical data and convincing etho-logic, O'Neill demonstrated that planets are swamplike gravitational wells, unwieldly spheres to which we cling like barnacles. The real eventual habitat for human beings is a luxurious, landscaped, gardened mini-Earth, fabricated by off-the-shelf current technology, showering back down solar energy and manufactured products possible only in a zero-gravity vacuum.

While at Folsom, I had written a book about space flight from Planet Earth *(Terra II)*—a stirring call for an expedition out of the solar system. O'Neill's proposal for mini-Earths was obviously the next step in human evolution, the next ecological niche into which DNA would push.

From that time I have been an active "booster" of the O'Neill project, serving as traveling advertising agent, alerting millions of young people to the next stage in the higher and faster human voyage.

To be candid, I now consider those who fail to understand the liberating inevitability of space migration with the amused curiosity with which we regard members of the Flat Earth Society or, at best, the gentle Amish who serenely turn their back on technological expansion of intelligence.

Exo-politics

The human species is exploding into hundreds of new sub-species. We're learning a great deal about genetic concepts that have to do with migration, the neurology of mutation, swarming, social castes, gene-pools, neoteny, and terminal adulthood.

In 1493, Columbus came back to Spain and said, "Hey, we can *live* over there," just as the astronauts came back and said, "Listen, the Moon and high space can be colonized." Now, when the word came back that there was a new continent, a lot of people said, "How dare you go over there? You're copping out. We should stay back here in Europe and build the dome of the Vatican; settle the wars of the Catholics and the Protestants; and fight with the Armada." Others said, "Life as we know it now can't exist over there. It's a primitive, terrible place."

The migration to North America was self-selective. William Penn and his group of dissenters wanted to get out of England, because they couldn't create Quaker reality there. The Catholic Lord Calvert led a group over because they were being persecuted by the Church of England. The Pilgrim mothers and fathers fled from England to Holland, mortgaged their possessions, and sailed the *Mayflower,* because they wanted a place to live out the kooky, freaky reality that they collectively shared. And there's no question the experiment is a success. Americans are freer than Europeans, and Californians are a new species evolving away from Americans—you're simply freer in California; there's more experimentation, more openness, more tolerance of differences, more future orientation in the West.

Now, the ecological puritans among us say, "Limit growth!" Well, you can't. Who are we to tell every have-not person in Asia, Africa, our country, and South America they can't have two cars, a color television in their garages, skateboards, and snow blowers? Nobody's come up with any plan for full employment, for getting a growth economy without inflation or a war. In the early 1960's Kennedy realized that he couldn't get the country going again unless he moved us up. He said, "We're going to the Moon."

One message we've learned from the DNA code is that population growth is out of our control. It's not within our power to really change an evolutionary process 2½ billion years old. We're just robot evolutionary agents, programmed to transport sperm-egg cargoes higher and faster and farther. Population is increasing. Within 10 or 15 or 20 years, some dictator will press a button, and who'd blame him? Space migration is the escape valve.

Within ten years after initiating space migration, a group of

1,000 people could get together cooperatively and build a new mini-world cheaper than they could buy individual houses down here. Within 25 years there'll be a High Orbital Mini-Earth for *your* vision of social reality. You have the right, duty, and responsibility to externalize that vision with those who share it. The only way you can do that is in a H.O.M.E. because there's going to be an increasing poverty of vision down here as we get more populated and energy decreases.

You better believe that the Russians are planning space labs. When they send up their crews, I don't think they are doing it to expand the plurality of human options. *They're going to steal the whole solar system from us,* unless we're alert.

Space migration is not another cycle of exploration/ exploitation. It's the only way our species can be assured a multiplicity of options in which the next series of experiments in human genetics can occur. When you've got new ideas you can't hang around the old hive. Pollution, crowding, and restlessness are the characteristic stimuli for migration. A lot of people in NASA don't want me going around talking to people about HOME's. They're afraid that you'll want it too soon; and get disappointed if they don't deliver. Still, within NASA there are young space freaks who sincerely want to get this planet moving and provide the increased freedom of space migration.

The fabrication of miniworlds should be voluntary. No government bureau should select who goes into space. Those that want to go, can try. Self-selection, not bureaucratic selection. Studies of social insects, herd animals, and human migrations all show that some migrate and some stay put. Some restless gene-carriers left the bogsides of Ireland and came to the New World. Most remained where, even to this day, they continue their ancient territorial-totem conflicts.

A simple ethological experiment anyone can perform: Ask the next hundred people you meet if they would like to inhabit large High Orbital Mini-Earths. Once reminded, for example, that the Russians are now manning a permanent station, at least half of those polled will embrace the idea. About 10% will be immediately enthusiastic. The younger the sample, of course, the higher percentage of aspirations for migration.

Such responses are probably genetic. The idea either does or does not trigger off an "Ah, yes" reaction. The same process has been occurring for centuries. When the Migration-to-America idea-signal was flashed in the 16th century, some nervous systems reflexively flashed "Let's go." Some will be impelled, compelled, obsessed, driven, fired, wired to move into space; others are bone-deeply, cell-essence horrified by the idea. We must listen to and respect these strong reactions. Those not fired-wired to go should be assured that migration benefits those who stay put in at least two ways:

(1) Migration is an escape valve that rids the home hive of restless outcastes; and

(2) allows for new experiments, technological, political, and social, in a new ecological niche far from the home hive. The stay-puts then benefit from the fallout of the frontier mutational experiments. (In this context, America can be seen as an enormous selective-breeding genetic experiment performed by Old World gene-pools.) If restless-mobile outcastes are allowed to move on, everyone benefits.

I find it useful to conclude discussions about space migration with an appeal to women. The swashbuckling argonaut-astronaut caste always forms the first wave. Once the mysterious frontier is demonstrated to be safe and inhabitable, then the religious and economic bureaucrats move in. But nothing happens until the women are activated. Space migration will explode when women realize that the best place to love, have children, fabricate new cultures, is in a High Orbital Mini-Earth of one's own design.

The introduction to this book clearly constated my early (1946) intention to understand my own behavior (and when possible, the actions of others) in terms of particle physicists. The logic seemed simple. Everyone agreed that nuclear physicists were the smartest caste of our species. They had, after all, transmitted matter into energy ($E=mc^2$). As far as I was concerned, the president of the American Physical Society should automatically double as president of the United States.

And now they were beginning to observe, measure, and establish friendly relations with basic units of energy-matter. Quarks seem to be units of information-intelligence. All grosser, slower structures—atoms, molecules, cells, multicelled organisms—were simply frozen bits of nuclear information. It seemed most logical that the behavior of human beings (including myself) might be explained and understood in terms of the characteristics of quarks.

It was delightful to discover Nobel Prize physicists discussing quarks in terms of charm, magnetic charge, strangeness, and *spin*—a new concept for psychology. The more I examined the implications of particle-spin for human meaning, the clearer it became that spin was a psychological idea whose time had come. Nuclear reactors and space technology had made us experientially aware that everything in nature, from galaxies to mesons to the drainage from your sink, is merrily revolving both around its own personal axis and in orbital paths around everything else.

For centuries, human beings had known that our planet rotates around its axis every 24 hours and around the sun one revolution per year. But not until recent satellite pictures could we "feel" the little sphere busily rotating from west to east. The amazing amount of survival data and evolutionary significance associated with East versus West orientation became a central theme of the next book in the Future History series.

The Intelligence Agents assembled data from many sources to orient the species to the importance of spin in preparing for the next stages of evolution. This volume carried the two preceding book–design experiments a step forward. By 1976, fewer Americans were getting survival information from books. Much more intelligence data was being transmitted in magazines—notoriously expensive and risky to publish. *The Intelligence Agents* was a successful attempt to publish a magazine in the guise of a book, or vice versa. Each chapter I wrote was designed to look like a magazine article written in the future by either a friend or an authority in the field. Also included were satirical porn-vignettes, advertisements, and sources of magazine-type illustrations.

Intelligence agents

Spinning Up the Genetic Highway

In terms of spherical geometry, the 30th to 45th degrees latitude (North and South) locate the runways along which gene-pools accelerate to Escape Velocity.

North-South is an Astro-Neurological constant based on magnetic charge; East-West, an Astro-Neurological constant based on spin. Rotational orientation relative to the home star determines the direction of Migrating Intelligence.

To experience the power of spin, imagine that you stand 50 miles (250,000 feet) high. Face west and sense the Earth moving you backwards. You would have to keep striding forward 1,000 miles an hour to keep the sun at the same angle—an easy stroll; 100 paces an hour would do it. Face east and feel that you are moving downward, pushed by spin-momentum, at 1,000 miles an hour. You are falling towards the sun, which will rise in front of you, below you.

Primitive organisms face the sun, ride passively towards the sun. More advanced organisms develop the mobility to chase the sun, to move against the rotational tide. When you greet the sun, after the night, you are facing Asia. The word *Asia* comes from Greek-Latin, "region of the rising sun"; *Europe* from Greek and Semitic, "land of the setting sun." When you face east, you are peering down into the past where our gene-pools came from. When you see the sun disappear over the horizon, you are looking up into the future. This basic attitudinal orientation based on spin is one of the fundamental define-characteristics of all energy structures.

The Hermetic Doctrine holds that what is so above, is so

below. Recapitulation theory holds that the same sequences re-evolve at all levels of energy. Neurologic thus leads us to expect *spin* to be a basic dimension of biological structure. To understand a terrestrial human, it is necessary to understand hir spin-caste, determined by how far west SHe and hir gene-pool have migrated—and at what speed.

Fore-Spin is moving west, pushing up against the rotation to develop mobility; to attain altitude. Moving into the future, ascending into empty ecological niches. Why was California explored and settled from Europe? Why didn't the wisdom of the East sail across the Pacific? Why today, in 1978, do the eastern countries compress into xenophobic centralized anthills, discouraging migration?

Because of *Back-Spin*—sitting, immobile, passively riding the down-wave. Occidental-orientation is actively pushing against rotation, continually being tested, shaped, formed by the airflow, your antennae continually probing forward for the next pathway opening up.

Only from post-terrestrial altitude can one realize that on a spinning sphere, against the spin is up. Turn a world map so that East is down. Then reexperience the long climb of humanity from East to West. The busy caravans shuttling up and down the Asian trade routes. The enormous ant-armies of Alexander overrunning the past (no worlds for him to conquer westward). Genghis Khan's fast-moving equine technology storming upward. The explosion of Muslim columns. Roman legions painfully pushing up into Gaul. Sense the movement of human swarms over the centuries—the empire-hives sending out the exploratory probes westward. For 1,000 years (A.D. 400–1400) the waves of mobile-elite sperm-eggs splashed up to the western-European beach-ledges and waited to scale the Atlantic Ocean—the greatest swarming phenomenon in human history! The port-cities of Cadiz, Lisbon, London teemed with migrants, explorers, space-travelers commanded by Genetic Directive to scale this mountain of water 3,000 miles high.

During the 10 centuries before Columbus, doughty Vikings and fervent Irish monks returned to tell the story of the new ecological niche. But the technology for lifting gene-pools into the unknown had not emerged. The Atlantic Ascent had to await the Protestant Reformation to free gene-pools from the Catholic-hive center. Only a society of self-actualized families, democratically linked together, was capable of pushing gene-pools into the storm altitudes of the North Atlantic.

A gene-pool is a species-unit capable of protecting its young over several generations. Marauding Francis Drakes and John Waynes and John Glenns are beginning probes, but nothing happens until the family units move together.

Genetic Intelligence is measured by the ability to move

gene-pools upward, angling always westward, pushing against, and being shaped, re-formed, activated, mutated by Spin-Pressure from the Future.

The Neurogeography of Terrestrial Politics

Terrestrial politics is based on mammalian competitions between neighboring hives that share the same neurotechnological level. Each quantum jump in neurotechnology increases the size of the political unit. Tribes are swallowed up by neighbors with superior artifacts. Higher-technology nations set up boundaries of greater extension. But China and Russia confront each other along a 3,000-mile border with the same nervous, bluffing postures of 4-footed mammals protecting turf.

Ideological differences are, of course, irrelevant. Neighboring gene-pools have to compete according to a relentless law of territorial (plus-minus) magnetism. To occupy any ecological niche is automatically to be "against" those who inhabit the neighboring one.

To illustrate the limbic (primitive-brain) nature of Old World politics in 1978, note that Morocco receives its arms from America; its neighbor, Algeria, obtains weapons from Russia. The border between the two neighbors is tense. The next country, Tunisia, receives arms from America and quarrels with both its leftist neighbors, Algeria and Libya. Poor confused Egypt, switched (in 1975–76) from Russia to America, but now manages to maintain hostile contact with both its neighbors—Libya and Israel, *regardless of ideology.*

Continuing down the zoo-cages of our animal past, note that with an amazing disregard for common sense or political principles, each country opposes its neighbors.

Such a renowned political theorist as Henry Kissinger was so totally robotized that he believed in the Domino Theory: If South Vietnam fell, then all the Southeast Asian nations would topple into monolithic communism. The paranoia completely disregarded the obvious. Once Saigon collapses, nature takes over! Cambodia attacks Vietnam, Vietnam raids Laos, Thailand snarls at Vietnam—and all Southeast Asian countries oppose their northern neighbor, China. Africa reveals the same confrontations. The political map of Africa conceals the fact that within countries arbitrarily defined by European colonists, tribal enmities rage on. Africa is a checkerboard of mammalian savagery. Ninety percent of African countries are ruled by assassins and military chiefs.

Until World War II, Europe was also a checkerboard of quarreling neighbors. The technological quantum-leap, which always increases the size of the gene-pool territory, forced a change. The Eastern Bloc nations were forced together into a monolith confronting the union of West European states. Border tensions no longer exist between nations but along the great East-West Iron Curtain. Note, also, that 90% of West European countries are ruled by elected representatives.

This North-South bifurcation of the genetic highway has produced a fascinating left-right division that perfectly parallels the cerebral hemispheric split. The "right-hand" northern countries developed logic, rationality, manipulation of artifacts and symbols. New technologies require harmonious collaboration. The energies of thousands must be linked up to maintain an automotive business or a Coca-Cola industry. Technology creates larger and more intelligent gene-colony units.

Why did the right-hand Europe develop the technology and carry the freedom-gene upward? Why did the left-hand Africa fail to produce mobility-freedom-gene-pools? Why did the genetic highway veer north instead of south when it burst out of the Middle East? Why did the northern Mediterranean centers—Greece, Rome, Venice, Paris, Madrid, Lisbon, London—light up in sequence?

Think of evolution as an ascent—literally a climb, a series of intelligence tests that activate the velocity-altitude-freedom circuits. From the Mid-East midbrain there are two pathways. The Arabs took the easiest, the southern route, slid off along the low road. Insectoid armies oozing from the east, sending soldiers and military bureaucrats.

The high-road North was a ladder to be scaled. Look at the map: first the Dardanelles to be crossed, then the prickly mountains of Greece, the fingered peninsulas, the Balkan mountains, the high Alps—rugged land, choked with geographic barriers offering refuge to ascending gene-pools. The story of evolution is the ascent of Celtic out-castes on the shoulders of the teeming Eastern autonomic-involuntary centers.

A glance at the map reminds us that the human race is exactly a competition of speed: small gene-pools racing to keep ahead of the engulfing wave of insectoid collectivism. Swarming pressures squirt small gene-pools into empty ecological niches where new realities (Plan-Its) can be created.

The issue is never in doubt, however. The primitive past lapping at the outskirts of the frontier is simply a signal to speed up. When Socialist-equality becomes dogma, genetic-elitism reappears among the Western out-castes, and new gene-pools assemble on the frontier outposts. Everyone on the frontier is self-selected for frontier behavior. The new ecological niche is always filled by those genetically templated for mobility, independence, and change. The ascent of gene-pools up the Atlantic was a gigantic genetic-selection process. Typically, each European gene-pool sent its best fertile stock. Once a beachhead had been established, more settled members of the gene-pools could follow. But in most cases, new gene-pools were formed by mutated migrants.

Structural and Temporal Castes in the Human Being

Caste Division is a most effective survival device. A species with caste differentiation and enculturation based on multistage imprinting (obvious examples: social insects and humans) divides its survival specialties, thus complexifying and expanding performance.

 Ethologists describe two forms of caste differentiation, structural and temporal. Structural caste is defined by genetic wiring: division into specialized functions (worker, warrior, drone, builder) that characterized hive organisms and civilized hum-ants. Structural caste in insects is easily identified by visible morphological (anatomical) differences. A drone bee looks different from a worker or queen. Highly complex neurological differences also characterize each insect hive. The nervous system of each juvenile worker-ant is imprinted with specific culture cues. But in humans, neurological differences are more important in determining the behavior of each caste. Genetic-anatomical templating produces involuntary-robot behaviors. Male and female is one structural caste difference. Big, muscled, hyperadrenalized aggressives are a separate caste—the warriors, the Amazons. Dainty, fragile, nurturant minister-types are a caste. Bobby Fischers, J. Edgar Hoovers, Bella Abzugs, and Marilyn Monroes are caste-exemplars. The caste distinctions are blatantly visible.

 But although these differences were taken for granted by earlier societies, discussion of genetic types is taboo among modern humans. Socialist countries forbid talk about genetic caste-differences because Marxism holds that society determines behavior. Western democracies deny caste differences because of commitment to equality. Revulsion against Nazi fanaticism also makes genetic caste discussions *verboten* among liberals—and most scientists are liberals. (It is interesting that uneducated, lower-class people readily accept the reality of racial and caste differences. Country bumpkins and illiterate farmers are aware of the effects of breeding.) Common sense suggests that new caste differences will emerge as *Homo sapiens* continues its accelerated evolution.

Temporal Caste refers to the process of maturation in which an individual metamorphoses from one form to another, performing different survival functions at each developmental stage.

In an anthill temporal casting assigns the young tasks of infant care. Slightly older ants are assigned housekeeping and hive-repair functions, metamorphosing into the more external functions of exploration, food-gathering, or warrior activity. An organism that has passed through temporal metamorphic sequences is simply more intelligent. Temporal caste means polyphase brain and thus multiple realities. The suckling infant is certainly a very different caste from the serious 10-year-old school child. The rock 'n' roll teenager is certainly a different caste than the tottering post-menopausal.

Until recently, our philosophers have been unable to understand temporal casting in humans—for very good genetic reasons. At each developmental stage, the individual must imprint the current hive reality for that stage. The infant is not concerned with teenage preoccupations. Each human accepts the reality of the current temporal stage hive-imprint, and almost totally represses the memory of previous stages. Senior citizens forget what it was like to be adolescents.

Think of the human gene-pool as a complex molecule that builds on new elements as it evolves. Temporal casting allows for temporal flexibility. Each generation is a wave moving through the gene-pool—contributing to the locomotion of the gene-pool through time. Does the Stage I suckling infant play a role in the human anthill? Oh yes! The infant's task is to trigger domestic responses in adults. The neonate performing its repertoire of activities is working just as hard as the auto worker or the dutiful parent.

If Mom's 11th brain is not cued by gurgles and cries, young Mother will be down at the dance hall swinging her hips—or horrors!—competing with men.

Thus the enormous neurogenetic significance of the Pill: An irresistible Women's Liberation Movement occurs one generation after voluntary birth control appears. Birth control is self-directed management of temporal caste sequence. Women can postpone Stage 11 matron-morality. The "youth-cult" which has produced middle-aged teeny boppers and married teamsters wearing Fonz hair styles is another by-product of the newly-won control of our neurogenetic brain sequences.

The school child (ages 5–11) plays a crucial role in keeping the educational industry going. The Teenager Caste plays a warrior role. Indeed, before 1960, every dictator knew how to keep restless students from rioting in the university—get them fighting on the border. In times of peace, urbanoid teenagers keep the police and the judiciary going. More than half of all reported crimes are committed by those under 18. Every caste has to be kept occupied. In "primitive" tribes, young children perform baby care. Older girls help with agriculture, older boys guard the flocks. Civilized society's technology and complex labor divisions have diminished the survival value of child-castes. Thus the elaborate extended education to prepare youngsters for warrior and post-warrior status.

The crucial scientific question is this: What are the stages of human evolution—both in the species and in the individual? Most human conflict and confusion could be sweetly solved if we understood that 92 percent of other human beings (and societies) are at developmental stages different from our own. To know all is to forgive all. We smile tolerantly at younger kids because we know we passed through those stages and that they will too.

A knowledge of human stages would allow us to smile at the hunter-gatherers in our society who expect welfare checks and are great at running and jumping; to tolerate the passionate, dramatic rhetoric of Mideastern midbrainers; to comfort domesticated parents worrying about their kids; to support advanced brain computer-electronic wizards who have activated brain circuits ahead of ours. The answer to all human problems is to recognize your genetic stage, go to the place where your genetic peers hang out, and in that secure place prepare yourself for the future stages inevitably awaiting you.

But first we need a scientific and psychologically convincing list of human states. This search must take into account the fact that for the last 5,000 years, the shrewdest ethologists and philosophers have been typecasting human behavior on the basis of extensive empirical evidence. These ancient classifications, which must have some validity, have produced the classic typologies of human castes—the 12 signs of the Zodiac, the 22 Tarot types, the 12 Graeco-Roman divinities—which clearly represent basic human modalities.

The Zodiac, for example, presents 12 survival tactics, each of which refers to a genetic technology and a development stage. Suppose we study the correspondences between the original sequence of the Zodiac and the stage of evolution which science defines for our species and us as individuals.

In the incoherent tangle of Zodiac ravings, we find three important items of neurogenetic wisdom:

Regular cycles influence neural development.

Each of us is controlled by rhythms we can decipher and harmonize with.

Each of us is born into a caste, or complex of castes, that we pass through as we mature.

To attempt correspondence between astrology and science is doubly risky. The scientists scornfully consider astrology as superstition. Astrologers prudishly resent scientists intruding on their symbols. But no matter. Let us assume for a moment that each of us represents one of the twelve intelligence-survival-solutions and each of us, in maturing, passes through and relives all twelve solutions. This clever tactic allows each of us to recapitulate evolution and to move ahead to create the future. Individual human beings evolve, stage by stage, as higher circuits of the CNS are activated. Our 24-calibre brain allows us to imprint (fabricate) temporal Realities available to every major life-form that has preceded us on the scene. We can creatively reimprint each of the 24 temporal realities.

The Twelve Primitive Reality Stages

Stage 1 (Receptive-dependent infant): Welcome to the planet. Your first assignment is to suck, float, turn your amoeboid receptors towards the warm breast and incorporate chemicals that will make you grow.

Stage 2 (Biting-squirming infant; 6 months): Now you can define yourself a self-mobile, incisive shark-like individual pushing towards and away from what you want to put in your baby mouth.

Stage 3 (Crawling Infant; one year): Hey, you made it to the shore-line-floor-line, ready to cut loose from Sea-Mother and slowly, steadily start to master gravity.

Stage 4 (Toddler; age 1–2 years): Congratulations! You can precariously stand up on your 2 legs and use your bipedal neurotechnology to scurry around like a clever, tricky rodent grabbing everything you can get your hands on when they're not looking.

Stage 5 (Territorial child; age 3–4): Oh ho! Now you're big and crafty enough to stake out and defend your little claim. Your crib, your doll, your room, your Mommy. Nervous, jumpy, possessive mammal. Feeling your size, especially with the littler ones. Just three years old and you're a mafia-capo, a treacherous lion, a power-jumpy Kissinger. More power to you, kid. Thanks for the smile.

Stage 6 (Show-off kid; age 3–4): Big deal, big shot. You've learned that gesture, grimace, cry, posture, exhibitionist noise can attract attention, signal your needs. You're talking, but it's monkey-

Zodiac Type	Speced Stage	Personal Stage	Tarot Card	I Ching Trigram	Greco-Roman Divinity	Ecological Niche
1. Pisces	Amoeboid	Sucking	Fool		Pluto-Proserpine	Water
2. Aries	Fish	Biting	Magus	Kun (Earth)	Neptune	Water
3. Taurus	Amphibian	Crawling	Empress		Ceres-Dionysus	Shoreline
4. Gemini	Rodent	Toddler	High Priestess		Hermes-Mercury	Low-land
5. Cancer	Carnivore	Territorial Kid	Emperor	Ch'en (Earthquake)	Vesta	High-land
6. Leo	Primate	Gesturing Kid	High Priest		Apollo	Trees
7. Virgo	Paleolith	Parroting Kid	Lovers		Diana	Caves
8. Libra	Neolith Metal-	Thinking Kid	Chariot	Kan (Toil)	Prometheus	Huts
9. Scorpio	age Tribal	Group (gang) Kid	Strength		Minerva	Village
10. Sagittarius	Feudal	Adolescent	Hermit		Mars-Venus	City
11. Capricorn	Home-owner Democracy	Adult—Parent	Wheel	Ken (Protec-tion)	Juno-Jupiter	Industrial society
12. Aquarius	Centralized State	Senior Citizen	Justice		Themis	Humanoid hive

Figure 10. The twelve primitive stages of personal and species evolution as listed and predicted by various ancient and scientific models.

noises and birdcalls. But it works, and you're pretty pleased with your power to communicate.

Stage 7 (Parroting mimicker; age 4–6): Now the fun begins: you learn word-magic. You catch on that you can speak or write certain words and, boy! something happens. You are now a six-year-old with the mind of a paleolith savage. You don't understand how or why, but the ritual action works. Most of the 20th-century humanity has remained at this pre-semantic level. At least 50 percent of Americans don't think for themselves; indeed they have been educated by society *not* to think for themselves, but to rote-learn and parrot.

Stage 8 (Thinking kid; age 6–8): You've learned how to use words as tools, rearrange them logically, invent new combinations, figure things out on your own. And think for yourself! As a seven-year-old, you have attained the mentality of a neolithic toolmaker.

Stage 9 (Group activity; age 9–12): Now you are learning how to play collaboratively, join groups, divide labor, take part in organized teams. You have reached the tribal level of species evolution. You are still a superstitious, treacherous savage, but you are on the way to becoming a civilized human-insectoid.

Stage 10 (Adolescent barbarian): Now you're really cooking. The sexual-courtship-mating circuits of your brain have been activated by RNA hormones. You're a teenage robot, obsessed with your identity.

You're romantic, intense, cruel, moody, emotional, fickle, not yet social-ized, wary, rebellious of those who wish to civilize you. And you love to laugh at the adults.

Stage 11 (Domesticated adult): Uh, oh. What happened? Suddenly you've been tamed. All at once, you of all people have become an adult. You've got a job, settled down, given up your wild, romantic dreams. The territorial circuits in your brain have been activated and you're a domesticated robot. You want to get a piece of turf, lock into a hive-task, be part of society and settle down. Build a little nest. Get married. The parenting instinct is going to lock you up. You are an adult.

Stage 12 (Senior citizen): Wow, where did it all go? It all spun by so fast. For twenty years you've been a parent-slave, obsessed with child-care, working, struggling to protect the young. Now they've grown and gone and the old energy juices aren't flowing. You've lost fire and vigor. You are no longer interested in change, competition. You sense aging, weakness approaching. You feel vulnerable and scared. You try to cling to the past, but it's all changing and you're not sure you like it. You can't protect yourself anymore. You look for security. You want a strong government, Social Security, and police-establishment to take care of you. You think you're gonna die.

This difference between *who you are* (basically, genetically) and *which temporal stage you are passing through* has always confused those who seek to explain human behavior.

You may be wired with a Stage-5 brain—possessive, control-ling, aggressive (society needs you for its protection). Or you may be wired with a romantic, flamboyant, intense Stage-10 brain. In either case, you go through the temporal stages. If your structural caste is 5, you may become a parent (Temporal Stage 11) and your parenting will be controlling. If you are Caste 10, when and if you become a parent you will raise your kids with a flashy, flirtatious style.

So far, this list of Temporal Stages of human life is fairly standard. But now we shall consider, possibly for the first time, a systematic prediction of twelve stages of human evolution to come! There have been sporadic previous attempts to forecast human devel-opment: the *Purgatorio* and *Paradisio* of Dante. Various utopian and science fiction writers have described their futique visions. (In particular, Robert Heinlein has constructed a Future History series.) But the next paragraphs present the first logical, empirical sequence of future steps; based on scientific facts and corresponding to sequences of ordinality presented in many philosophic systems of the past, including the I Ching, the Tarot-numeration, the Zodiac, Greco-Roman divinities, He-brew alphabet, as well as the ordination presented in the Periodic Table of Elements, the unfolding chronology of scientific and technological discoveries in neurology, biochemistry, microgenetics, and quantum physics.

A discussion of these future stages of our evolution will be found in the books *Exo-Psychology* and *Game of Life.* The latter book is entirely devoted to establishing the astonishing correspondence between the classic, occult sequences of ordination, the Mendeleyev Periodic Table, and the sequential unfolding of the post-Einsteinian sciences. In relating avant garde science to arcane, mystical techniques such as the Tarot, I Ching, Greco-Roman divinities, and the Zodiac, I was trying gamely to reassure the nonscientific traditionalists by relating their occult models to the novelties of science.

I hoped it would comfort astrologers and orientalists to learn that the ancient systems did, indeed, predict to the scientific future. This courtesy did not work. Most Tarot readers and zodiac experts were offended by the extension of their systems. They don't want to change. The reader will recall that at the outset of our researches in consciousness-expanding drugs we revised the Buddhist-Tibetan Book of the Dead and the *Tao Te Ching* and even the Catholic ritual of the mass to fit into modern brain-change. The experts in these fields tended to dismiss our bridging gestures as "sacrilege."

If scientists believe in the orderly evolution of knowledge, they, too, should be pleased to discover that the most up-to-date concepts of wholistic body consciousness, neuroelectronics, genetics-sociobiology, and quantum physics were anticipated, however, metaphorically, by the occult systems of the past.

The following list of prognostication is also immediately and practically applicable to your life. It sets up a specific sequence of self-growth. This is, therefore, the first program of individual development to specify how the intelligent human can follow a schedule of inner development correlating with the astonishing and liberating advances in external science.

Now that we have mastered those first twelve primitive, survival techniques and can handle 20th-century social realities, we are ready to pass through the steps of post-cultural, post-bureaucratic, self-confident, self-contained self-direction.

Twelve Future Stages of Post-Cultural Evolution

Stage 13 (Hedonic consumer): Your ability to avoid, compassionately and humorously, the limits of your social-hive, allows you to define

Figure 11. The twelve future, post-cultural stages of personal and species evolution.

	Zodiac Type	Specied Stage	Personal Stage	Tarot Card	I Ching Trigram	Gredoi Roman Divinity	Ecological Niche
13.	Pisces II	Hedonic Consumer	Me-generation	Hanging Man		Tethys	Receptive Body
14.	Aries II	Hedonic Engineer	Body Intelligence	Death	Tui (Joyous Lake)	Oceanus	Self-managed Body
15.	Taurus II	Tantric Union	Hedonic Link-up	Temperance		Rhea	Body Fusion
16.	Gemini II	Neuro-electronic Consumer	Neural Self-Indulgence	Devil		Theia	Receptive, Post-hive Brain
17.	Cancer II	Neuro-electronic Intelligence	Brain Wizard	Tower	Li (Fire)	Cronus	Brain-computer Link-up
18.	Leo II	Fusion with Other Brains	Synergic Mind-link	Star		Hyperion	Space Colonies
19.	Virgo II	Genetic Consumer	Sperm Intelligence	Moon		Phoebe	RNA-DNA
20.	Libra II	Genetic Intelligence	Egg Wisdom	Sun	Sun (Wind)	Mnemosyne	Genetic Engineering
21.	Scorpio II	Genetic Symbiosis	DNA Linkage	Judgement		Crius	New Species Moving Through Galaxy
22.	Sagittarius II	Quantum Consumer	Singularity	no card		Coeus	Moving to Galaxy Center
23.	Capricorn II	Quantum Intelligence	Gravitational Engineer	Universe	Chien (Cre-ative-Heaven)	Iapetus	Moving to Galaxy Center
24.	Aquarius II	Neuro-atomic Fusion	Absorbtion in Black Whole	no card		Themis	Center of Galaxy

yourself as an aesthetic consumer. Your body belongs to you. You must learn to relax, transcend the guilty-pessimism of prescientific religions, become a sensually receptive, artistically indolent, passively-hip pleasure-lover. Rejoice in your ability to live as an esthetic dilettante, a neurological gourmet, a happy-go-lucky nigger-hippie, wandering through the Judeo-Christian garden of eden.

Now you must resist 2,000 years of grim pressure to make you into a slave of society. Hedonic consumerism is a stage you are going through. Like sucking infancy, like careless adolescence. You are not going to remain at this level forever. But you must master the sensual, erotic instruments of your body, use your sensorium as a complex mosaic of rapture, understand how to indulge and pleasure yourself.

Then, when you are clever enough, and diligent enough to get your sensory-somatic scene together, you can advance to:

Stage 14 (Hedonic artist): This next step is simple and playful. You have taken the great, basic step by freeing yourself from the hive-morality of submission-suffering. Now you start creating an esthetic environment around you. You will have lots of help. There are thousands of texts, manuals, courses, teachers to assist you, to offer leads and methods. The only danger is that you might get caught in one style. In your liberated exuberance, you may sign up too quickly in one mode of self-actualization. Scout out the field. For thousands of years the most intelligent, free, strong people have been fabricating personal esthetic realities. Don't fall for the first neighborhood master. Remember, to keep developing in the future, there is only one trap to avoid: loss of faith in yourself, your own tough, innocent, potential to grow.

You will learn to make your life a work of art, a quiet, smiling dance of growing beauty. There is no hurry. Each esthetic yoga takes time—the complexity of your somatic and neural equipment is infinite and unique. Also, as you continue to evolve, you will constantly add to your esthetic style. Indeed, each stage beyond simple Esthetic Mastery requires that you go back and improve, simplify, complicate your growing singularity.

Stage 15 (Esthetic linkage): After you have located the source of virtue and pleasure within yourself and learned how to create external projections of your inner style, you are ready to take the next logical step in personal development. Link up with another or others.

At this point we can look back and see that the Consciousness movements of the 1960's brought millions of Americans and Western Europeans through Stages 13 and 14. If you remain at Stage 13, you're a lazy hippie. If you remain in lonely splendor at Stage 14, a narcissist. Both are steps to pass through. The inclination to club, to fuse, to link-up with others who share your esthetic style is the obvious progression. Symbiosis, grouping is the way that isolated DNA organisms formed the first cells. Social grouping led us from the caves to a new order—linkage based not just on economics or territorial defense but for shared esthetic vision. A new social connection of free, confident individuals whose aim is to enhance personal growth, to stimulate in each other inner development, to turn each other on, to add to each other's hedonic progress.

The ancient name for this stage is tantra, fusion of the erotic-spiritual-psychological. Usually this occurs *au pair*—two enlightened people discover that one-times-one equals infinity. Often larger groups assemble for esthetic-lifestyle sharing: communes, intentional communities, esthetic groups who work-play together around a common artistic task.

The stages to come make great demands upon one's strength and confidence. It is almost impossible to maintain a solitary life of continual mutation-metamorphosis. The support and balance and broadened perspective of the shared-voyage require conscious fusion. These linkages need not be possessive. Often two or more people join, exchange the energy-insight needed to master the stage and then, lovingly, part to explore varied new realms of the future.

Stage 16 (Neurological-electronic consumer): At rare and wonderful times in human history, societies have emerged affluent-secure enough to allow certain intelligent individuals the freedom to explore the three stages just described. The history of art and civilization is the story of what can be done with the body, its sense-organs, and musculature. Lucky you! You're living in the greatest electric-brain boom of all time.

Since World War II an entirely new dimension of human neurotechnology has developed. Radio, television, high-fidelity reception, high-speed calculators and computers have activated dramatically and advanced your brain-response—accelerated and expanded the scope of your reception, integration, and transmission of signals. The suburban child of five has experienced a million times more realities than the most educated-traveled aristocrat before 1940. The revolutionary advances in transportation, including extraterrestrial rocketry, have also stretched human neurology.

The sudden explosion of brain-activating drugs in the 1960's is a natural consequence of this neuroelectronic information processing. While around four percent of those growing up in our electronic computer culture are genetically equipped with brains that can instinctively harmonize with accelerated computer rhythms, the rest of us require chemical assistance, a brain-activating drug which will free our brains to move at the speed and breadth of the information presented by electronic devices. We need neuro-acceleration aids to keep up with the computer whiz kids.

During the sixties, millions of people ingested brain-accelerating drugs and exposed themselves to mind-blowing audio-visual overloads. This *wow* produced a now-generation of passive neuroelectronic consumers who grooved on the McLuhan multiplicity, *2001* Space Odysseys, who saw protean realities flash on their cerebral projectors, but could not make it work in our own lives. Thus the great retreat back to hot-tub, wholistic hedonism.

But we didn't quit, did we? We were just taking a Me-generation breather. We haven't come this far to spend the rest of our lives as spectators of the cosmo-genetic moving-picture show. So we mutated to . . .

Stage 17 (Neuro-electronic artist): Hey, hurray! We've sudden-ly realized that the universe is not a heavy, gravitational mosaic of stellar-stones or solar-fusion-furnaces, but a web of radiant information. $E=mc^2$; and Energy is not Newtonian force-work, but bits of fast-moving decipherable intelligence. Reality is moving pictures filtered through a wide-lens brain, and God (i.e., you) directs the action, writes the script, selects the locations, casts the players, arranges the distribu-tion and promotion.

The successful consumer of external electronics (TV) and internal signaling (acid) is no longer satisfied to be a passive recipient. To evolve in harmony with the times, we must learn how to master the fast-moving equipment—neuro-computers actively assessing the librar-ies of the world, transmitting via home video, playing complex computer games, using bio-feedback circuitry, accelerating our brains to faster rhythms.

We must all become Cronkites and Coppolas. These days there are swarms of Tesla-type "idiot savants" and 17th-stage, 21st-century brains popping up, producing amazing advanced, futique neurological tools. Let's use them.

Stage 18 (Neuro-electronic linkage): And once we start man-aging high-speed information transmitters, we are free from our land-locked, terrestrial status. Now that intelligence (not fire-power, man-power, land-power) is the key to survival, we are ready to leave the surface of the planet and move into high-orbit. Our species could not have reached the moon if we did not have mastery of long-distance, high-speed communication. The landlocked social groupings to defend turf or to control natural resources are no longer relevant once we have access to unlimited space and the natural resources of the moon and asteroid belt.

Intelligence is high-speed communication and transportation which allows us to form more efficient linkages with others of our kind. This is a definition of love. High fidelity fusion. Aren't we wonderful!

Stage 19 (Genetic consumerism; sperm intelligence): Ever since the first neolithic agricultural settlements we have understood the importance of breeding to produce desired life forms. It was the herdsman tribes which developed the first moralities and social structures based on kinship, protection by males of the egg-supply of the tribe.

For millennia humans have manipulated sperm-egg exchanges to protect and control. Not only our sexual mores but even our theories of evolution have been based on grabbing egg-supplies. The Darwinian theories of evolution suggest that male competition for breeding dominance was the mechanism of evolution. Natural selection is a concept of genetic consumerism; take what is there.

The deciphering of the DNA code (which occurred exactly at the time when physics decoded the atom, pharmacologists decoded and synthesized brain chemicals, and electronic information-processing emerged on the scene) initiated the era of Genetic Consciousness. The Biological Revolution! Like jubilant adolescent schoolboys, our scientists started recombining DNA strands, cloning, histocompatibility typing, developing DNA repair techniques. Whoops. By reshuffling the chromosomes we can select the new species that we desire. Most exciting is the probability, indeed, the inevitability, that we can decipher the aging sequences and inoculate ourselves against aging and death.

Consumer access to DNA is the ultimate dream of primitive human life. We have attained the status of the Old Testament God-the-Father, the immortal creator and controller of life. Welcome to the club.

Stage 20 (Genetic intelligence; egg wisdom): But wait a moment. In our enthusiasm to breed our animals, manage our family gene-pool, manipulate the codes of life, we have made that same classic consumer error—which we committed when we accepted word magic, feudal power, body rapture, and electronic passivity. Sperm intelligence is a stage through which we must joyfully pass. The next step in our development is to realize that there is a biological wisdom that fabricated DNA, that designed us so that we could become smart enough to decipher the code.

Here we return to the pre-urban, pagan wisdom that recognized that there is a genetic intelligence that provided us with the DNA toys with which we play. Scientific paganism, a worshipful respect for biological intelligence, for the Gaia principle which we are now coming to specify and understand.

We discover that this green, lush planet, protected all comfy and cozy like a cotton womb, with exactly the right temperature and atmosphere and the flow of chemicals arriving exactly where they are needed for DNA to build bodies, is not an inexplicable accident. A wonderful intelligence has been at work to terraform a rocky lunar-like sphere into a Garden of Life.

Gaia scientists like Lovelock and Margulis have demonstrated that there is one DNA tree of life which operates basically at the unicellular level and which constructs larger organisms as transportation organs to move cells and chemicals around. Whoops, what's happened? We suddenly realize that we humans are not Father Gods, but humble and grateful agents of the great Life Web. We are in the wonderful position of being the nervous system of the Biological Energy. SHe sees what SHe is doing across the galaxy and around the planet through our eyes. We are Hir chauffeur-pilots. We get to look at the maps of Hir continual expansion and to share Hir delight in the endless variety of Hir beautiful forms.

Now isn't that the best job we've ever been offered? Conscious Evolutionary Agent! Isn't that the best role we have been cast for in any of the philosophic scenarios? And it's all based on up-to-date evolutionary science!

Stage 21 (Genetic symbiosis; DNA linkage): After we got control of our bodies, we linked-up and got access to our brains. After we got control of our brains, we linked-up and got access to DNA. Now that we understand our genetic function, we can and must link up to continue the process of our own evolution. Symbiosis is the secret of life. Each single cell is the clubbing of at least three separate DNA species who form cooperative arrangements to construct and maintain that incredible urban complexity—the single cell. The logical momentum of our journey so far and our scientific knowledge of how DNA operates leads us to the conviction that symbiosis, at the DNA level, is an inevitable step in our growth.

I have felt comfortable and clear about the first 20 stages of evolution presented in this book because I have experienced them and science has confirmed my intuitions. But DNA symbiosis is a stage which I have not reached yet and which our geneticists have not worked out yet. In preparing myself for this wonderfully loving step, I have tried to open myself up to unicellular wisdom and DNA collaboration. I have exposed myself, cautiously, to the widest range of geographical, biochemical, interpersonal environments. I have seen every disease, every evil, every taboo, every danger as a form of Hir creativity to be allowed warily, affectionately within my body-brain envelope, so that I can be inoculated and immunized by what my previous ignorance led me to fear or avoid or destroy.

I carry around in my body-brain, and probably in my DNA, a little piece of these alien DNA strands. And I await the discoveries of the geneticists which will teach us how to increase our symbiotic ability. Is this not the love of all life?

Stage 22 (Quantum consumer): Here, and in the two stages to come, we are beyond the objective knowledge of our species; but we can resonate in harmony with the best speculations of our boldest and smartest minds—the quantum physicists. Quarks are probably cluster-clouds of information bits defined by the basic coordinates of particles moving through space/time. Of these our material world is made: and can be remade by us. Quantum consumerism is the heady discovery of Heisenberg Determinacy—our brains define the basic nature of nuclear reality.

Stage 23 (Quantum intelligence; gravitational engineer): Our nuclear fusion physicists have created small stars. Our astronomers and gravitational physicists have detected Black Holes. Our mathematicians have produced equations for fabricating the universe, manipulating fusion and black hole energies. We await with interest the discoveries and technologies which will allow direct translation of our biological-neural equipment to nuclear-atomic form.

Stage 24 (Neuro-atomic fusion): And when we have defined and translated ourselves into basic particle form we shall link with other like quantum minds in a wonderful, totally revelatory, celebratory fusion. We look forward with delight to that which awaits us on the other side of the Gravitational Gate. What a wonderful universe we are part of!

Evolutionary Agents working the frontiers of human hives inevitably make temporary alliances with groups of "outsiders" struggling to present or defend a necessary caste against the disapproval of the gene-pool's conservative inertia.

Thus during the 33 years this book covers, it was necessary for me to ally with psychologists against medical psychiatrists, with humanist psychologists against impersonal-experimentalists, with dopers against the police, with leftist militants against Nixon, with Black Panthers against the FBI, with scientists against liberals, with space advocates against Naderites, with geneticists against leftists, with longhairs against the crewcuts, then with Beverly Hills razor-cuts against the indolent hippies; always, always, with the Egg Trust against the Sperm Bank.

The reason for this continual shifting of alliances is built into the nature of the change system. The Intelligence Agent is concerned in the process of continual change. The outcaste groups with which SHe collaborates want, of course, to get inside, become respectable, and push everyone else around.

During the 1970's, the outcaste group that stirred up the most scandal, shock, and subversion of hive morals was the homosexual. Like other repressed minorities that preceded them, the gays began to stand up, flex proud muscles, and rock the gene-ship. The same street-corner newspaper racks that in the past vended hippie-underground papers and Black Panther and radical pressings now presented the new alternate-lifestyle newspapers. Gays were the embattled outcaste heroes.

Thus I was not surprised when Dean Gengle, brilliant, satirical columnist for the gay paper *Advocate,* asked me for an in-depth interview. Those who have played the media game know that an interview can never be better than the interviewer. Dean Gengle's high-altitude questions taught me a lot (always the hope of the interviewee) and produced a burst of survival information not often found vended in the machines along Santa Monica Boulevard.

Socio-biological musings

(The physical setting is Leary's writing refuge in West Hollywood. Leary went over the transcript to clarify the vocal transmissions. It is quite simple to enter Leary's model. It is quite another thing to try to leave, once it's been entered.)

The paradox: You can only begin to de-robotize yourself to the extent that you know how totally you're automated. The more you understand your robothood, the freer you are from it. I sometimes ask people, "What percentage of your behavior is robot?" The average hip, sophisticated person will say, "Oh, 50%." Total robots in the group will immediately say, "None of my behavior is robotized." My own answer is that I'm 99.999999% robot. But the .000001 percent non-robot is the source of self-actualization, the inner-soul-gyroscope of self-control and responsibility.

Of course, there's paradox at every single level of this genetic enterprise. The more freedom you have, the more responsible you have to be. The higher you go, the more precise your navigation must be. I am totally committed to doing something about my own robothood and the robothood of those around me, sending out signals that will activate singularity.

If you're really interested in the mutational sequence of ideas and how they're passed on, old ideas can be fun. For example, in 600 B.C. Buddha was saying things that were as far as you could go in the caste society he came from. His nervous system had advanced 7 or 8 circuits ahead of his times. He simply could not communicate more precisely because he didn't have the technology.

We can be intelligently conscious only in terms of the technologies that we have externalized. Our machines become the metaphors for understanding and getting control of our bodies and brains. Once atomic particles and electronics were discovered, it became possible to apply the Buddhist metaphors.

Well, then, how does de-robotization take place?

Simple: You migrate to ecological niches where the genetically selected Intelligence Increasers are found. If you are an emerging butterfly, locate the members of your species and hang out with them.

How about simply establishing communication with those persons exhibiting the clearest and most intelligent signals then apparent to you?

That gets complicated, though, because we are at different stages. Fifty percent of Americans are basically Paleolithic. They believe in repetitious magic. If you gave the "average American" total political power, (s)he'd act like Idi Amin. What sense does democracy make if all members of society are robots from different genetic castes? Each gene-pool produces, just as in a termite colony, exactly the number of caste-workers needed to perform survival functions, which keep changing.

If there's a war and a lot of warrior ants are killed, the queen will produce nothing but warrior ants to balance the colony. Each gene-pool has to produce its warriors, its diggers, its teachers, its artists. If you don't see that *all* castes are necessary to the whole, it's because you're caught in chauvinisms—the equivalent of worker ants scorning warrior ants.

Since homosexuality has always been a part of every society, you have to assume that there is something necessary, correct and valid—genetically *natural*—about it.

How do you respond when people accuse you of reductionism, as some accuse the socio-biologist point of view?

In chemistry, you have to study the basic elements before you can get the right combinations to create the forms that you want. You are not imposing on the chemicals anything that they don't want. Hydrogen is down there, just ready to start making it with oxygen. Sodium is begging to date chloride. In order to understand the synergy, you have to reduce and reduce, but there's no ultimate essence. Even in the nucleus of the atom, you are confronted with unique complexities.

Don't you worry when you contemplate the human condition?

I'm delighted at the way things are unfolding. Relax. Evolution is working out on this planet exactly the way it is supposed to. Anyone living today is being hurtled through a remarkable historical sequence of changes. The fact that anyone has survived these mutations is a ringing endorsement of DNA. So it makes me smile when anyone starts to come on with this worry and danger stuff.

Might there be "cosmic abortion" of larvals that simply didn't get to the point where they could migrate off the planet's surface? Why must we assume that all such organisms survive to term?

There is one life-organism on this planet, Gaia. Its shape is spherical: a scum-film on a round rock. Its very clear aim is to incubate itself and slide over the entire planet, both watery and terrestrial; and to continue to push up and out like a vegetative thing. The whole human species gene-pool represents the neurological aspects of the biosphere. Can this planetary/spherical biointelligence, called Gaia, make "mistakes" so that one part of it can destroy the rest or abort the whole process? Anyone preaching danger, human error, or ecological naughtiness is talking about him- or herself. Gaia is foolproof.

Personal philosophies concerned with mortality, failure, wickedness, lead to generalized projections of doom because each society senses that it is outmoded. The Ayatollah Khomeini and Ronald Reagan are old men who know their way of life is over. Each society creates agents who jump ship and create new gene-pools. The future is fearful and gloomy only if you are committed to the *current* social structure. I'm robot-wired to explore better ways of ship-jumping to carry the Celtic genes into the future.

This leads to continual accusations of treason and betrayal from frightened members of the old gene-pools. My poor, dear Mother didn't understand the very different future into which I was carrying her seed. That's the poignant chagrin: the change-agent helps a genetic jump to the next point, and then evolution moves beyond. My grandfathers moved my seed from Irish medieval bogs to Western Massachusetts. My mother rooted. I continued the migration.

I'm interested in those "quantum jumps" in evolutionary intelligence.

Anything written before the last two or three years, did not include the Gaia hypothesis atmosphere; unified life-intelligence of which species are simply robot sperm-egg vessels. There is an irreversible logic, a predictable sequence, and a navigational direction to this life-intelligence, and the more you understand its basic principles and rhythms, the better you feel about the whole life situation. You can worry about your own personal situation, sure—and to the extent that you're a hive-centrist rather than a hive-outcaste futurist, you've got a lot to worry about.

For 3,000 years, our most intelligent stoics believed that their social system, therefore everything, was doomed. "All we can do," they said, "is keep our ship going for another generation." Doom/gloom is honorable and genetically necessary. To keep a gene-pool surviving in the present, you have to have a lot of heavy-duty stoics who oppose changes.

Everything's going exactly according to plan. Hitler and Stalin were important warning signals that everybody picked up. Hiroshima/Nagasaki ended mammalian territorial warfare on a mass scale, didn't it?

So far.

Why has talking about mind-altering psychedelics become a new cultural taboo?

Taboos are the most fascinating issues in any gene-pool. If you visit another society, you ask, "What are the taboos?" and you locate the genetic tension between the future and the past. Future realities interface with present and past realities at the taboo. Cannibalism, for example, is a taboo against the past. The taboo about LSD wards off the future. It concerns self-directed tampering with your own neurology.

Well, space colonization isn't taboo, yet. In an article in Mother Jones, *the author states: "Turning to space seems a way of not solving a problem, but evading one."*

I'm bored with talking about space colonies, just as in 1965 I got bored talking about the marijuana legalization. You simply have to wait around until the present left-wing welfare establishment pisses off. The stay-down-here-and-suffer-equally people can't see that migration is always the way to solve survival problems. So we just sit here marking time until space opens up.

We're being squeezed into space by some genetic imperative, the need to establish new ecological niches for cultural plurality, new solutions, new technologies, lifestyle plurality, consciousness diversification. For example, in 25 years we could have miniworlds in space made up of just bisexual vegetarians. They can do what they want in their world. That's what evolution is all about—new ecological niches to try our new lifestyles, being smart enough to migrate and not fight. For those who want to change, there will be *many* worlds of bisexual vegetarians, voting about nudism versus glitter. And *their* new outcastes will migrate.

What might be the neurogenetically programmed function(s) of gay people?

Well, I think they play caste roles in fashion, communication, and outcaste perspectives. Obviously, the gay caste is going to be pushed out of the center of that domesticated nuclear family. They're simply more sophisticated in picking up nonverbal signals, signs, symbols, in seeing through the limitations and vulgarities of the dominant species. So they're going to be the sharpest critics, the best observers. A domesticated father-robot simply isn't going to be looking ahead into the future and predicting alternative societies. On the other hand, you have to understand the irritation of domesticated robots who see this "gay" minority dancing around, heating up the sexual situation with all sorts of campy new twists and making fun of the domesticated. No wonder the poor Anita Bryant types are pissed off.

But all these cultural frictions will disappear when Space Migration allows different castes to build different social realities. Abortion, for example, always becomes an issue just before migration to a new ecological niche. When a territory is underpopulated, DNA turns up the baby-dial. When a niche is overpopulated, DNA turns down the egg-machine and switches on the restless migration buttons. Abortion is unnecessary when we have unlimited real estate in High Orbital Mini-Earths. If you can live for 500 years and build thousands of Plan-Its to fill with people, then no one will mind taking off a century or two to breed 25 kids. More gay people will become wonderful parents when we realize parenthood is a very demanding but brief sequence to pass through.

Cloning is another taboo, scary to terrestrials crowded together on an overpopulated planet. But with unlimited HOME's being built, cloning will be a natural technique.

Nuclear energy is another controversial issue. As soon as solar-satellite power stations start beaming down energy, nukes won't be needed within the atmosphere of the womb-planet. But nukes are needed in high orbit. All taboo controversies occur at the interface of change.

The gay controversy heats up now at a period of pre-migration swarming. It is a temporary problem. When we can live for 500 years, kids will grow up knowing that they have endless options for future worlds.

You see, all terrestrials are basically unhappy because we know we are trapped on a prison planet with a short life-span. This tends to make us grumpy, chauvinistic, fearful of change and suspicious of differences. When we live long enough to build and inhabit many different Plan-Its, these new options will ease the horrible terrestrial depressions.

It would seem we are nearing the point where we will be able to alter the DNA code itself.

Well, to the extent that we can alter DNA, we are preprogrammed by DNA to alter it. DNA monitors what happens to it. It's like the center of the midbrain, which is supposed to keep the body temperature at 98.6 degrees. Built-in protection mechanisms assure that as soon as the temperature gets too high, a series of operations go into effect to bring it back down again.

No group of humans can interfere with a 3-billion-year evolutionary process. The system can break down at the individual level, but that doesn't mean that the DNA design is in any way invalidated. As a matter of fact, even that breakdown is anticipated. Every entity with the illusion of individuality and free choice can break *itself* down. The option of individual error is not a problem of free will or determinism, it's both.

However, the strategy of DNA is continually to activate stages prematurely in a few individuals. Different organisms, or different people, can have future brain circuits activated way ahead of current technology. This accounts for the extraordinary variety of human nervous systems within human society. So it's possible that if you know the fixed, predictable sequence of evolution, you can locate your own gene-pool in the time context.

Also, every gene-pool or species is a conglomerate mixture of what you'd call the central tendency of the species, plus a lot of the past and some of the future built within it. Consider the American gene-pool just for illustration. I estimate the American gene-pool is now perhaps 50 percent Paleolithic or more primitive. Although the average American is a Paleolithic caveman, monster, the society is happily run by castes more advanced than that. Why? Because the more advanced levels are smarter and can get the powers of transportation and communication.

In other words, they can understand how the system works and thereby get to whatever level they aspire to—depending on real understanding, of course.

Well, they're one or two steps ahead of the past. The politicians and bureaucrats who shuffle symbols are one step ahead of the average American, who, if you let hir, would just go out and kill and loot and rape. So there is that thin veneer of neurogenetic intelligence that guides gene colonies into the future.

Kind of like the guidance and control system?

That's right. I call the guidance and control center of the gene-pool the DOM species. Now ahead of the DOM species, there's a predictable, layered sequence of futique species who are in competition to see which way they are going to move the sperm-egg ship next. And always making up the mass of the gene pool are the swarming neolithic and paleolithic and primate humans who give the biological motive power to the crafts and keep them going. They're the worker ants, the warrior ants.

No matter how advanced, you have in your nervous system the Paleolithic, the primate, the barbarian. So I'm not talking about an elitist "us" against an animalistic "them"—each of us has the whole sequence in our own nervous system. You have to make honest peace with your own reptilian and Paleolithic centers before you can activate future circuits in yourself or signal the realities of those behind or ahead of you.

I *intend* to sound cold-blooded and impersonal and inhuman. The paradox is this: Your compassion, empathy, and identification with any other form of life depend entirely upon your neurogenetic ability to maintain this evolutionary perspective.

You have to be ultimately inhuman, post-human, to have a

shred of intelligent compassion for the freakiness of other human beings. Another paradox is that you can only be as futique and post-terrestrial as you have been successful in dealing with past terrestrial realities. In prison for four years, I had to learn how to master the mammalian savageries that I floated above as a Harvard professor.

How far into the future have you intuited?

It's easy to see into the future. Simply find the futique robots that every gene-pool is throwing up. California is swarming with futique prophets. On the other hand, you can move into the future only as far as you have successfully mastered the past. Nervous systems activated to future realities 5 or 6 jumps ahead are in danger of losing touch with the present. Sometimes they can't manage an intelligent sexual encounter or even make a living. So it's not just how far into the future you can see, it's how much future can you practically harness to the survival issues in your life right now?

Would it be useful to say that each human plays the part of a mobile neuron in this emerging organism identified as Gaia?

Exactly. You can also say that a gene-pool is a plexus of neurons, that a solar system is a neural circuit. As long as we operate with brains, there's no way that our understanding of the universe can be anything but neurological. We are both limited by and guided by our brain; the brain is always the observational platform from which these maps are being drawn.

How do you keep yourself open to a continual updating?

It becomes a neurological habit after a while. I'm a genetic robot: I was programmed to be changeable, which has its risks as well as its advantages.

EPILOGUE

(Scientific superstars)

Every branch of science currently is exploding with theories, techniques, and discoveries that dramatically change our concepts of the universe. I hope that by writing this PR puff for scientific intelligence, I can contribute to the recognition of those upon whom our future rests. Because the grim bottom line is this: Science and only science can solve the problems of the past and produce the improved future.

Let's put it bluntly: Scientists should stop shirking their responsibility and take charge of human affairs. When we were territorial primates we were naturally led by barnyard politicians. We now understand that spaceship Earth is a delicate, complex web of energy processes that must be understood and harmonized if we are to survive. Politics has become too important to be left to politicians who cannot and will not comprehend the situation. Our rulers in the future must be people with scientific training and with brains wired to handle relativistic complexity. We would not let the controls of a 747 fall into the hands of congressmen. Our officials should be selected the way our athletic teams are chosen—on the basis of recorded performance, of demonstrated excellence.

As a modest step in the process of intelligence increase, I nominate for adulation, acclaim, stardom, the following scientists who have recently overturned stupifying taboos of the past:

1. The Self-Organizing-Dissipative-Structure Theory of Ilya Prigogine

Ready for another Einstein? Well here's a Nobel-prize-winning chemist who has freed us from the death sentence implied in the Second Law of Thermodynamics.

The task of presenting Prigogine to the nonscientific community was begun by Marilyn Ferguson. Here is her summary of Prigogine:

> *How did life develop in a universe of ever-increasing disorder? How do order and complexity emerge from entropy? Now Ilya Prigogine, a physical chemist, offers a startling explanation, complete with mathematical proofs: Order emerges because of entropy, not despite it!*
>
> *Open systems, in which a structure exchanges energy with the surrounding environment are what he calls "dissipative structures." Their form or pattern is self-organizing, maintained by a continuous dynamic flow.*
>
> *The more complex such a structure, the more energy it must dissipate to maintain all that complexity. This flux of energy makes the system highly unstable, subject to internal fluctuations—and sudden change. If these fluctuations, or perturbations, reach a critical size, they are amplified by the system's many connections and can drive the whole system into a new state—even more ordered, coherent and connected. With each new state, there is greater potential for change. With new levels of complexity, there are new rules. As Prigogine puts it, there is a change in the nature of the "laws" of nature.*

Brain-Mind Bulletin. May 21, 1979

By showing how complex systems can arise from less complex ones, he helps bridge the gap between biology and physics, a contribution towards the unified field theory that Einstein sought vainly to find in his equations.

2. Neil Goodman and the Self-Deterministic Narcissism of Quantum Physics

Most 19th-century physicists were highly conventional thinkers living in and influenced by Judeo-Christian monotheism: the barbarous notion that there is One-and-Only-One-God (a male, of course) who made the universe and rules over it like a Middle-Eastern sultan. God, or some other grim lawmaker, had fabricated the universe out there. All that "mankind" could do was to decipher, step by step, what was already writ, passively examining the entrails of birds, performing scholastic translations of the great text of nature.

The problem with this servile approach to knowledge is that

many different groups arise, each claiming to represent the One-and-Only, each demanding the right to destroy all others as heretics. Monotheists love ominous terms such as "external laws," "laws of nature."

Quantum physics has changed all that. The philosophic implications of multiple realities have been thoughtfully discussed by J. A. Wheeler ("the universe is preselected by consciousness"), Nobel laureates Eugene Wigner and Brian Josephson ("consciousness is at the root of the quantum principle from which space-time-mass arise as secondary structures"), and Jack Sarfatti ("the physicist is an artist who molds atomic reality with the aesthetic integrity of his intention"). Popular books by Fritjof Capra and Gary Zukav have demonstrated the correspondence between ancient Oriental philosophies, especially Zen, and the flux of quantum physics.

The most probing examination of the implications of multiple-reality determinism has been provided by Harvard philosopher Neil Goodman.

> *"From Goodman's perspective, it . . . makes more sense to think of various characterizations of reality that might be presented in words, pictures, diagrams, logical propositions, or even in musical compositions. Each symbol system captures different kinds of information and hence presents different versions of reality.*
>
> *"In Goodman's view, works of art (like the models of physicists) can also be profitable viewed as samples. Just as certain fabric swatches accurately reflect the whole bolt, so may certain works of art accurately reflect . . . important forms, feelings, affinities, and contrasts from the fabric of life."*

The above quotes are from an article by Howard Gardner, a Harvard psychologist.

3. The New Generation of Brain-Drug Researchers

Custodians of public morality denounce all drugs as "escapes." From their standpoint, they are correct. The Russians and Irish spend over a third of their income on strong alcohols to escape brutal reality. Moral custodians fail to understand that personal subjective realities are in many cases superior to the grim social rigidities. The freer, the richer, the higher the quality of life, the more technologically advanced the culture, the more varied the brain-drug options available. In China there is no drug problem because there is no "problem" of individuality, or creative dissent. In sophisticated centers where intelligent, creative, innovative people swarm together, you will find a gourmet range of botanicals and chemicals that activate the widest scope of brain circuits.

Today, the average suburban 18-year-old knows more about the brain-drug option than the most sophisticated scientists did twenty years ago. More and more people are using more drugs with less furor and confusion and accident. The next rational step is to improve the chemicals so that they are safer and more efficient, more precise in duration, and brain-function activated.

A new breed of psychopharmacologists is producing new drugs that will provide the individual with fingertip access to and control of his own nervous system. There is no mental function or dimension of consciousness that cannot be intensified, accelerated, expanded. Work on receptor sites and beta endorphins is isolating chemicals naturally produced by the body that simulate the effects of the most common "head" drugs like morphine or LSD. This research encourages the speculation that soon one can have one's blood typed or one's spinal fluid assayed to isolate and then synthesize precisely the chemicals that one's brain is geared to use as fuel.

4. Genetic Engineering: Chakrabarty and Kennedy

Here is the ultimate step in active, confident, self-determination. Humanity is taking charge of the evolutionary process and writing the life script. No longer need we cower in helpless fear, victims of a blind genetic destiny. We can now create new forms of life, correct faulty DNA blueprints, use the amino-acid language of life to write the prescriptions preventing aging and death.

J. R. Chakrabarty and Ian Kennedy merit distinction because they have created *controversy!* It started when the Indian chemist, via recombinant DNA methods, created in the General Electric laboratory a new mutant bacteria that eats oil spills. His claim for a patent was turned down by the U.S. government. Chakrabarty appealed and the Supreme Court in June 1980 issued its decision. Chakrabarty was legally credited as owning the life form he had created! The Pope promptly denounced gene splicing as heretical and he was right.

The Chakrabarty decision gave genetic engineers a license to step up their work. Brave New Life Forms!

Ian Kennedy is even more controversial. Working in a "safe" laboratory at U.C. San Diego, this British virologist cloned the semliki forest virus, although he had been given government permission to replicate only the sindbis virus. The semliki forest virus is not dangerous. Dr. Kennedy surely knew this better than the federal officials who classify risk potentials. Four of Kennedy's graduate students exposed the existence of the unauthorized bacteria to the administrators. Kennedy hinted that the substitution of species might have been an act of sabotage. An investigating committee suggested that Kennedy was guilty of a cover-up, and the brilliant researcher was barred from his own lab. Cover-up of what? Kennedy exposed the most dangerous disease now troubling our species—bureaucratic, political interference.

5. Roy Walford: Immunization-Inoculation as Keys to Evolution

When Roy Walford was a child, he pondered about the alleged invincibility of death. Being a thoughtful, intelligent cub, he resolved to devote his life to the cure of this lethal disease. His studies in the histocompatibility locus antigen (HLA) system have "happily merged" with other work on the biology of aging: immunology, DNA repair, free radical biochemistry, and hormone studies.

Aging may be partially caused by a failure in the autoimmune system. You age because your immune system starts producing antigens against your own cells. In other words, you begin to reject yourself. (Makes sense when you think about it.) As of September 1980, some researchers in the field of prolongevity were already testing new antiaging drugs on themselves and their parents! When two developments occur in a science—(1) a convergence of many competing cures and (2) the experts dosing themselves—the breakthrough is usually close at hand.

Like other new-breed Smart Ones, Roy Walford is a multi-disciplinary, wide-gauge thinker. He's sexually magnetic and that's apparently important. It's becoming clear that philosophers who can't master their bodies and esthetic energies can't help but give us a crippled world view. Like other Smart Ones, Walford has systematically opened up his intuitive, relativistic right brain by means of the standard yogi techniques. Roy Walford has made the future his home town.

6. Edward Wilson: Sociobiologist

Edward Wilson, distinguished Harvard biologist, was delivering a scientific paper at the 1978 meeting of the American Association for the

Advancement of Science when a band of militant feminist academicians poured a pitcher of water over his head. As he stood by the lectern at a prestigious scholarly meeting!

Clearly Wilson is doing something right. Anytime a young, respected, attractive frontier scientist gets mugged because of his data and theories, we're alerted to a Prometheus script.

This historical drama started with a romantic South African physician, Andre Marais, who, disillusioned with human behavior after the bitter Boer War, returned to the Transvaal and spent the rest of his life shooting morphine (from army supplies he had salvaged) while living with tribes of natives, troops of baboons, hives of bees, and colonies of termites. He discovered that a profound intelligence coursed through these alien societies. Their basic behavior patterns roughly duplicated in almost all respects the social behavior of humans. Indeed, these so-called lower species had succeeded in solving many urban and territorial problems in the evolutionary cycle.

These successful species (the termites have been flaunting the same melodramatic lifestyles for 150 million years) seemed to be guided by some sort of collective genetic intelligence that uses individuals as preprogrammed units necessary for collective security. Individuals are apparently harnessed to their divisions of labor by means of imprinting that releases their specific innate mechanism.

Now enter Edward Wilson, who writes a classic textbook on the behavior of social animals, *Sociobiology* (Harvard University Press, 1975). We confront the notion of genetic intelligence, species planning, biological wisdom—heretical, vitalist, creativist notions that we considered in the Gaia section. There may not have been a genetic intelligence in the past, but there sure is now! It's us! The emergence of the science of sociobiology becomes an irresistible, irreversible mutational event. We become the genetic intelligence.

Once you start thinking at the level of species intelligence, you raise your perspectives from personal realities to a broader space-time frame that makes the future a most exciting place.

We can start asking the simple but powerful navigational question: Where is evolution taking our species? The answer: In any direction, fashion, style, mode that we—led by the New Scientists —choose.

To be continued. . . .

Index